TARA WINKLER is the Managing Director of the Cambodian Children's Trust (CCT), which she established with Jedtha Pon in 2007 in order to rescue fourteen children from a corrupt and abusive orphanage.

Tara has led CCT through a number of significant organisational changes, including the closure of the initial CCT orphanage in favour of a holistic model of programs and services to help Cambodian families escape poverty, while ensuring family preservation. Tara now speaks out against the spread of orphanages in developing countries, caused by the good intentions of foreign donors, and of harm that comes to children when they are separated from family and left to grow up in institutions.

In 2011 Tara was awarded NSW Young Australian of the Year in recognition of her work with CCT and she has been featured twice on *Australian Story*.

How (Not) to Start an Orphanage is her first book.

HOW (not) TO START AN ORPHANAGE

...by a woman who did

TARA WINKLER
& LYNDA DELACEY

ALLEN&UNWIN

SYDNEY · MELBOURNE · AUCKLAND · LONDON

Dedicated to Sinet and Sineit Chan

First published in 2016

Allen & Unwin
83 Alexander Street
Crows Nest NSW 2065
Australia
Phone: (61 2) 8425 0100
Email: info@allenandunwin.com
Web: www.allenandunwin.com

Cataloguing-in-Publication details are available
from the National Library of Australia
www.trove.nla.gov.au

ISBN 978 1 74237 628 8

Set in 12/17 pt Minion by Post Pre-press Group, Australia
Printed and bound in Australia by Griffin Press

10 9 8 7 6 5 4 3 2 1

MIX
Paper from
responsible sources
FSC® C009448
www.fsc.org

The paper in this book is FSC® certified.
FSC® promotes environmentally responsible,
socially beneficial and economically viable
management of the world's forests.

Contents

Preface

If you're reading this book, I'm guessing it's for one of three reasons:

1. You heard about the twenty-one-year-old Aussie girl from Bondi who rescued fourteen kids from a corrupt orphanage in Cambodia. You're inspired by the idea of helping people in a developing country and you want to know what it's like (or at least, what it's been like for me).

2. You're cynical about charities and you're reading this to, you know, feed the fire. (Because don't we all do that sometimes?)

3. You're already a supporter of the Cambodian Children's Trust (CCT), the non-government organisation that this book is about, and you've bought a copy because the proceeds help to support our work.

If your reason is number three . . . thank you! It's because of people like you that CCT exists at all. Even though I'm often the one out front receiving the praise, CCT's work is very much a team effort. This team includes our incredibly generous supporters, as well as CCT's amazingly dedicated staff in Cambodia and volunteers in Australia. So this book is a story about a journey that you are also a part of.

If yours is the second reason, I get it! You'll probably find a few reasons to be rather pissed off with me in parts of this story. But hopefully you'll come to see that at CCT we are really good at learning from our mistakes, listening to constructive criticism and taking positive action to do better. There's no gold standard or silver bullet in the fight against poverty, but I do believe CCT, working hand-in-hand with some other exemplary organisations, is helping lead the way in Cambodia.

If your reason is the first (you want to know more about my story), I'm going to walk you through my experiences—the good, the bad and the ugly. Sharing my story in such a public way is not something that comes naturally to me. I'd give almost anything to remain behind the scenes and out of the spotlight. But I do understand that when people decide to support a small grassroots operation, they need to get to know and trust those who are running it. So it's essential at this stage that I play a much more public role than I'm entirely comfortable with.

But of course, for inspiration I need only look at the resilience and courage of the kids and families I work with in Cambodia; if they can soldier on through so much adversity with big, bright smiles still intact, then I can find the courage to share my story with the world.

As the American researcher Brené Brown famously said: 'The original definition of courage, when it first came into the English language—it's from the Latin word *cor*, meaning heart . . . was to tell the story of who you are with your whole heart.' That is what I will endeavour to do in this book: to tell you my story, from the heart, honestly and authentically.

I do need to state that I've changed the names of many of the people and organisations that appear in this story to protect both the innocent and the guilty alike.

And I should warn you, this is *not* a book about a saintly individual who runs an orphanage. In fact, CCT is not an orphanage anymore.

As I write this, CCT, though only eight-years-young, is a well-respected Cambodian non-government organisation (NGO), whose work is made possible by a small but loyal base of generous supporters. We're all about empowering the next generation of Cambodian kids to reach their full potential—because at the end of the day, solving Cambodia's problems is not a job for one small NGO. It's not even a job for all of the NGOs in Cambodia (and there's no shortage of them). It's a job for an entire generation. We believe CCT's job is to empower that generation.

We are dedicated to helping Cambodian children to escape the intergenerational cycle of poverty—for good. And, though this may come as a surprise to some, orphanages are not the answer. They are, in fact, a big part of the problem . . . (I could go on and on about this, and I will! But later . . .)

For the last few years, we've been achieving our goal by focusing on family. We ensure that some of the most vulnerable children in the world have access to top-notch healthcare and a well-rounded education, while enabling them to stay with their families where they belong. This approach helps to prevent them from being trafficked and subjected to child labour, and from being separated from their families and ending up in orphanages. We do this because it's better for the kids, better for the adults they'll grow up to be, and better for the communities they are a part of.

Sometimes, I have to pinch myself when I look back and reflect on how far CCT has come. It seems just yesterday I was standing at the gate of a very different organisation, with fourteen desperate kids running towards me.

And I have to remind myself of how far *I've* come too, from the nineteen-year-old backpacker landing in town with a pair of over-sized Dolce & Gabbana sunglasses on my head, thinking South-East Asia would be a cool place to hang out for a few months until I went back to real life to continue building my career in the film industry. (Spoiler alert: that never happened.)

So. Here we go.

STEP 1

Meet some orphans

1

I grew up in the eastern suburbs of Sydney in a not-so-average family. Peter, my dad, is a Hungarian-Australian musician, circus performer and bad-joke-teller. He loves Leonard Cohen and wombats. Sue, my mum, is a professional storyteller, preschool teacher and dog-lover. She loves gardening and listening to ABC radio.

I've never called them Mum and Dad. They've always just been Sue and Peter to me. They never referred to themselves as 'Mum' and 'Dad', so I didn't either.

I was very aware (and sometimes rather embarrassed) that Sue and Peter were a little more left-of-centre than most parents. They were proud of being part of the 'counterculture' and made sure that my little sister Noni and I were very aware of it. Both Sue's and Peter's political and idealistic views of the world mean they are still fundamentally hippies at heart. They've been in a committed relationship for over thirty years, but never married and have never intended to.

When Sue was a young woman, she spent five years living in a pink caravan in Bellingen, with a pink cockatoo, a golden labrador and a little horse that she once rode to victory in a country horserace (wearing jeans and a wedding dress!). She left Bellingen to travel the world for two years. She has always given to charities, and always planned, in her retirement, to volunteer her time to a charitable cause.

Peter spent his youth in a travelling circus as well as performing in bands. Like Sue, he was a passionate traveller. At twenty-three, he was backpacking through India when he got very sick with hepatitis. A local family took care of him while he slowly recovered. He often stayed with them in his years of travelling through Asia. When he came back to Australia, he returned their kindness—by helping them out financially for the rest of his life.

Peter and Sue adore little kids. Peter loves telling the story of the first time he met me—especially when I'm being stubborn. Sue went through a long, painful labour with me and when I was finally dragged out with forceps, I was whisked off to intensive care to clear my lungs of fluid. Peter followed me down there. When he finally got the chance to pick me up, he says I looked up at him with eyes that said: 'Watch out! I'm gonna give you hell!' He loved that about me.

I remember early childhood as an endless summer of daisies and music and My Little Ponies, with my little sister Noni by my side and my small, tight-knit family all around. My dad's sister Eva and her family lived in the flat upstairs, and my grandparents lived nearby.

My grandmother Joan, Sue's mum, was a diehard social activist. She stood for election as a candidate for the Democrats. She rode on floats in the Mardi Gras, and wrote a book arguing against the prohibition of illicit drugs. She was pretty much the coolest granny ever. But I didn't call her 'Granny'. I think she might've punched me if I tried. She wanted to be recognised as an individual, not just a role, so Noni and I grew up calling her by her name, too.

I've always been fairly headstrong. As a kid, once I had decided on something, that was that. Much to Sue's dismay, I went through a phase in primary school of being a strangely fussy eater. At one point, the only thing I'd agree to eat for breakfast was fairy bread. So this was what I made (way overloaded with hundreds and thousands) every morning. But then I decided I didn't like butter, so I had a rather hard time keeping all the hundreds and thousands on the bread. Then I discovered smoked salmon and cream cheese bagels and decided I wanted to eat those every morning instead.

Growing up, my cousin Sarah, Noni and I used to spend every Thursday after school with my Hungarian grandparents. We'd eat pickle sandwiches and play My Little Ponies all afternoon. I was very close to my grandmother Nagy (Hungarian for 'biggie' as in 'big mama') and I never tired of hearing her stories. She had a lot of stories to tell. She survived the Holocaust as a young woman and was interviewed by Steven Spielberg's research team for the archival project 'Survivors of the Shoah'.

Her stories were very vivid in my imagination. Being ordered by the Nazis to play piano for them before boarding a train to Poland. Arriving at Auschwitz, lining up in the freezing cold. Watching as people in the line ahead were casually divided—some sent left, some sent right. Having no idea what was coming except that it was bad. Coming face to face with Josef Mengele, the notorious Angel of Death, and being taken by how handsome he was, immaculately dressed with striking dark hair and eyes. The wave of his cane, sending Nagy and her younger sister to the right. Holding her mother's hand and pleading for him to let them all go together, but still he waved left. Which meant that was the last time she ever saw her mother.

Nagy's stories entered my dreams and, in a strange way, became my memories. She would always end her stories by reminding me how grateful she was for the life she had now—in a beautiful country, surrounded by her beautiful family. She was never bitter or angry. But Peter was. He had a lot to say on the subject. And Peter's anger and grief became my anger and grief. This is how intergenerational trauma works. You can look it up. It's a thing.

But anyway . . .

During the school holidays, Sue and Peter liked to take us off the beaten track, and would drag us (sometimes protesting) deep into the Australian bush, or to remote villages in Indonesia or tiny islands off Vanuatu—places where breakfast was served with an attractive sprinkling of bugs, and where there wasn't a smoked salmon bagel for miles. We climbed active volcanoes and swam with dugongs. We learned from a young age to embrace foreign cultures and form lasting friendships with local people.

We were also lucky enough to be brought up in an animal-loving family. My first dog, Pepper, was a scruffy mixed terrier. She was two when I was born, and was my constant companion for the next sixteen years. As a toddler, I was often to be found curled up in Pepper's kennel. To me, home just doesn't feel like home without a dog. We also had pet mice, fish, cockatiels and, best of all . . . horses.

I was six months old when Sue took me on my first horse ride. Poor Sue. I'm sure she had no idea what she was getting herself into. She's a good rider herself—thanks to her farming background—but she hadn't had much experience with the advanced equestrian disciplines she would soon be hearing about, twenty-four hours a day. Though it was expensive, she and Peter did their best to support my passion for horseriding. And I was about as passionate as they come.

I was nine years old when I got my first job with horses at a riding school near Sydney's Centennial Park. The school's owner, Caz Stubbs, let me muck out stables and lead beginners around the park in return for riding lessons. I hero-worshipped Caz—who'd started the school at just twenty years of age—and hoped I'd grow up exactly like her.

I did have other interests as a kid; I took piano lessons, learned guitar from my dad, I loved drawing and painting and surfing down at Bondi Beach. But in the end my passion for horses took over.

After years of ferrying me to and from the stables, Sue and Peter decided to use part of an early inheritance they received from my grandmother Joan to buy twenty-five acres on the south coast, three hours from Sydney.

'Can we get a horse now?' I asked hopefully.

'Yes,' they agreed (somewhat brokenly). 'You and Noni can each have a horse.'

They built a small weekender on the land, and for the next three years I spent every single weekend there, so I could ride, train and compete. It was heaven.

When I think about it now, I don't know how Sue and Peter did it. Horseriding is not a great sport for a middle-income family in the city. But they made sacrifices. I remember watching the opening ceremony of the 2000 Sydney Olympic Games with Sue from a little caravan in Parkes Showground in south-west New South Wales, where I was competing in an agricultural show. That wasn't exactly Sue's idea of a great time, but she didn't complain. (Well, not too much, anyway . . .)

~

In my early high school years, having my life split between the city and the country was a challenge for the whole family. Every Friday, as soon as the afternoon bell rang, I'd bolt out the school gates, rush home and grab my riding gear, then either Sue or Peter would drive me the three hours down the coast so I could ride my horse all weekend. Finally, Sue and Peter (with help from Joan) agreed to send me to New England Girls' School (NEGS) in Armidale, six hours north of Sydney. There I could combine my passion for horses with the last three years of my secondary education.

I remember feeling as if all my dreams were coming true as we drove up the pretty New England Highway to NEGS. For the first time in my life I would be able to live on the same property as my horse, Theo, and be entirely responsible for his care.

I missed my family and felt a bit bad about leaving Noni, but boarding at school was quite fun, kind of like one big long slumber party. Rain, hail or shine, I'd be up at the crack of dawn every morning to feed, water and rug Theo before classes. I could ride as much as I wanted in my free time. It didn't do wonders for my grades, but I didn't care.

NEGS was great for me in all ways but one: the food.

The culture surrounding food at NEGS was light-years away from the healthy, organic food I was used to at home. Each day we had a buffet breakfast, followed by a cake at morning tea, then another buffet-style hot lunch, then another sweet thing for afternoon tea, then dinner and dessert, then a cake for supper. We were given so much food we'd have silly eating competitions and food fights.

In my first year at NEGS, I finally hit puberty. I was unaware of how integral having a streamlined tomboy's body was to my sense of self. But the fact was that my body was changing. A very strange feeling came over me . . . a feeling of deep, profound discomfort with my changing shape.

Over the summer holidays, I decided to go on a health kick and lose the kilo or two I'd gained at school. I attacked the project with my usual gusto. My grandmother Joan went to the gym every day, so I started going with her. I counted every calorie I put in my mouth, and restricted more and more of my food intake.

By the time I went back to school, I seemed to be winning my personal war on puberty—I was super fit and shaped like a broomstick. And food and me . . . well, let's just say we were developing a very unhealthy relationship.

I was determined to keep the curves away. The problem was that I couldn't control my food supply at NEGS. I could only ever count on breakfast to be a reliable source of low-calorie food. 'No problem,' said the dysfunctional part of my brain, which was in the driver's seat by now. It had me eating fat-free cereal or toast at breakfast to kick-start my metabolism and then starving myself the rest of the day. I was also running and riding every day.

This obsessive diet meant that I quickly dropped to a dangerously low weight. The sensible part of my brain knew that what I was doing wasn't healthy, but by then I was firmly in the grip of anorexia nervosa and had no idea how to free myself from it. Every day became a fierce battle to hide my inner turmoil from the rest of the world.

Eventually, Sue called me from Sydney. 'Hi, sweetheart . . . how are you?' Her tone was very gentle—the tone she uses when she's concerned about me. 'We got a call from the school. They're worried about you being very thin . . .?'

'Huh? Who called? What did they say?' I demanded.

'They're worried you might have an eating disorder,' she explained. 'They sound quite concerned about it.'

'Oh god. They're such idiots!' I spluttered. 'I'm just eating well and training hard and not eating the unhealthy crap they serve up all day long! Just because I don't eat ten pieces of cake doesn't mean I've got a fucking eating disorder!'

'Well, it's good to be healthy,' Sue agreed. 'But everything in moderation, okay?'

That afternoon the nurse called me down to her office.

'Have you been vomiting?' she asked, as she gestured for me to step onto the scales.

'No!' I told her truthfully. 'Really, I'm fine. I just don't eat junk food and I get a lot of exercise.'

I pushed aside the anxiety and stepped onto the scales, trying to look like I didn't care. My weight had dropped even lower since the last time I'd checked. I hadn't expected it to be quite that low, but I did my best to hide my shock. I stuck to my story about healthy eating and intense training schedules and eventually she let me go.

I decided from then on I'd keep my weight just a little higher, thinking that if I could achieve that, I could prove to myself that I was fine. What I didn't know was that at that weight, I had already gone way too far. I didn't get my period for over a year and I've since discovered that I was doing irreversible damage to my bones, which would cause major problems later in life . . .

The issue never came up again, but for the rest of that year I lived in fear of being called back to the nurse's office. The sick part of me craved hearing people tell me I was thin. But at the same time, whenever I heard it, I felt threatened, exposed and defensive.

Poor Sue and Peter were confused and at a loss as to how to help. I was riddled with shame and did everything in my power to keep it all very secret. The only way I knew to help myself was to keep doing what I was doing. As long as I was following the eating and exercising rules I'd set for myself, I was reasonably happy.

I should make it clear that I don't blame puberty or NEGS or anyone else for giving me anorexia. Eating disorders are complicated mental illnesses with a bunch of abstract social, psychological and genetic triggers that I think were waiting inside me, like a time bomb.

~

As I moved into my final years of school, I met the pressure to bust my gut studying with an eye roll. I never bought into the stress of the HSC exams and the idea that the set of marks you get when you're seventeen years old will determine your fate. I believed that a successful life could be made with or without university. And I knew that the well-beaten path was probably not going to lead to the sort of life I wanted anyway. A 'normal' life looked pretty boring to me—I craved adventure.

So instead of studying every waking hour like many of my friends, I decided to take up martial arts. I had a great trainer, Anthony Kelly, and eventually ended up attaining my black belt. But I wasn't particularly interested in belts. I just wanted to learn how to fight. Anthony, who had six black belts and several Guinness World Records, would inevitably pin me every time, but he never went easy on me. Training was always a highlight of my day, and a great antidote to all the crazy HSC-related stress flying around the boarding house. It was also the only thing that helped quiet the voice inside me telling me that I wasn't good enough until I was thin enough.

As the end of year twelve loomed closer, and after much deliberation about my future career path, I decided not to pursue riding professionally. I wanted to keep horses as a hobby, something I would always love to do, not something I *had* to do. This meant I'd have to part with my beautiful horse, Theo, after school finished. It was a decision made with many tears, but I knew horseriding wasn't the right path for me and that he'd bring endless joy to another young, ambitious rider.

In the last few months of year twelve, I had an idea that would make it possible to combine all the hobbies I loved: I decided I wanted to be a stunt actor! I roll my eyes over that ridiculous plan now—I would've hated stunt acting—but at the time I thought it would be a great way to combine my skills in martial arts, horseriding and surfing, and spend my life flying to exotic places and jumping off moving trains and galloping round on majestic black horses.

The first step in my plan was to get my foot in the door of the film industry—and I was prepared to do whatever it took to make that happen. So while everyone else was studying, I was making phone calls and sending emails to every film production company in Sydney.

Eventually Rosemary Blight, one of Australia's leading independent film producers, agreed to give me work experience with her production company. I'd be working for free, but that was fine. I planned to make myself so indispensable that after the production wrapped they'd just *have* to give me a job.

~

Graduation Day was great, mostly because it marked the end of my childhood—the end of a chapter and the beginning of an exciting new one where *I* was in the driving seat. Much to my surprise, I did okay in the HSC—I even topped my grade in Information Technology.

I packed up my life at NEGS, said a very sad goodbye to Theo and to all my friends—who were mostly heading off on schoolies week— and made tracks back to Sydney. I moved in with my grandmother Joan, so I could keep my independence without actually having to pay any rent. (Yes, I know, I'm incredibly lucky to have such a supportive family.)

Despite the generation gap, Joan and I made excellent housemates and fell into a routine like an old married couple. We went to the gym together and to Politics at the Pub and to meetings of the Council for Civil Liberties. But Joan let me live my own life. She never worried about me being out late and gave me the space I needed to do my own thing.

I started working for Rosemary as a runner in the art department on a telemovie they were making called *Small Claims*. After talking to some of the other crew, I quickly realised that stunt acting wasn't such a brilliant idea for me, after all. But I was still very inspired by the film industry, especially by the art department and the possibility of using my IT skills in computer-aided set design.

By this time, my weight was back in the normal range, not because I had recovered from the eating disorder but, rather, I had moved into a different phase of it, which my new therapist called 'disorderly eating'. I don't think it's always easy to fit eating disorders into neatly defined categories. At this time I was somewhere between anorexia and bulimia—sometimes restricting, sometimes bingeing, but without the purging. This eating pattern pushed me up into a normal weight range, but at a normal weight I felt disgusting. I found getting dressed in the morning a particularly horrible ordeal and often didn't want to leave the house. But, with an iron will, I pushed the dark thoughts aside so as not to screw up the exciting opportunity I had landed in the film industry.

The vibe on set was great and I genuinely loved every day of filming. I was working with a great group of people who said they were really impressed by my work ethic and can-do attitude. The positive feedback I got from them was a great boost to my self-confidence.

After production on the telemovie wrapped up, the art director and art department team bought me a beautiful gift—an engraved Leatherman pocketknife that I'd been eyeing off for a while. And, even better, they invited me to join them as a paid member of the team on their next job. I was in!

Our next job was for a TV commercial. My role was to assist with set-dressing and props-buying. The money was good—great, actually, for someone who wasn't even eighteen yet. But this job wasn't as satisfying as the last. In fact, it was unbelievably stressful.

Most of the job involved racing all over Sydney in my little green Mitsubishi sourcing, buying and then returning props. My boss, the art director, would regularly remind me of the grave importance of my role and of the consequences if I fucked up. And when I did fuck up, boy did I hear about it! Oftentimes, the entire crew would also hear about it as I was scolded on set or at a wrap party. As a perfectionist, this was a hard pill to swallow. I would regularly drive home from work in tears.

I slogged it out for a year, working on commercials for things like soft drinks, dog food and incontinence pads. One of the best set designers in the country had also taken me under his wing and was teaching me to use a CAD (computer-aided design) program. But I wasn't happy and the stress aggravated my eating disorder. I was killing myself over this job and all for the sake of helping multinational corporations to make even more money. It didn't feel right. Not at all. My great big dreams for my successful career in the film industry felt like they were fading before my eyes.

And then one afternoon Peter called me in a terrible state of shock. 'Your grandma has died,' he said, his voice trembling. 'Nagy has died.'

The thunderbolt of shock was followed by a wave of nauseating despair.

Peter picked me up, his face horribly pallid, and we rushed down the road to her house. The ambulance was parked outside. My Uncle Gil told us she'd just finished getting all dressed up to go to the opera when she sat down to lunch and just . . . died.

I stood next to the ambulance feeling like shreds were being torn off my heart. A warm wash of guilt came over me. Nagy adored her grandchildren and I'd spent so little time with her since I finished school and started working.

The last conversation I had with her was about going to a jeweller together to buy a chain for a special little gold pendant that she wanted to give me. It meant a lot to her. She had kept it since child-hood—even buried it in her yard in Hungary during the Holocaust years. It was still sitting in her jewellery box. It was her last wish for me and I'd never made the time.

In a fit of remorse I darted into the house to get it from her room, only to see Nagy lying dead on the carpet. I froze, feeling as if all the air had been sucked out of my body. Then I turned and ran. I wanted to scream at someone for not telling me Nagy was still there. Dead! On the floor! But by the time I got back outside I was choking on tears and couldn't catch my breath to speak.

Auntie Eva went into Nagy's room and got the pendant for me.

~

Losing Nagy was the point where everything finally unravelled. This was my first real experience of loss, and it was awful.

My eating disorder went into full flight. The episodes of bingeing and starving got much worse. I'd go for days surviving on as few calories as humanly possible, but eventually something would snap inside me. I'd lose control and then proceed to consume an obscene amount of food. When I physically could not fit another thing into my mouth, I'd rush to the bathroom and attempt to throw it all up. Sometimes I'd follow up by swallowing an entire packet of laxatives, just in case the purging didn't get everything. This living hell all happened in a shroud of secrecy and shame. The cycles of starving, bingeing and purging led me to a very dark place.

Being so out of control terrified me. Despite the lengths I was going to, I also wasn't losing weight, I was gaining it. I felt so utterly hideous and miserable I was often unable to leave the house.

These were trying times for Joan. She had no idea what was going on but was worried about me and didn't know how to help. Sometimes, in her frustration, she'd fling my door open and say things like: 'Tara, the state of your room is indicative of the way you're living your life!'

I'd pull the bedcovers over my head and wait until she left. I knew she was right, but I was powerless to do anything about it. I needed help, but was too ashamed to ask for it. I hated that I'd turned out to be a person who suffered from a 'body image' disorder. Even the shame was shameful.

To some, the solution to eating disorders can look rather simple: 'Just don't be so vain! Just don't buy into societal pressure to be thin!' But, actually, it's got nothing to do with vanity. It's the opposite, in fact. It doesn't represent what I value in life or what is important to me, or even what I consider to be beautiful. It's an illness, perpetuated by thoughts that I know are irrational, but which I still couldn't fully control. The actual suffering associated with eating disorders and body image disorders is as horrific as any other mental illness.

As a naturally slim woman I also carry feelings of guilt, knowing that other women sometimes perceive my struggles as a personal slight against them. They sometimes reason that if I think I'm fat, and they're bigger than me, then surely I must think they're grotesque? I know this has affected some of my friends over the years, and I'm truly sorry for that.

The truth is, when I see other women torturing themselves over their weight, I just want to reach out and tell them they're beautiful and to fuck the impossible (literally impossible) standards of beauty that our society demands we meet. But despite everything I've tried over the years, I still struggle at times to extend this same compassion to myself. I do better with it today, thanks to years of therapy, a healthy lifestyle, and a daily mindfulness practice that has helped immensely. But when I'm under a lot of stress or pressure, I still put tighter controls around my diet, just to keep the strange cycle of unhealthy thoughts and behaviours at bay.

The main reason I'm airing this extremely personal issue here is because I don't feel I could've told my story genuinely without it. Also because, over the years, some people have told me they see me as a positive role model—particularly for young women. My secret battle with eating disorders has made me feel rather unworthy of that title. So the best I feel I can do to compensate is to be honest about my struggles.

~

I tried everything to pull myself out of the darkness I had become trapped in after Nagy's death. I spent more time with my family and friends, more time with the horses. I got a Jack Russell puppy and went back to my therapist, who put me on antidepressants.

Nothing helped. I was in too deep to find my own way out. I needed a circuit breaker.

And then, out of the blue, it came.

As a combined eighteenth and twenty-first birthday present, Sue and Peter gave me a choice of a big party or a trip overseas.

I think they knew full well I'd opt for the trip. (In fact, their tone was: 'Would you like a (yawn) big party or a (YAY!) TRIP OVERSEAS?!') This was my big chance to climb out of the abyss I'd fallen into.

Soon, I was bidding a teary goodbye to Sue, Peter and Noni at the airport. As I walked through the departure gate, I felt horribly vulnerable and a little unsure I'd made the right decision. In my hand was the ticket for an Intrepid tour that would take me through South-East Asia—from Thailand to Laos, Vietnam and finally Cambodia.

2

The air in Bangkok in May 2005 was hot and heavy and infused with the familiar spicy scents I remembered from our family holidays to Indonesia. I felt none of the anxiety I'd feared I might about being in a foreign country on my own. In fact, it felt like the ultimate escape.

All that doona-diving I'd been doing was ultimately in search of this exact feeling. No one knew me in South-East Asia. I was suddenly free of all that had been weighing me down in Sydney. I was still very uncomfortable with my body at the size that it was, but here in Thailand, I felt like I was wearing Harry Potter's invisibility cloak. I was practically skipping with excitement as I wove my way down Khao San Road to meet up with my Intrepid Travel group.

I found twelve people—from Australia, the UK and the US—waiting for me in a hotel foyer. I plonked myself next to a lovely girl with a gorgeous Afro hairstyle from East London named Alicia, who was closest to my age in the group and fast became my new bestie. Our group leader gave us a basic rundown of our itinerary, and then we set off.

Over the next three weeks, we made our way through Chiang Mai, Chiang Rai, then down the Mekong and into Laos. We trekked through forests, shopped the night markets of Luang Prabang, dive-bombed into waterfalls and got riotously drunk together.

~

Cambodia was the final stop on the tour and I expected it to be much the same as Thailand, Laos and Vietnam. Like so many young westerners, I didn't know much about Cambodia and was only vaguely aware of the country's devastating history.

We travelled from Ho Chi Minh City into Cambodia in an old minibus. As soon as we crossed the border, everything changed. Suddenly we were travelling long dusty roads through empty fields, spotted with tall palm trees.

Brown-skinned farmers were hard at work in the midday heat, with red-checked scarves wrapped around their heads to shield them from the burning sun. Young boys tended water buffalo in the shallow canals that ran alongside the road. Tiny rows of crude wooden huts squatted alongside tall, elaborate Buddhist pagodas that seemed to drip with money. It was a strange, almost medieval new world.

The poverty was undeniably in-your-face. I felt slightly uncomfortable about being 'on holiday' in such a place. But the attitude of the people made up for it. Everywhere we went, no matter how hard life looked, we saw local people laughing, playing and enjoying life. We started a game—counting how many smiling people we could see from the bus window.

After several hours, we reached Phnom Penh. The city hummed with the sounds of construction work and mad, cheerful, chaotic traffic. We soon had cars, trucks, motos, bicycles, dogs, cows, buses and tuktuks coming at us from all directions.

Cambodia's tuktuks are a cute take on the auto rickshaw. Seen from a distance, they resemble tiny horse-drawn chariots, except with motos instead of horses.

We also saw a few cyclos, an earlier cousin of the tuktuk, careening through the traffic. The cyclo is basically what you get when a bicycle mates with a wheelchair. The chair sits over the front wheel, so the passengers can get up close and personal with the hair-raising Phnom Penh traffic.

But the family vehicle of choice in Cambodia is definitely the moto—that 125 cc motorbike/scooter hybrid that seems to be everywhere in South-East Asia. And I don't say 'family vehicle' lightly. Whole families get around by moto, with babies, grannies and little kids wedged in a row between Mum and Dad.

The road rules in Cambodia seem to be:

1) It's hot, so why walk when you can ride?
2) Don't worry about rules, just drive very slowly and try not to crash into anything.
3) Beep your horn cheerfully at everyone so they know you're coming.

As the sun sank that evening, we settled on the balcony of a beautiful French Colonial hotel looking out into the street and the river beyond—a vast body of water where the Mekong and Tonlé Sap come together.

The riverside is the centre of Phnom Penh's colourful nightlife—everywhere we looked, we saw street vendors peddling noodles, car parts, Buddhist trinkets, balloons . . . Everyone seemed to be chatting, yelling, laughing and bargaining. They greeted and thanked each other with the traditional *sampeah*, a prayer-like gesture and head bow I'd seen performed throughout Thailand (and in the occasional yoga class).

The tuktuk drivers, leaning on their chariots and smoking with raffish, bad-boy charm, jumped to life whenever a tourist passed by with a cheerful: 'Tuktuk, lady?' Young women sold sugary treats from their street stalls to boisterous little kids who chased each other up and down the promenade, stopping now and then to hit up passing tourists for a dollar.

I was enthralled. Cambodia was wild and I liked it.

~

The next morning we set out in a convoy of tuktuks to visit the Tuol Sleng Genocide Museum.

Travelling through the streets by tuktuk is crazy fun. It's like a lazy version of motorcycling, with the wind in your hair and the roar of the engine (tuktuk roughly translates as 'putt putt'), but with a roof over your head and a cushy bench seat to lean back into.

We threaded through the city centre with its bustling shops, massive hotels and French Colonial pubs, past the ubiquitous street markets and food stalls selling sugar cane and noodles and coconuts and fried tarantulas.

I was so entranced by the journey, I didn't spare a thought for the day's itinerary. The words 'genocide museum' didn't sink in until we spilled out of the tuktuks. I had done a little bit of reading on Cambodia's genocide when I booked the trip, but when we headed through a set of high concrete gates, I had no idea what I was in for.

The atmosphere inside was immediately sombre.

The museum is a former high school, and looked to me like a typical Aussie public school—if a little broken down. In the 1970s, the school was renamed 'Security Office 21' and then 'Tuol Sleng Prison' and became the main—and most notorious—office and torture facility for the Khmer Rouge.

It's impossible to understand Cambodia today without understanding what happened there between 1975 and 1979.

The Cold War and the Vietnam War of 1962–1975 were in many ways a clash between western capitalism and eastern communism. Throughout the war, the popular Cambodian head of state and former monarch Prince Norodom Sihanouk tried desperately to hold onto power and keep Cambodia from being drawn into the conflict raging just over the border. There was a pervasive fear in Cambodia that, if drawn into the conflict, the country would lose its independence and disappear from the map altogether.

Sihanouk allowed North Vietnam to establish bases in eastern Cambodia. He also let China use routes through Cambodia to send military supplies to North Vietnam. The US and its allies (including Australia) responded by carpet-bombing vast tracts of eastern Cambodia.

History books call this the 'secret bombing'—US president Richard Nixon authorised the operation without the knowledge or approval of the US Congress. For five years, they targeted the bases and supply routes and deliberately bombed civilians, to put further pressure on the Cambodian government.

By 1970, many of Sihanouk's colleagues in Phnom Penh had lost faith in him and the decisions he was making. Many of the people who lived *outside* Phnom Penh were also unhappy with Sihanouk, the USA and, indeed, city people in general. They felt they'd been abandoned to suffer through the US-led bombings, which had created serious social upheaval. It's not clear how many Cambodian civilians died in the carpet bombing. But estimates range from a few tens of thousands to over 600,000. Hundreds of thousands more were displaced, leading to famine and terrible suffering.

Sihanouk was deposed by the pro-western Cambodian general and prime minister Lon Nol, who was rumoured to have CIA backing. The self-proclaimed president of the Khmer Republic had his work cut out for him. From day one, his army was locked in conflict with the guerrilla forces of Cambodia's communist Khmer Rouge. The tough, mostly rural-raised Khmer Rouge army was headed by a shadowy group of leaders, which included the French-educated Pol Pot. These leaders were huge admirers of communism—particularly Stalinist and Chinese Maoist communism—and dreamed of creating a proud new empire in Cambodia . . . a return to the glory days of Angkor Wat.

Before the bombings began, the Khmer Rouge had little support within Cambodia. But four years of carpet-bombing had created serious socio-political upheaval, and the Khmer Rouge's popularity grew.

The Khmer Rouge's vision of a proud and prosperous Khmer empire was not unappealing to some of the people. And sympathies for the Khmer Rouge were further swayed by patriotism when the deposed Prince Sihanouk and his wife joined the Khmer Rouge. Many people joined them, saying that they were 'fighting for their king'.

So now there were two major political factions in Cambodia—one led by the pro-western Lon Nol in Phnom Penh, and the other led by the pro-communist Khmer Rouge army, which was aided and supported by China, North Vietnam and the communist guerrilla fighters in South Vietnam, the Viet Cong.

When hundreds of victorious Khmer Rouge revolutionaries marched into Phnom Penh in April 1975 to overthrow the Khmer Republic and take control, many people cheered. But only at first. Almost immediately, the Khmer Rouge forces set to work, emptying every school, hospital, workplace and home in the city at gunpoint. They marched the former inhabitants out into the countryside to work on collectivised farms. Anyone who was too weak or sick to work was killed, as were many who admitted to having worked for the defeated Khmer Republic.

Pol Pot's vision of a self-sustaining agricultural utopia, 'purified' of the corrupt influence of the west, turned out to be a slave empire. The Khmer Rouge burned money and destroyed modern technology. They destroyed all prior tradition and culture in Cambodia, and reset the calendars to Year Zero.

By August 1975, the innocuous high school in Tuol Sleng was a house of horrors. At first, it was a prison and interrogation centre for members of the former Lon Nol regime. But soon Tuol Sleng, or S-21 as it was also known, was repurposed as a secret prison, where anyone who voiced opposition to the regime was sent and subjected to slavery, starvation, torture, and eventually death. Among those detained were politicians, academics, doctors, teachers, engineers, artists, students, foreigners and monks. Around two thirds of those killed at Tuol Sleng were Khmer Rouge cadres themselves, so obsessed were the Khmer Rouge with hunting out 'the enemy within'. Over its four years of operation, Tuol Sleng saw an estimated 14,000 people pass through its gates. Only *seven* are known to have survived.

Throughout their internment, these men, women and children were subjected to extreme torture—too appalling to detail here. Most people confessed to all kinds of nonsense to escape the torture, and then found themselves transported to the Killing Fields at Choeung Ek to be executed.

Tuol Sleng was one of a chain of 200 such centres across Cambodia where enemies of the Khmer Rouge were taken to be interrogated and killed.

The overall number of people who died during the reign of the Khmer Rouge is hard to pin down, as so many also died from slave labour, disease and starvation. The number tends to hover around 2.2 million, in a country that had, at the time, a population of roughly 7.3 million.

~

Tuol Sleng, the Phnom Penh high school turned torture prison, is now a monument to the madness of that time—a permanent reminder of just how far human beings can go.

To say that visiting Tuol Sleng was a sobering experience is putting it mildly. The twelve of us drifted through the buildings together, united in speechless horror. It's impossible to walk through the converted classrooms with their empty metal torture beds and bloodstained floors without imagining the terror that the inmates must have felt at the time.

Then we came upon a display of black-and-white photographs of the prisoners who passed through the gates. That was my undoing. The mug shots of thousands of prisoners, with their haunting stares, seemed horribly familiar. The Khmer Rouge's meticulous record-keeping reminded me of the extensive documentation procedures of the Nazis. It took me back to those Thursday afternoons when I'd pull out Nagy's old shoebox of photos of her friends and family who had died in the Holocaust and make her tell me the story behind each of them. In my mind, I could almost smell the putrid stench of the overcrowded train as Nagy, her Mum and her little sister Eve were shunted towards Auschwitz . . .

I realised with a shock that the tour had moved on without me and I was standing alone in front of the photos. I suddenly felt a bit sick. I found the first exit and stood dully in the shade by the side of the building. I didn't want to see any more.

I've been back to Tuol Sleng once since that first trip. On neither occasion did I make it through the whole museum.

~

In a far more subdued mood, we travelled on from the prison into the countryside outside town, to the Killing Fields at Choeung Ek.

I wasn't particularly looking forward to the next stop. I felt I'd already seen enough. But I wanted to stick with the group, so I gritted my teeth and prepared for the worst.

But, to my surprise, the grounds at Choeung Ek at first seemed nowhere near as confronting as I'd feared. It was a peaceful grassy spot in the countryside. The grass was green and covered by shady trees. The bucolic air began to dissipate, however, when we came upon the main focus of the memorial: a large mausoleum filled with thousands of excavated skulls from the surrounding mass graves.

Grim reality set in when we began the tour through the grounds behind the memorial. 'Killing Fields' is an appropriate label for this place. The remnants of mass graves formed deep sunken depressions in the earth across the fields, with narrow dirt paths weaving around them. Of the 129 mass graves, only 86 had been exhumed. Signs beside the graves matter-of-factly proclaimed the ghastly truth about what lay below.

MASS GRAVE OF 450 VICTIMS.

MASS GRAVE OF MORE THAN 100 VICTIMS, CHILDREN AND WOMEN, WHOSE MAJORITY WERE NAKED.

MASS GRAVE OF 166 VICTIMS WITHOUT HEADS.

One chilling sign read: KILLING TREE AGAINST WHICH EXECU-TIONERS BEAT CHILDREN.

As the Khmer Rouge gained power and reach across Cambodia, hundreds of thousands of people from all over Cambodia were taken out to killing fields around the country and executed. At first, these were people suspected of colluding with the west and being 'against' the new communist regime. So city dwellers, the middle-class and educated people were immediately suspect. But as the Khmer Rouge's utopian vision failed and food became scarce, practically anyone could find themselves being accused of anything and sent to the killing fields. Whole families, including children, were killed so they couldn't grow up to spread their middle-class poison, or seek revenge for the deaths of their fathers . . . or for no clear reason at all.

On 25 December 1978, Cambodia's traditional enemy, the Vietnamese, invaded Cambodia supported by hundreds of Khmer Rouge defectors and drove the Khmer Rouge from power. In 1979, Vietnam put a puppet government in place and though the Cambodians initially saw them as liberators, their views changed when the oppressive nature of the occupation unfolded. It is said that the Vietnamese denied the Cambodians food sent by aid organisa-tions and instead used it to feed their own troops. This contributed to a widespread famine in Cambodia, which led to approximately 650,000 deaths in the year following the fall of the Khmer Rouge.

It then took years before the rest of the world offered a helping hand, and many more before the country began to recover.

Even today, Cambodia is one of the poorest countries in Asia, and the poorest citizens still go hungry.

~

Our Khmer tour guide said: 'After rainy season we see many more bone come out. Look, you will see so much bone in the ground. We never can pick it all up!'

We all looked down. Until that moment, none of us had noticed all the human bones scattered through the dirt beneath our feet. My nausea returned—I told myself the heat was getting to me. I went and sat by the gate and waited for the rest of the tour to finish.

While we should all be made aware of the horrors of war and take some strong lessons from it, the experience at both the Tuol Sleng Museum and Killing Fields had been extremely intense and felt too close to home for me. I could only stomach so much at one time. Especially when I considered that the holocaust that had wiped out nearly a quarter of the population had happened only three decades earlier. In sociological terms, it's barely the blink of an eye.

That visit to Tuol Sleng and the Killing Fields changed something inside me quite profoundly. On the tuktuk ride home, looking at the early evening activity on the streets, I couldn't see any sign of the bitterness or darkness I might have expected from those who had undergone such horrific trauma so recently. All I noticed was the kindness and cheerfulness of the Khmer people around me, and I felt an enormous respect and admiration for them. With their warmth and contagious smiles, they seemed to embody the spirit of Nagy.

~

The next day, we travelled for seven hours to Siem Reap, home to the famous Angkor Wat temples. I was still recovering from the awful things we'd seen the day before. Everywhere I looked, I couldn't help imagining the horrors of the bombings and the Khmer Rouge years. The crumbling huts, the roaming gangs of kids, the desolate rice fields . . . these sights outside the window of the bus didn't seem to be just about poverty now—they seemed post-apocalyptic.

The following morning I overslept and stumbled, blinking and fuzzy-headed, out of my hotel room. I met Alicia, in a similar state, in the hallway.

'Where is everyone?' Alicia croaked.

I looked at my watch. It was 9.30 am. 'I think we've missed the six o'clock bus to Angkor Wat,' I said.

The only thing to do was catch a tuktuk out to Angkor Wat on our own.

As it turned out, our laziness was rewarded. Even though we had to put up with the midday heat, and missed some of the temples on our itinerary, we had avoided the hordes of other tourists who flock to the temples in the cooler hours of the day. We had the temples virtually all to ourselves!

Angkor Wat is a source of great pride for the Khmer people. A thousand years ago, it was a gigantic, thriving city linked with canals—the Venice of South-East Asia. Today only the incredible stone temples that once studded the city remain. We wandered through Ta Prohm, a temple that has largely been reclaimed by the jungle, and marvelled at the enormous, muscular tree roots that snake their way through the exquisitely carved stone walls.

There were no walkways or barricades in 2005, so we explored the enchanting temple like a pair of shorter, sweatier Lara Crofts. We attempted to parkour our way over the ancient rubble and through the temple walls until the heat caught up with us and we decided we missed our friends—and air-conditioning! There is no doubt whatsoever that Angkor Wat has earned its place as one of the Seven Wonders of the World. It is truly, magnificently awe-inspiring.

~

That afternoon we drove out of Siem Reap to visit a small NGO called the Akira (or Aki Ra) Landmine Museum. The museum, established by Akira, an ex-child soldier, was really just a wooden shack, displaying literally thousands of deactivated landmines and unexploded ordnances (UXOs). Most of the bombs had the letters *USA* printed on them.

A red-headed English volunteer named Ethan gave us a very casual tour through the shack. He told us the names of all the different types of landmines and explained their different purposes. It was a little unsettling how haphazardly the landmines had been arranged for display. Ethan assured us they were all safe and, to demonstrate, he picked up three anti-personnel mines and juggled them for about three seconds before reassuringly dropping the lot. One rolled and bumped into my foot. I bent to pick it up but a young boy on crutches appeared out of nowhere and snatched it up.

'Hey! Thanks!' I said, impressed by his dexterity. Then I added, in slow, unintentionally patronising English: 'My name is Tara. What is your name?'

The boy flashed me a confident smile and replied in fast, fluent English: 'You're welcome! My name is Vanna.' He was an athletically built boy with a gentle face, who looked about fourteen years old.

'Vanna, why don't you tell everyone about yourself and the other kids who live here at the museum?' Ethan suggested.

'Me and twenty more girls and boys are living here with Akira,' the boy said, beaming. 'Akira, he is like our father. He care for us and we can study here and have good life. All the girls and boys here, they are like my brother and sister. They also have problem with the mine.'

He hiked up his trouser leg to show off his prosthesis. It was confronting to see that prosthesis on such a young kid's leg.

'When I was young boy I work in the field and I step on the mine,' he said in a matter-of-fact tone, smiling his bright smile again. 'Akira, he is good man. He have hard life too but his wish is to help many Khmer children.'

Later, Ethan filled us in on more of Akira's story. He did indeed have a hard life.

'Akira was born in the jungle and was basically brought up by the Khmer Rouge,' Ethan explained. 'They killed his parents and, as soon as he was big enough, he became a soldier. When the Vietnamese invaded, he was taken into the custody of Vietnamese soldiers, and eventually ended up in the Kampuchean People's Revolutionary Armed Forces under the new government. He planted thousands of landmines himself—because that's what they made him do. He never had a family, or an education, or a childhood. All the poor bugger knew was war and fighting and doing what he was told to stay alive. Can you imagine what that does to a kid's head? But when he left the army, he started working as a de-miner for the UN. After he left the UN, he went back to the villages where he'd planted the mines and dug them up all by himself, defusing them with handmade tools. He still spends hours out in the fields on his own, working to clear Cambodia of landmines. He cleared all the landmines you see here. And he started this NGO to help these kids.'

I was impressed. It was such an incredible story—an amazing way to turn around a life filled with tragedy and misfortune.

Impulsively, I asked Ethan, 'How did *you* get involved with the museum?'

'I just wandered in and asked if I could help,' Ethan said. 'They're always looking for volunteers here to help with the tours and teach the kids English and such.' He then added perceptively, 'Why, you thinking of volunteering?'

The three-week Intrepid tour was due to wrap up in Bangkok in two more days. I'd budgeted for eight weeks away, and it suddenly seemed frivolous, ridiculous, to go on with my holiday, to sit on a beach and forget everything I'd seen and heard in Cambodia.

'Well,' I said, 'I've got a few weeks up my sleeve, and, well, yeah—I am!'

3

Back in Bangkok, the members of the Intrepid group exchanged sad goodbyes. This was the end of the holiday for most and they were heading back home. Not me though. As far as I was concerned, my trip was just about to get exciting! I was impatient to get back to Cambodia.

I organised a one-month Cambodian visa starting on the first of June, and jumped on the next bus to Poipet, the Thai–Cambodian border crossing.

I decided I'd stop for a day or two in a province called Battambang, located in north-west Cambodia, between Siem Reap and the Thai border.

Battambang, I was told, was the 'real' Cambodia, without the flocks of expats and tourists. The province's riverside capital, also called Battambang (pronounced Bat-tam-bong and affectionately known as 'the Bong'), is the second largest city in Cambodia, and was formerly a Khmer Rouge stronghold. In Cambodia, the city is renowned for its lovely French Colonial architecture and its rich cultural history. It has produced some of Cambodia's greatest singers, actors and painters.

The bus trip from Bangkok to Battambang was a bit 'authentic' (meaning 'bloody hard going'). So the first time I laid eyes on Battambang, I was not at my best—but neither was Battambang.

This was a particularly hot, dry season, and the flat plains on the outskirts of the city were scorched and barren. The roadside was dotted with scrawny dogs that looked a little like dingoes, dilapidated buildings and skinny Brahman cows all covered in thick layers of red dust from passing traffic.

The outskirts thickened into shop-lined streets, but I was somewhat surprised when the bus screeched to a halt beside an old tin shed that turned out to be Battambang's bus station. This was the centre of Battambang city? I now understood what was meant by the 'real' Cambodia. I wasn't expecting skyscrapers, but Battambang was hardly a city. It was just a dusty little country town, practically rolling with tumbleweeds.

A tuktuk driver awaiting business grabbed my bag and rushed for his vehicle. I followed, saying, 'Teo Hotel, Teo Hotel,' hoping I was pronouncing it correctly. He nodded, not breaking his stride.

It was hot. *Really* hot. As I stepped into the tuktuk, with beads of sweat rolling into my eyes, I suddenly felt overwhelmed with exhaustion.

The tuktuk carried me to the Teo Hotel, and I dragged my bag up to a tiny, windowless room, had a cold shower and fell straight into a deep sleep.

~

Lonely Planet told me that Battambang 'city' was walkable, so the next morning I decided to brave the heat and spend the day exploring at a slow, easy pace.

Old yolk-coloured buildings with cute blue shutters lined the streets. They were dilapidated but beautiful. I imagined how grand the quiet, shady boulevards must have looked long ago.

It felt good to observe real Cambodian life—not the show put on for tourists. I passed a vacant lot where a group of young boys were playing a spirited game of volleyball. About fifty saffron-robed monks filed past them, stopping at a local eatery to receive alms. A dainty pony trotted down the street hauling a heavy load of coal.

Battambang was a strangely antique world—quaint and other-worldly. After the crazy hustle and bustle of Phnom Penh, Siem Reap and Bangkok, I revelled in its quiet, laidback atmosphere. But Cambodia's poverty seemed much more apparent here, or perhaps just less hidden from tourists' eyes. There were, of course, lots of kids begging from tourists in Siem Reap and Phnom Penh, but here I saw groups of little kids working, dragging big plastic bags around, shoving discarded cans and bottles into them. Older women, dressed in rags, pedalled through the hot streets with heavy loads of junk strapped to their bicycles.

When the sun started to throw red-gold light across the town, I stopped at one of the slightly tattered stalls along Stung Sangker River to buy a cold mango shake.

A tired-looking girl about my own age served me. She was carrying a newborn baby. Her hair, like mine, was long, dark and tied back in a ponytail. I noticed that her face was gaunt and sunken, and her teeth were stained brown.

This is me, I thought guiltily, *in another life.*

My privileged childhood flew into sharp focus. While I was at school, riding horses and scoffing smoked salmon bagels, what was she doing?

The fruit shake cost less than fifty cents but, impulsively, I handed her $5 and gestured for her to keep the change.

Her expression switched from confusion to gratitude. She pressed her palms together and thanked me profusely. I felt a little uncomfortable. Did $5 really mean so much to her? I felt suddenly ashamed of the wealth I had done nothing to deserve. I was just born in a different country . . . that was all.

When I got back to my hotel, a driver who'd been lying in his tuktuk by the gates, waiting for business, jumped out to greet me.

'Hello, miss. Oh, you come back so late! Cambodia real dangerous in night-time! You must be so careful! Next time you call me, okay? I can come get you!'

He handed me a small piece of torn paper. His number was scribbled in pencil with *Mr Chan TUK TUK* written underneath.

'Thanks, maybe tomorrow,' I said, keen to make my escape into the hotel. Tuktuk drivers were always offering up tours in Cambodia—I'd become quite used to saying 'No thanks, not right now, maybe later.'

But Mr Chan was not to be brushed off so easily. 'Oh, yes. Sure! Tomorrow I wait you! Mr Chan! My name Chan. I wait you!' His face was now alight with hope, his smile stretching from ear to ear. I warmed to him in that moment. It was clear he badly needed the work.

'Okay!' I said, smiling. 'See you tomorrow then, Mr Chan.'

I turned into the gates when he called out again 'Sorry! Miss! What your name?'

'Tara,' I called back, making an effort to roll the r.

'Oh! Tara. You look same Cambodia people and your name is Khmer name, too! It name of special star!'

I laughed and made my way into the hotel.

~

I slept late the next morning and forgot all about meeting Chan. But, sure enough, when I finally made it out of the hotel gates, there he was, waiting patiently.

'Tara!' he called out, waving to me with that big warm grin of his.

He handed me a very carefully written note outlining his plans for our tour. It read something like: *Bamboo Train. Old temple. Stop for eat lunch. Kamping Poi Dam, bat cave.*

'Sounds great! Let's go!' I said, jumping into the tuktuk.

'Okay!' Chan cheered, clapping his hands together. 'We go!'

And with a splutter of the engine, we were off on our tour of Battambang's attractions.

We stopped first at a roundabout on the way out of town to pay our respects to Battambang's local deity—a huge black statue of a giant king brandishing a staff.

'Battambang mean "lost stick",' Chan called over his shoulder as we pulled up beside the frankly completely-fucking-terrifying-looking statue. Chan explained that a cowherd found a magic staff and used it to overthrow the king. The cowherd-king's skin turned black and he grew to be a giant. But then he lost his staff in battle with the old king. The victorious king made him serve as the bodyguard and protector of Battambang.

People were lighting incense and praying at the statue's feet. 'Khmer people here all pray to him to pass exams and win lottery!' Chan grinned and kicked the tuktuk's moto back to life.

We rattled out through dusty roads to the countryside, stopping in a small village of little houses on stilts to visit Battambang's famous 'bamboo train'. The 'train' was basically a square bamboo platform with a two-stroke engine attached that travelled on a single set of rickety old railway tracks. The bamboo train is a functioning mode of transport used by locals, but even though there weren't many tourists visiting Battambang in 2005, it was still one of the city's main attractions.

I climbed on top of the bamboo platform for a 'magic bamboo carpet' ride across fields and jungles. Whenever another bamboo train came up the track from the opposite direction, the driver of the least-laden vehicle (usually ours) dismantled the bamboo platform, engine and wheels and pulled it off the track, so the other vehicle could pass. Then he'd put it all back together again and continue on. It was kind of ingenious.

After that little adventure, Chan and I visited pretty pagodas, a pre-Angkor Wat-era temple called Banan at the top of an incredibly steep mountain, and a half-finished statue of the Buddha that juts out of a mountain beside a cave that was filled with millions of bats.

It was all quite fun, but mostly I just liked hanging out with Chan and hearing about everyday life in Battambang. At lunchtime, he took me to eat at a local restaurant. It was basically just a cluster of small bamboo huts with thatched roofs set in a big paddock, with some rather strange statues of things like swans, pineapples and zebras scattered around the place. We entered one of the huts and lounged on the hammocks strung up on either side. A young waitress came over and Chan ordered.

I couldn't read the menu but politely reminded Chan that I was vegetarian. He waved his hand and said: 'Don't worry, you will love this food so much! Real Khmer food!'

Predictably, both dishes that arrived had meat in them. One was stir-fried chicken with vegetables and the other, a bean dish with raw beef. I picked around the chicken at the vegies doused in loads of soy sauce and, as tactfully as I could, steered the conversation away from my lack of interest in lunch.

'Chan, I will stay in Battambang for two more days,' I said. 'What do you think I can do here?'

'Maybe I can take you to see some other village in Battambang?'

'Okay, great! And I would like to do something small to help some of the poor children I've seen here. Is that possible?'

'Oh! You are so kind girl! Yes, I take you one or two hour from Battambang. We can go to market to buy some book and school clothes for the children who are the poorest in the village. It not cost much money. I can also take you to visit some children in orphanage. They real need help too!'

'Okay, yeah, that sounds like a good plan, Chan.' I was impressed by his enthusiasm to help people poorer than he was. And not even a whole lot poorer, as I later discovered.

~

The next morning we set off early for the market and filled several garbage bags with second-hand clothes, school uniforms, schoolbooks and pens. Chan did all the haggling, so the whole lot cost just a few dollars.

'We must take moto to the village because it is dancing road!' Chan said with a high-pitched chuckle. 'Very bumpy. No good for tuktuk.'

We piled the bags onto Chan's bike: some in front of him, and the rest stacked high behind him, leaving the tiniest little space for me. I spent the next hour with my arse hanging off the back of the bike, my face mashed awkwardly against the hot, black garbage bags, which I had to embrace so I could cling by my fingertips to the sides of Chan's shirt.

We slalomed around the bends and potholes of that dusty red road with the burning sun beating down on us. When we finally pulled up in a tiny rural village, I wasn't a pretty sight, and getting myself unstuck from that precarious position on the back of the bike wasn't easy.

I tried to slide off the back of the moto without losing the contents of the bags. In doing so, I accidentally slid off the wrong side and got a nasty burn on my leg from the exhaust pipe. The red dust had stuck to my sweaty skin and my arse was totally numb. I'm not sure if you've ever had the privilege of experiencing a completely dead bum, but let me just say it makes walking rather difficult. To top it off, I realised that somewhere along the way my Dolce & Gabbana sunglasses must have fallen off my head.

I was dangerously close to falling down in a heap on the dirt road and having an I-feel-sorry-for-my-dirty-numb-burnt-sunnyless-self meltdown. But the sound of about thirty chattering village kids heading our way snapped me out of it.

Most of them weren't wearing shoes, many wore only shorts and some little ones weren't wearing any clothes at all. Their teeth were brown and their hair was ratty, but my god, there was so much joy in their little faces.

There was a lot of pointing and giggling.

'They excited to meet a foreigner!' Chan told me, while trying to dab my weeping burn with a minty smelling white paste.

'Is that toothpaste?!' I exclaimed, pulling my leg away. 'Please, Chan, I'm fine,' I said. 'Let's just hand out these clothes.'

'Toothpaste is very help the burn,' he explained. 'But maybe no good for foreigner,' he shrugged. 'We go to doctor when we back in Battambang. Now time to make the kids so happy!'

Dozens of little faces beamed up at me as we opened up the garbage bags and started handing out the contents. The kids went bug crazy—it was like I was Oprah, and I'd just announced that they'd all won a free car or something. They clapped and cheered and jumped up and down. More and more kids came running, and some mothers came too, reminding the kids to say 'thank you' and pushing the tiniest kids' hands together in the traditional Khmer gesture of thanks. When the bags were empty, I watched the kids trying on the clothes and comparing the books and pens as if it was Christmas morning.

A couple of the kids came and held my hand and looked up at me with bright eyes and sweet, shy smiles.

Their warmth and openness was like nothing I had ever encountered in Australia. The experience reconfigured my whole mental map of the world.

In that moment, all the discomforts and annoyances that had bothered me just minutes earlier were gone. All that remained was a humbling, spine-tingling sense that I had just glimpsed what is truly important in life.

It felt wonderful. It felt real. It felt significant. And it had been so easy to do so much.

Or so I thought . . .

~

Without the overstuffed garbage bags the trip home was a *lot* more pleasant. But I couldn't help bombarding Chan with questions about his ideas on poverty, the war, the government, corruption, the NGOs he'd worked for, and the future for Cambodia. He seemed delighted to answer all my questions, and I was impressed by how open all his responses were—all while navigating the incredibly dodgy road.

Chan had never attended a day of school in his life and spent most of his childhood in a refugee camp. Many Cambodians lived in refugee camps to escape the ongoing fighting and the famine that continued after the fall of the Khmer Rouge. In fact, for a long time, the largest settlement of Cambodians outside Phnom Penh was a refugee camp on the Thai border.

Despite the rough start, Chan kept his family together through street smarts and a strong work ethic. Most of his English education had come from practising on the foreigners he ferried around Battambang.

It had been a life-changing day for me. I was tired but still glowing with a deep sense of satisfaction. I had a lot to digest, a lot to think about.

~

Early the next morning we made the same trip to the market to buy things for the orphanages Chan had arranged for us to visit. This time we filled three garbage bags with clothes, books and pens. And this time we were travelling in comfort—the tuktuk felt like luxury after hours perched on the back of Chan's old moto!

The first orphanage, which was on the outskirts of town, struck me as a rough place for kids to live. The buildings were dilapidated and dirty, and the grounds dry and dusty.

But the kids seemed incredibly happy. They came bounding out of the building like excited puppies to greet us, their eyes bright with curiosity. They crowded around me while Chan and I opened the garbage bags and distributed the goods, accepting them with a polite *sampeah* and a big beaming smile.

Soon they were clinging to my hands and arms like I was a long-lost relative. One of the little girls tried to engage me in a giggly game of rock–paper–scissors. They really were very sweet. I found it quite remarkable to be treated with such affection at our first-ever encounter.

After I'd spent a few minutes with the kids, Chan introduced me to a thin, bookish-looking man who was the orphanage director.

The man thanked me for the gifts in broken English and then lapsed into silence. I suddenly became aware that there had been no staff around when we arrived and so we had not asked permission before handing out the clothes and books. Was that a faux pas? I wasn't sure.

I was suddenly very uncomfortable standing there, unable to make conversation, surrounded by kids and staff who stared at me like I was a big green Martian.

'I think maybe they want small donation from you,' Chan whispered to me.

'Oh . . .' I said, feeling very awkward. I whispered: 'Chan, I just spent my day's budget on the stuff we got at the markets.'

'Oh, don't worry, don't worry,' he said, but I was flustered by now and pushed a US$20 note into his hand. Chan presented the $20 to the director with two outstretched hands. The staff and kids pressed their hands to their foreheads and sang what I assumed was the standard thankyou response.

I felt rather embarrassed. I wished I'd had more money to give them. From the state of the place, it was clear they needed cash—of course they needed it. It was an orphanage.

And now that I'd given them all that I could, hanging around any longer felt pointless. I turned to Chan. 'So,' I said brightly—too brightly. 'Should we get going then?'

As we walked back to the tuktuk, Chan made a call to the next orphanage to let them know we'd be arriving a little early.

'Chan, I don't have any more money to give to the next two orphanages,' I told him. 'Is that a problem?'

'No problem, no problem! I make clear when we arrive. Clothes and book is enough! No problem!' he assured me.

'Okay . . .' I replied doubtfully, not sure how this could possibly be the truth.

The next orphanage was bigger, and seemed a bit better off. The children were waiting in a line at the gate, as if the Queen of England was about to arrive. A girl of about twelve greeted me, put a paper necklace around my neck and took my hand.

The director was a jovial middle-aged man. 'So nice to meet you,' he said. 'Ah! You bring gift for the children! Do you want to give them now?'

'Oh, yes, okay,' I said, feeling rather awkward. The books and clothes I'd brought felt like rather a paltry response to the warm reception they were giving me. I doled out the books to the kids. They squealed and jumped up and down in excitement as they received them. Some of them squeezed my hand in gratitude.

'I wish I could give more!' I said to the director.

'Oh, you are a very kind lady,' he said, nodding. 'We thankful for all the donation! Now the children will show you around.'

I let the cluster of kids lead me around the compound. They were incredibly charming and intelligent, and spoke a little more English than at the first orphanage.

They showed me their open-air classroom—a fairly empty room with a few wooden desks and a blackboard—then we moved on to a larger room with rows and rows of beds. A far cry from my childhood bedroom, filled with stuffed toys, books and colourful artefacts from our family holidays. There was rubbish everywhere in the big dormitory and I could smell the toilets over the other side of the room.

Next they led me to a pigpen, where they were raising two big sows and some very cute piglets. I stopped to scratch the piglets' noses. They closed their eyes and made soft little grunting noises, and pushed each other aside for a turn.

I started to feel a bit sad—for the pigs and for the kids. I didn't imagine that any of them had a very promising future.

I was feeling more than a bit emotional by the time we got back to the orphanage gate. I took a deep breath and swallowed the lump in my throat.

'You want to take some photos with the children?' the director asked me. 'You can show your family and friends when you get home.'

Damn. 'I didn't bring my camera,' I said apologetically, feeling like I'd failed again.

'That okay!' the director said. 'Thank you for your kind gift. Come back again soon.'

Sitting in the tuktuk on the way to the next orphanage, the wheels in my mind turned over, trying to process why I was feeling so uncomfortable. After all, I was 'doing my bit', giving as much as I could honestly afford.

Slowly, I began to see the problem. If I didn't make a decent-sized donation to these orphanages—which I didn't have the money to do— then this whole day was just an empty exercise in self-gratification. This was just me buying a few books and pens so I could feel like a good person . . . It was a token gesture—especially when I hadn't even thought to find out if books, pens and clothes were what the orphanages actually needed.

I was feeling pretty disheartened by the time we pulled up outside the third and last orphanage on our list.

The compound of Sprouting Knowledge Orphans (SKO) was surrounded by a tall fence with a big, dark wooden gate chained up with a padlock. Through the cracks I could see only two little wooden shacks. The rest of the compound was barren and dusty and eerily quiet. It didn't look like children lived there at all.

Chan beeped his horn a few times and finally a tall, lanky, young Khmer man came to open the gate for us. About twenty or so kids trailed behind him. I was struck by how solemn and listless they all seemed compared to the bouncy, happy kids at the other two orphanages.

They were all very thin, and some of them seemed to be suffering from some sort of skin infection that covered their limbs and faces. The young man introduced himself as a member of staff. 'My name is Reaksmey,' he told me. Then he immediately launched into a long rave in Khmer.

Chan translated: 'He say they have big problems to get enough money. Not enough food for the children for long time now. They eating scrap food left over from monastery down there.' He gestured down the road. 'One girl has HIV . . . she takes tablets from hospital, but she gets sick a lot, but no medicine, because not enough money. No money for doctor for any of these kids . . .'

Reaksmey, trailed by the flock of kids, showed me their dormitory, which was about the size of my bedroom at home in Sydney. The kids showed me how they slept—more than twenty of them lined up like sardines on the dirty tiled floor. No mattresses, no blankets, not even any mosquito nets—here, where mosquitoes carried horrible diseases like dengue fever and malaria.

One of the older girls, a pretty teenager with a thick braid down her back, dunked a metal cup into a big old urn, thick with wriggling mosquito larvae, and offered it to me. 'Uh, no thank you,' I said as politely as I could. She drank the water herself.

I wanted very badly to get away from this place. It was all too desperate for words. To speed things up, I started robotically handing out the clothes and books from the remaining bag. The kids smiled as they accepted them, but seeing smiles on their solemn little faces didn't give me any comfort at all. I was trying to hold back tears—and not quite succeeding.

Reaksmey talked to Chan in Khmer, his tone urgent. I looked at Chan, my eyes begging to leave. Chan said: 'He's asking if you will stay to volunteer, Tara,' he said. 'He say the children real need the help. You could teaching some English and help with some writing to get the funding.'

The sweat on my back turned to ice. I was way out of my depth now. Cruising around on Chan's moto handing out treats to excited kids now seemed ridiculous. These kids had real problems, and needed real help. There was a girl here with HIV. I'd never even met a person with HIV before, least of all one who couldn't even afford treatment. I felt totally overwhelmed, and I felt guilty for feeling that way.

I started to stammer, brushing a rogue tear away. 'Oh, Chan . . . I can't. I want to. I really want to. But I can't. Tell him I'm sorry.' I blinked at the tiles as Chan translated. I knew I was too young and inexperienced to deal with all this. It was too big—far too big—for me. The three of us stood motionless for a long moment while the translation happened.

Reaksmey made some understanding hums—it was clearly the response he expected. And something about this response just did me in. My mouth opened impulsively.

'When I go home I will help to raise some money for the children,' I blurted.

Even as I made this promise, I had no idea how I could keep it. Chan translated again. Reaksmey nodded and attempted a smile, but I saw the scepticism and disappointment on his face.

The look on Reaksmey's face made me all the more determined to keep my word. I looked him in the eye and said firmly, 'Please can I have the contact details of the director of SKO? I will contact you again from Australia.'

Chan translated again and Reaksmey's eyes brightened. He bowed, palms pressed together, and then scuttled back to the shack to scribble an email address on a scrap of paper.

I waved goodbye to the kids, who were all still standing quietly behind Reaksmey. They waved back.

As we pulled out of the orphanage gates in the tuktuk, I asked: 'Why is SKO so poor, Chan?'

'I not sure also,' he replied.

I knew corruption was a problem in Cambodia, so I asked: 'Do you think there is corruption at SKO?'

'Can be,' he said. 'Yes, maybe I think you can be right.'

'But, the kids, they shouldn't have to live like that,' I said, unable to stem the flow of tears any longer.

'Yes, they real need the help,' he agreed. 'But now you must stop to think about this. Make you too sad. Tonight you come to eat rice with my family for your last night in Battambang. My wife, she cook very nice vegetari food for you!'

~

And so I got to meet Chan's beautiful, soft-spoken wife, Mina, and his three gorgeous children—ten-year-old son Ponlok and daughters eight-year-old Bopha and three-year-old Chea. They seemed like the perfect family for a nice man like Chan and I took to them all immediately.

Their home, set on a tiny block of land in a crowded Battambang 'suburb', was a simple, one-roomed structure with a dirt floor. It was humble, but clean and comfortable.

Mina made me feel very welcome as she bustled around preparing food and laying it out on a straw mat in the middle of the floor. She smiled and gestured for me to sit. 'In my country, we like to sit on the floor to eat food,' Chan told me. 'Even the king sits on the floor!'

Mina was an amazing cook. It was a meal fit for a (vegetarian) queen.

There were bowls of morning glory fried with chilli, tom yam soup with fresh mushrooms picked from her own small garden, fried tofu with bean sprouts, and green mangoes sprinkled with salt, sugar, chilli and my all-time favourite Asian condiment: delicious, delicious MSG. I love MSG—umami is the fifth (and the best!) taste. When restaurant menus boast *No MSG!* I go: 'Dammit! I love that stuff.'

Mina sat next to me, with her legs tucked politely to one side in the traditional Khmer way and her hand resting on my knee. Her warm smile crinkled the corners of her eyes as she encouraged me to keep eating until I could barely sit upright.

When the dinner plates were cleared, I retired to a hammock that was strung up between the two poles that supported the little house. The kids then set about impressing me with endearing dance routines they had choreographed themselves, an entertaining combination of hip-hop and line dancing. Chan, Mina and I laughed and clapped all through their performances.

Despite their obvious poverty, this family seemed to be a shining example of the resilience I was learning to associate with Khmer people. They looked for ways to be happy instead of reasons to be sad. It was clear to me that these kids were the product of good parenting. They were intelligent, polite, inquisitive and playful. Their English was pretty good, too.

When it was time for them to go to bed, I said a heartfelt goodbye to the family. Chan drove me on the moto through the dark streets of Battambang back to the Teo Hotel. At night, Battambang was like a ghost town. All the shops were shut up with big steel grates pulled across the front and there was almost no one in sight.

'See you in the morning, *P'oun srey*,' he said.

'Hey?'

Chan smiled. 'It mean "little sister". You are like my family now. You can call me *Bong*. It mean "older brother".'

'Goodnight, *Bong*. Thank you for a wonderful night. I like your family very much.'

He waited until I was safely inside the gates of the hotel then I heard the splutter of his motorbike engine starting up and moving off down the road.

I took a deep breath of the warm night air. Visiting Chan's family had somehow revived me. I made up my mind that I would try to help his family somehow, too, after I got back to Australia.

~

The next morning, bright and early, Chan picked me up and drove me to the bus stop by the Stung Sangker River. Just as I was stepping onto the bus he handed me a note in the formal Khmer style, with both hands outstretched and a little bow of the head.

It was similar to the note he had given me when we first met, which already felt like a lifetime ago.

It read:

> To P'oun Srey Tara,
> Thank you for come visit my country. It is my happiness to know you. I keep you in my good friend for a long life. I never forget, I keep in my mind. I hope you come back to Cambodia again.
> Love,
> Bong Chan

~

After the confronting and heart-rending adventure I'd had in Battambang, it was a relief to head back to Siem Reap and the relative familiarity of the Landmine Museum.

When I pulled up in my tuktuk I was met with an eerie sight. There was a young boy standing at the gates, dressed as a Khmer Rouge soldier in green military fatigues with the traditional red-checked scarf wrapped around his head. I was startled—had Cambodia jumped back in time thirty years while I wasn't looking?

'Hello, Tara!'

It was Vanna!

'Vanna, why on earth are you dressed like that?'

'For the tourists! I'm happy to see you again! You come to volunteer like you say? Let me help you.'

He took my bag and led me inside.

'Is Ethan still here?' I asked, as Vanna led me towards a cluster of simple Khmer structures.

'No, he go home. But Jilly is here now.'

Vanna was incredibly agile despite his prosthesis. He led me to the side of the tin shed that housed the museum, and carried my bags up a tall ladder to a tiny tree house. It was maybe four square metres, and its walls fell about a metre short of an old tin roof, but it had a nice view, looking down into the museum compound from the treetops.

There was already a bag and a makeshift bed set up in the tiny space. Vanna put my bags down beside them.

'Is Jilly sleeping here too?' I asked, feeling a little awkward about sharing such a small space with a complete stranger.

'Yes,' Vanna said. 'We can fit two volunteers here, no problem.'

Julia (or Jilly as the kids called her) turned out to be a lovely Irish girl a few years older than me. She had arrived a week earlier and, like me, she was on a tight budget. But, in return for volunteering, we were provided basic accommodation and food.

Akira, his wife Hort and the twenty kids lived simply, of course, so for the next three weeks Julia and I slept in the tree house with no electricity, showered out of a bucket and ate cucumber stew with rice three times a day.

There were no creature comforts in sight, but I barely noticed because life at Akira's was really fun—possibly because I was a little enamoured of Julia.

Julia was completely at ease with Cambodia, as if she'd been living there for years. She'd sweep up her skirt and hop side-saddle onto the back of a moto, just like the locals did. She knew everyone's names and had the script for the museum tour and all the kids' clapping games down pat. She had even managed to pick up an impressive amount of basic Khmer. She was very beautiful and smart, completely capable and sweet and everyone adored her—including me.

I threw myself into the routine at the museum with gusto, partly motivated by my experience in Battambang and, if I'm being honest, partly to impress Julia. In a couple of days I had learned almost as many words as Julia, and I, too, had the clapping games and the museum tour down pat.

The tours were always the most sobering moments in my day. I often had to explain to the tourists that stepping on a landmine isn't like it is in the movies. You don't hear a click and then have time to plan a 'Houdini escape'. You just put a toe on these things and boom. You're toast.

The landmines seeded across Cambodia in three decades of war were usually designed to maim, not kill. Injuring one soldier means that two other soldiers are put out of action, because they're forced to stop and help the injured soldier. Pol Pot called the mines his 'perfect soldiers' because they never slept, and they didn't need to be fed or clothed or given toilet breaks. And, sadly, Pol Pot was just one of the many warmongers from all sides of the conflict who laid these horrors in Cambodian villages, farms, footpaths and fields. It meant that for decades to come, kids like Vanna stepped on the mines.

Today it's estimated that around 40,000 Cambodians are living with landmine-related injuries. For a long time, the economy and social development and mental health of Cambodian people was badly damaged by the landmines. But thanks to the many de-mining projects being run by the Cambodian government, de-mining NGOs, and people like Akira, Cambodia's landmine problem is slowly being resolved.

After the tours, most people were kind. Their donations covered the costs of running the museum and looking after the kids.

~

Hanging out with Julia and the kids was fast becoming the highlight of my trip. Julia and I got on famously. It wasn't long before my infatuation with her turned into a full-blown crush.

I had never really had a crush on a girl before. And, luckily for me, it turned out she quite liked me too. We embarked on one of those holiday flings that casts a rosy glow over everything. We'd go on romantic dates to Angkor Wat in the late afternoon when entry was free and all the tourists had gone. Sometimes I would take my sketchbook and try to capture the play of light on the mystical statues. Other times we'd just sit quietly together, absorbing the awe-inspiring atmosphere.

After the sun slipped below the walls of the temple, we'd jump back in the tuktuk and head into town. We'd sneak into one of the big hotels' swimming pools and go skinny-dipping, have a drink at a little expat bar, then we'd head back to the museum, slightly tipsy, before the 9 pm curfew and sleep under the stars in our little tree-house home . . .

It was all doomed, of course—she had a life in Ireland, I had a life in Australia. But a bit of doom isn't so bad when you're nineteen years old. It just makes everything even more romantic.

~

When we weren't busy with tourists, Julia and I gave the kids casual English lessons or took them into town to internet cafes to teach them computer skills. The kids at Akira's were enthusiastic students and learned astonishingly fast.

I was struck by the disparity between the kids at Akira's and at SKO. There was such a marked difference between Akira's small but thriving enterprise with all these happy-looking kids and that broken-down orphanage in Battambang.

Seeing what Akira had done was incredibly inspiring. It gave me hope that somehow I'd be able to make good on my promise to SKO. It's so easy to be overwhelmed by the problems posed by poverty. But Akira seemed to be living proof that, with a little bit of money and enough motivation, something can be done.

The Akira Landmine Museum—known these days as the Cambodian Landmine Museum—is now backed by a US charity and an Australian war veterans' group.

I still hear from Vanna and some of the other kids from time to time. They all seem to be doing well.

4

After my holiday was over, I returned to Sydney full of energy—I was *back*! The trip seemed to have been just the circuit breaker I needed to loosen the grip the eating disorder had on me. There had been no time for those starve, binge, purge cycles, so I had inadvertently established better, healthier eating habits. The negative thoughts were not gone completely, but they were quiet enough again to make me feel like I was finally ready to jump back into my life again.

I had a mental list of everything I wanted my life to look like: I would get back into martial arts, keep practising meditation, take more piano lessons, resume my fledgling career in the film industry, travel the world, learn a new language, support SKO and Chan . . . It was a long list.

I restarted piano lessons with one of Peter's old students, the musician and keyboard player Carolyn Shine. She was great—smart, funny and well-travelled, strikingly beautiful with a gorgeous boyfriend, doing a job she loved with all these exciting creative projects on the side . . . When I looked at her life I thought to myself: *That's the life I want.*

I thought about Cambodia constantly, and I couldn't stop thinking about SKO and the sad little kids who lived there. Anyone who'd listen got an earful of my stories about the landmine museum, Chan and his family, and the SKO orphanage.

I was hoping I could support SKO from Australia in much the same way that my dad supported his friends in India. But I was only just making enough to support one life. How was I supposed to make enough to help all those kids?

I picked up a few jobs working on commercials, but no matter how hard I tried, I couldn't get back my enthusiasm for the film industry. The reality of life in Sydney and working in a job that I didn't love started to pull me down again. I conceded that maybe the film industry just wasn't for me. So I set out to find another way to make money.

I decided that, if I was to help SKO, I needed to understand more about how the NGO world worked. So I volunteered for a while at Oxfam and UNICEF, hoping it would lead to something paid and permanent.

Meanwhile, to support myself, I taught horseriding for my childhood hero: my first riding instructor, Caz Stubbs.

It was great to get to know Caz all over again as an adult. When teaching people to ride, Caz would say that a rider's hands should be steady but soft, firm but giving. And that was exactly what Caz was like as a person.

In between lessons we'd talk about my recent travels.

Caz was enthralled by my stories. Soon, we were dreaming up ideas to raise funds and fulfil the promise I'd made to the SKO orphanage.

At first, I thought these were all just pipe dreams. Caz's ideas for running a fundraiser involved finding a venue, getting people to donate art for auction, finding musicians, caterers and volunteers all willing to donate their services. To me, it was like saying: 'I'll just pop off now and scale Mount Everest.' But Caz is a doer. If anyone was going to make our fundraiser happen, it was her.

It wasn't easy. Australian law governing fundraising for a charitable cause is a mire of complexity, involving registered names and great piles of paperwork. Getting it wrong could leave us open to huge fines.

After many frustrating and confusing phone calls, we decided the safest way forward would be to hire a charity consultant to set things up for us. It would cost us $2000, but we figured it was worth it to get it right the first time and steer clear of legal trouble.

The consultant recommended we register as a 'charitable trust fund'.

I was in the middle of teaching a group of horse-obsessed ten-year-olds when Caz appeared, phone to her ear. 'Tarz, quick, what do you wanna call the trust? He needs the name now so he can submit the paperwork.'

We'd been throwing around ideas for names for weeks, but nothing had stuck. All our ideas were either too corny or too vague.

'I dunno,' I said. 'How about Cambodian Children's Trust? Keep it simple?'

'Okay then, Cambodian Children's Trust it is!' Caz grinned. When she got off the phone she said: 'CCT, eh? This is the start of exciting things to come. Now let's raise some money!'

~

If I had a time machine, I'd go back now and scream: 'Nooooooo—call it something Much. More. Original!'

Actually, this is a perfect moment to stop and just make something very clear: We are *not* the Cambodian Children's *Fund*. Our name is the Cambodian Children's *Trust*. T for Trust. Got it?

Okay. We can move on.

~

About a week later, I was in the middle of a group lesson in the main arena when Caz raced up to the gate. She was beaming.

'Guess what?' she cried. 'It's sorted! My friend Maxine Hawker is on board to help us make this fundraiser happen. We'll hold it at my mate Stephen Mori's art gallery on the first of December. He's going to ask all his artists to donate a work. Max is going to sort the catering through her work. We should be able to raise heaps! We'll go and meet Max and then check out the gallery tomorrow. How cool's that? It's all happening!'

'Oh. My. God!' I stared at Caz, awestruck by her ability to make things happen.

My heart began to soar. I realised in that moment that, very soon, I'd be back in Cambodia! I had too many concerns about the transparency of SKO to just send over the money we raised. I would have to save enough cash to buy a ticket back to Cambodia and make sure that every cent donated was spent on the kids. I also had to save enough to help Chan and his family.

In that moment I decided to tighten the purse strings for a while. No more shopping. No going out. No more Bondi brunches with friends.

'Tara!'

One of my young students snapped me out of my reverie. There was a pile-up of ponies in the corner of the arena, all placidly ignoring the flapping legs of their small riders.

'Pull your right rein!' I called. 'Nope. That's your left rein. Pull the other one and keep kicking. That's it . . .'

I turned back to Caz. 'We're going to need volunteers—and musicians!' I said. And as soon as the words left my mouth, I realised I had great contacts for both. After all, my dad was a musician and my friends and family were already keen to help. 'I'll get on to organising it. Far out. I can't believe it's really happening!'

~

With the wheels now in motion, I signed up for a Teaching English as a Second Language course in the city. The qualification meant I could teach English to the kids at SKO without feeling like a total fraud. Hopefully, I could help them learn to speak English just as fluently as the kids at the Akira Landmine Museum.

Feeling motivated, I saved for the cost of my flight and managed to put away some funds for Chan, too. I remembered him telling me what a great asset cows were in Cambodia. He said that Cambodian families who owned cows were 'rich families'.

So, I decided to buy Chan a cow.

'What a brilliant idea, Tara!' I hear you say.

I know, right?

I sent him an email telling him of my plan to return and asked him how much it would cost to buy a cow for his family. I was a bit shocked to see his reply a few days later—it turned out that a full-grown cow could cost as much as US$1000. *Geez, is that more than a cow would cost in Australia?* I wondered.

Nevertheless, I trusted Chan and I was committed to the idea now. He sounded very excited about it but pointed out that if he was to keep his own cow, he'd need to build a solid two-metre-high fence, which would cost another US$150.

'Sure. Fair enough,' I thought. And I promised to send him the money as soon as I had it.

Chan's email also included a very warm invitation for me to stay at his home for as long as I liked. Even though I couldn't really imagine how or where I'd be sleeping in his single-roomed home, how could I say no? I thanked him and said I'd certainly stay for a few days when I first arrived.

~

The fundraiser at the art gallery went incredibly well. Sue's friend Hugh Wade was our MC for the night, and he did an amazing job revving up the crowd. He gave it his all and literally resorted to auctioning the shirt off his back to raise a few more bucks. Thanks to Hugh, Caz, all the artists, and volunteers and the generosity of the friends and family who attended, we raised about $20,000 for the SKO orphanage.

A lot of people were inspired by the night, and put their hands up to help. Some of my old school friends started buzzing with excitement about saving up to come over to volunteer at SKO for a while.

And Sally Power, a film production manager I'd become friends with through my work in the industry, also stepped forward to help.

Sally had long nurtured a dream of setting up an eco-village in the developing world, so when she heard of my plans with SKO, she was hooked. She offered to manage all CCT relations in Australia. This was great news for me, as I couldn't manage admin in Australia *and* work in Cambodia, and Sally is very good at what she does.

She bought me a decent video camera. 'We're going to need the best footage you can get of the kids so we can let people know where their money went,' she said. 'And you should make a video diary of your time there, too—we might use it on the website or to get corporate sponsorship or something.'

Uh—okay. The thought of turning the camera on myself was never going to be appealing to me. Ever since I was sixteen and had first developed an eating disorder, I've never enjoyed having my photo taken or being filmed. But I decided to be brave and embrace the discomfort. I trusted that Sally knew what she was talking about when it came to the power of photography and film.

~

In the weeks that followed, life was all about my upcoming trip to Cambodia. I sent Chan the money I'd promised via Western Union, and soon got an excited email from him with photos of a shiny new fence and a very handsome white Brahman cow.

I also wrote to SKO to let them know I was coming back with some funds that I'd raised, and I was now qualified to teach English.

I got a reply from a man named Jedtha, who introduced himself as the new director of SKO. His English was a bit better than that of Reaksmey, the staff member I'd met when I visited SKO. He said he was very happy to hear of our successful fundraising efforts and looked forward to meeting me. He said he'd arrange an affordable place for me to rent for the three months I planned to stay in Battambang.

~

It was an exciting time and I felt like I was on top of the world. Except for one thing. A good friend of mine from school, Fiona Reynolds, was very sick with a brain tumour. Fiona, or Fee as we all called her, was exceptional in every way. She was down-to-earth, good at every-thing and adored by everyone. She was both school captain *and* dux of the year in year twelve.

Fee was in hospital recovering from her third operation, which hadn't gone so well. She had already suffered setbacks from the previous operations, but this time she was suffering paralysis down the left side of her body.

I visited her in hospital before I left, bringing my guitar and a songbook.

No matter how sick she was feeling, she'd sing along as I played. I felt terrible saying goodbye and heading off overseas while lovely, vibrant Fee was stuck in a hospital bed. But I was certain that if anyone could beat it, Fee could.

~

It was dark when I stepped off the plane in Phnom Penh in late November 2006, but the thick warm air that embraced me as I walked across the tarmac felt wonderful. My spirits lifted as my head filled with visions of coconuts, sticky rice, tuktuk rides and $5 massages.

I checked into a cheap hotel by the river for the night, and the next morning hopped on the first bus for Battambang.

I could hardly believe the change in the Cambodian landscape. In just six months the dry, dusty brown countryside had transformed into a tropical paradise of swaying palms, sparkling waters and rice fields in vibrant shades of bright green, emerald and gold . . . it was like I'd tumbled down a rabbit hole, into Wonderland.

I stared out the window all the way, mesmerised by the beauty of it all. I've learned it's impossible not to fall in love with Cambodia towards the end of the year. The weather is divine and the sunsets turn the sky into a real-life Monet.

Before the bus even came to a stop in Battambang, I spotted Chan, Mina and their kids. They were standing together on the kerb, scanning the windows of the bus for me.

'*P'oun srey*! So happy see you!' Mina embraced me, with little Chea in her arms. Chan's smile was so wide he looked like the laughing Buddha.

He grabbed my bags from the bus boys and swung them into the tuktuk. Ponlok and Bopha took my hands and we all climbed aboard, arranging ourselves awkwardly around my luggage.

When we arrived at Chan and Mina's place, Chan proudly opened the gates of the new, rather ominous fence around his tiny home.

Inside the house, I immediately noticed that their wooden bed, which was previously covered only with a grass mat, now had a new single mattress on it. It was adorned with a crisp, pink frilly satin sheet and a lumpy hard pillow with Hello Kitty on it.

I was excited about staying with Chan and his family, but I felt terrible that they'd gone out and spent money on me, the spoilt foreigner. 'Oh, wow, Chan, this is very nice of you,' I said, 'but where will you all sleep?'

'Oh, we just sleep on the floor,' he said with a proud smile.

I could feel the smile on my face fade. 'Chan, I don't want you to sleep on the floor while I'm on your bed! I can stay at a hotel.'

'No, *P'oun srey*!' he snapped in a surprisingly stern tone, almost a shout, before switching straight back to the higher-pitched, friendly manner that I was more familiar with. 'You not understand. We always sleep on floor! It is Khmer way.'

This strange moment lingered in the air. I felt suddenly a little woozy and disoriented. I understood I'd insulted Chan.

I said softly, 'Thank you, Chan. You're very kind to me.' Then I changed the subject. 'Where's the cow?'

'Oh.' He looked down, his demeanour completely changing again. 'We sell the cow already. I hope you not angry me! It was so nice cow. But the cow, he make our house smell so bad. It not easy for Mina to clean every day. But we get so good price! Now we think, if you are happy, we can buy one small car.' He looked at me imploringly. 'I'm sorry I not tell you before, *P'oun srey*! I not want you to angry me!'

'Wait—the cow was living *in* your house?!' But of course it was! I should have realised when I saw the photos of the new fence around their house. With barely a metre-wide strip of land surrounding the modest house, where else were they going to keep the cow but inside with them—like an extremely large, cloven-hoofed, methane-excreting dog.

'Uh—yeah!' I cried. 'The car's a much better idea!' I knew Chan could make good money by driving a car as well as a tuktuk and moto.

I realised how foolish it was to assume that a cow would be appropriate for a city-dwelling family of non-farmers. My steep learning curve had begun.

Mina prepared dinner on the red-hot coals inside the ceramic stove, while Chan and I made plans to go to SKO first thing in the morning. I told Chan that SKO's director, Jedtha, had said he'd arrange a house for me.

Chan shook his head sceptically. 'I can get you house, *P'oun srey*— more cheap, good house and close to my home, too.'

'Oh . . . well, we'll see,' I said, trying to be diplomatic.

I didn't sleep much that night, partly because I could feel the wood through the thin foam mattress, and partly because I was excited and nervous about going back to SKO.

Before I went back to Australia, I wanted to make sure the $20,000 we had raised for SKO was used effectively. I just didn't know what exactly that would look like. Something that would make a good, sustainable difference—not like the tokenistic bag of old clothes and books I had donated last time. I hoped this director, Jedtha, would turn out to be a sound guy with good ideas about how to do that.

I look back now on the earnest youthful certainty I felt that night and just cringe. We'll talk more about the whys and wherefores of that later. But for now, please remember not to mistake the story I'm about to tell you for an 'inspiring' story. It's a good story, I hope. But ultimately, it's a cautionary tale.

~

When Chan and I arrived at the orphanage gates, SKO looked just as quiet, just as bleak, as it had looked the first time. I suddenly felt a bit nervous.

Chan beeped the tuktuk's horn a couple of times and a tall, serious-looking man came to the gate. He wore clean beige trousers and a white shirt. Wordlessly, he touched his palms together and greeted me with a very formal *sampeah*. When his hands fell away from his face, his smile was kind, but his eyes seemed to brim over with sorrow.

'Hello, I am Pon Jedtha, director of SKO orphanage,' he said in very precise tones.

'Hello.' I hopped out of the tuktuk and shook his hand. 'I'm Tara—I emailed you ...'

'Yes, I remember. You will volunteer here and also teach English. We are so happy to have you. Please come in, we can talk more.'

Jedtha opened the gate wide to allow the tuktuk to enter. The grounds and buildings were even more desolate than I remembered— but there was an extra building now, and a set of shiny playground equipment.

'Oh—a new building,' I said.

'Yes,' said Jedtha. 'A German organisation help us build it for the children to sleep in.'

We followed him on foot into an old wooden shed. It was dark inside, except for a few shafts of sunlight that speared in through the ridged edges of the corrugated-iron roof. Chan and I pulled up a pair of feeble cane chairs while Jedtha went to get us some drinking water.

The room seemed to serve as an office, but there were no shelves or drawers or office supplies. The walls were bare except for a large flowchart displaying the hierarchical structure of the organisation, labelled in Khmer.

There was a photo of a man with a very round face at the top, and then below that, on the second level, there was a photo of Jedtha. And below that, I recognised Reaksmey from my first visit to SKO. He was on the same level as two women I hadn't met yet.

I was puzzled to notice Jedtha was only on the second level—wasn't he the director?

Jedtha came back in and handed us each a bottle of water. It was lukewarm.

'We have no ice today,' he explained. He switched on a rusty ceiling fan and said something to Chan in Khmer. Chan nodded abruptly and said nothing, which meant the three of us lapsed into a long silence.

I sat stock-still, not knowing what to do next. I've since found that Cambodians are comfortable sitting together in silence in a way that westerners rarely are. The fan's metronomic whoosh filled the room. Bright flecks of dust drifted around in the shafts of sunlight. I thought: *Oh dear—I was hoping this was going to be easier.* Just to break the silence, I pointed at the chart on the wall.

'Jedtha, you are the director of SKO, right?' I said. 'So who is the man at the top here?'

'Oh—that is Rath,' Jedtha explained. 'Before he is director, but he can't speak English so he have problem to find the funding. Then he ask me to be director. You will meet him later. He's coming with the children.'

'How many children?'

'Twenty-four.'

'Are they learning English at school?'

Jedtha looked apologetic. 'I'm sorry,' he said, 'not very much English. They only learning French at school.'

I'd forgotten for a moment that Cambodia still had close ties to France. 'So, they speak French?'

Jedtha grimaced and confessed: 'Also, they not learn very much French.'

I couldn't help laughing at this and was happy to see a tentative smile appear on Jedtha's face.

'Would the children like to learn English?' I asked.

'Oh, yes. Of course!' Jedtha replied enthusiastically.

'Okay, when would you like me to start teaching English? And where? Do you have a place in mind?'

I couldn't help suspecting that there was no set plan in place for me at all.

'Up to you,' said Jedtha. 'Maybe today.' He gestured out the door towards a small open hut across the compound. 'You can teach them there.'

The hut was basically just a corrugated-iron roof held up with rough-hewn wooden poles. It had some rickety wooden school desks facing a wall where a whiteboard was nailed.

'Do you have any English books that volunteers have used before?' I asked.

'Hmm, no,' Jedtha said. 'We have volunteers come to play with the children only for one or two day usually.'

'Do you have pens and paper?'

Jedtha shrugged helplessly. 'No—not enough money.'

Okay, so that was where I could start, I guessed. 'Shall I go get some?' I asked him. 'And is there anything else you urgently need?'

Jedtha replied: 'Up to you. Whatever you feel you help, you help.'

I was a bit confused by his response. But English lessons seemed to be a good place to start. I was trained now, after all.

Clearly, it was time to spend a few of those precious Aussie dollars that Caz, Maxine and I had raised.

~

Chan headed off for the day to find some work in his tuktuk, and Jedtha and I headed into town on the back of his moto. On the way, I remembered that horrible moment when the young girl with the thick braid had offered me a drink of dirty water out of SKO's big, concrete urn.

'Jedtha, do the kids have clean water to drink?' I asked.

'No. If we can buy some water filters too, it would be so good,' he said, sounding pleased and surprised.

I expected to find downtown Battambang familiar, but within minutes I was totally disoriented. We made a few stops, and I couldn't help being amused by the strange way things seemed to be done in Cambodia. The bookstore is also the place you buy your exercise equipment. It's apparently totally normal for water filters to be sold at the light shop, and the place you buy a hammer is not the place you buy the nails.

Go figure! But this was life now, 'down the rabbit hole'.

We bought exercise books, pencils, pens and the only Khmer English-teaching textbook I could get my hands on (which unfortunately seemed to have been written by someone who learned English from a parrot). We also bought four large water filters that Jedtha assured me were the best.

Our first shopping mission was a success, and by now I was really looking forward to seeing the kids.

When we got back from the markets they were home. The youngest kids, all boys, came running up to the moto. They were still ragged and unkempt-looking, but they'd heard a foreigner had come to volunteer, so they were bouncing around with excitement.

I ran and grabbed the suitcase I'd brought with me that morning, full of stuffed toys I'd brought with me from Australia—mostly my own careworn childhood toys.

As a little kid I was obsessed with stuffed toys. I loved them, tucked them in at night, and fretted that they couldn't breathe if they were packed into a toy box. So, for me, it was a real *Toy Story III* moment to see them being loved again by a new generation of kids.

The first to be claimed was one of my childhood favourites, a big, lifelike, velociraptor that went to a bright-eyed little boy who seemed about to explode with happiness. The littlest of the boys reached up to pull out another of my favourites—an oversized, bottle-green crocodile. His smile was just as wide as the crocodile's. To my relief there were enough for everyone. Even the older teenage girls exclaimed and giggled over their new toys.

Kids are so easily impressed, I thought wryly, as they beamed up at me like I was the world's best person ever.

If I wanted to start our first lesson on a positive note, there couldn't be a more perfect moment.

'Can I do a lesson now?' I asked Jedtha hopefully.

'Yes! Yes! Please, you do!' he said, with a wide grin on his face. It's a lovely thing, the contagiousness of joy.

I heaved the big bag of books and pens I'd bought over my shoulder. The littlest boy, who had an adorable little raspy voice and a cheeky grin, grabbed hold of my free hand as I walked towards the makeshift outdoor classroom. All twenty-four kids huddled around, giggling and whispering, while I laid out piles of books on the rickety wooden desks.

Jedtha appeared at the back of the classroom, flanked by Reaksmey, a tall Khmer woman and another Khmer man. I left the kids peering into the bag while I stepped over to greet them.

'Hello, Reaksmey! I'm Tara. Do you remember me?' I said carefully, not able to recall how much English he spoke.

'Yes, I remember,' he replied. 'I am so happy you come to help us.' Reaksmey was taller and thinner than I remembered. His pronounced jawline was accentuated by how gaunt he looked. Was he ill?

'I'm very happy to help,' I told him as warmly as I could. 'Your English is very good. Where did you learn?'

He grinned bashfully. 'I learn at the pagoda,' he said.

'Reaksmey was a monk, same like me,' said Jedtha. 'He is my cousin. He help so much with the kids but we not have money to pay him so he sleep and eat here for free. And this is Savenh.' Jedtha pointed to the tall, statuesque woman on his left. 'She is SKO social worker, and this is Rath, SKO accountant.' He gestured to the man standing to his right.

Savenh, the social worker, had a stern look on her face, but she smiled and gave me the traditional Khmer greeting, which I hoped was a good sign. Rath followed suit. He was shorter than Jedtha, Reaksmey and Savenh, with a stocky frame and a round, impassive face. I recognised him from the organisational structure on the wall in the shed. He was the man at the top of the chart—the previous director.

The kids were becoming increasingly impatient to see what was going to happen with all these books. It was show time. I stepped up to the whiteboard, thinking: *Crap. Wish I'd had a chance to properly prepare a lesson. I guess I'll just wing this first one.*

To my delight, the kids were enthusiastic students. The forty-five-minute lesson flew by and the kids went away repeating the phrases I'd taught them. I was amazed by their motivation to learn—and I was relieved to think that I would finally be able to start doing some good here.

5

My next task was to find somewhere to live. It would have to be large enough for me and several others, as I had checked my email at an internet cafe in town and discovered, to my delight, that some of my old school friends were flying over to help out. They were coming quite soon, and would need somewhere to stay.

Chan and I went to look at the house Jedtha had picked out for me. It looked big on the outside, but when we stepped inside we realised it was beyond big—it was massive and completely unfurnished.

Chan's boisterous voice echoed off the polished tiles. 'This no good, *P'oun srey*! I get you something better. You tell "the Venerable Pon Jedtha" this too big. And too expense.'

I looked at Chan in surprise. There was something quite scornful in his tone whenever he talked about Jedtha that was at odds with his usual friendly persona.

But he wasn't wrong about the house. A day later, he drove me to a much smaller house in his own neighbourhood—a cute little pink villa. It was clean, fully furnished and reasonably priced. I agreed to take it on the spot.

Chan was over the moon. 'You see! I get you much better house!' he crowed. He'd get a small commission for securing a tenant; I knew—and completely understood—that this was part of the reason he was so pleased. He added: 'And Mina can come and cook for you and your friends and help you with the washing!'

'Oh no, Chan,' I said. 'I can't ask you and Mina to do that.'

'You are my family!' he protested.

I hesitated. I only had a little money to live on. But, on the other hand, Chan and Mina really needed some extra income. And I can't cook to save myself . . .

'Yeah, okay,' I agreed. 'But I'll pay Mina—my friends and I will share the cost.'

We were both quite pleased with the new arrangement. Having his family around would also make the house feel more like a home.

~

After I moved into the little pink villa I was free to concentrate on my work with SKO. I had started teaching two lessons a day. Cambodian primary school kids go to school either in the morning or afternoon, so I had one lesson in the morning with the afternoon-schooled kids, and one in the afternoon with the morning-schooled kids.

I remembered the Khmer words I'd learned at the museum and was picking up more every day—mostly from listening to the kids.

Spending time in the company of most Cambodian people is so effortless. Their sense of humour is second to none. They'll laugh at everything and anything and their joie de vivre is infectious. I was particularly enjoying getting to know the kids.

There were several teenage girls at the orphanage. Sinet, the girl who had offered me water when I first visited SKO, was easily the most confident and capable of the lot. In keeping with the Khmer custom of giving siblings quite similar-sounding names, her older sister was named Sineit. Sineit was very sweet and motherly but also a very quiet little soul, which I partly put down to the fact she was

HIV-positive and not always very well. There was sophisticated Kolab and her sister, gentle, innocent little Kanya. And Kanya's best friend Maly, who was fiercely intelligent. Many of the younger kids, who seemed to dominate SKO, were their siblings.

The girls all mothered the younger kids to some extent, but Sinet was definitely the unofficial 'boss'. She helped and supported me from the start. If I was struggling to get something across, she almost always picked up on it first and helped communicate it to the others. It was clear from the outset that she was quite exceptional.

~

By now, I was enamoured with life in Battambang. I bought a second-hand retro bicycle from a shop in town and rode it to SKO early each morning, past soft green rice fields. I loved how the locals, young and old, would wave and shout 'Hello!' with incredible enthusiasm as I passed by. I got a thrill out of listening to the meditative chanting and the traditional *pinpeat* orchestral music wafting from the monastery down the road. I often found myself lost in these moments. I couldn't remember feeling this content since my days of being on the back of a horse, galloping through the Australian bush.

I was also starting to get the hang of the English teaching thing. I enjoyed the whole process of drawing up lesson plans and preparing my classes on big sheets of butcher paper, knowing that the kids would eat it up like it was the most fantastic, most interesting thing they'd ever encountered.

When word got out about my lessons, other kids from the local neighbourhood and nearby villages started appearing at the gates, begging to join in. Jedtha told me they came from a slum community just down the road from SKO. I opened the door to all of them. Why not? I ended up teaching three classes a day, then four—until I was teaching up to eighty kids a day. The days were tiring but so rewarding.

The kids had such a natural appetite for learning. *With kids like this*, I thought to myself, *Cambodia's future must be bright!* The words of Nelson Mandela kept running through my head: 'Education is the most powerful weapon which you can use to change the world.' In my own little way I thought I was changing the world. *Insert face palm here*—but it felt good and, at the time, there was really no way of me knowing otherwise. I had a lot to learn about the potential harm that can come from volunteering with vulnerable children.

~

Some of the kids from outside the orphanage seemed even worse off than the kids at SKO—dirty and skinny, like they'd come in from the wild. I often wondered about their circumstances. A couple of times, I doubled one or two of them home on the back of my bicycle after the lessons were finished. It gave me brief insight into their home lives.

The huts in the slums were like cubbyhouses, cobbled together from corrugated iron, barbed wire, tarpaulins and plastic bags. The kids I'd been teaching lived in these 'cubbyhouses', often in large family groups with many younger siblings. Piles of rubbish littered the pathways between the huts, spilling over into the waterways. Many of the slums' inhabitants looked sick, which was hardly surprising. The kids were filthy and all of them were lice-ridden.

It was awful to see it. Try as I might, I just couldn't imagine waking up every day with that as my reality. No one should have to live like that. *How do they find the strength to keep on going?* I wondered. I felt ashamed of all the complaining about 'first world problems' that I'd done in my life. It's amazing how things are put into perspective when you see that sort of hardship. I wished that there was something more I could do for the kids from the slums.

But at least these kids still had family, I supposed. The kids at SKO were all alone in the world, and that broke my heart in a different way. The way they latched on to me so adoringly—it was nice at first, but they had only just met me. The more I thought about it, the more their implicit trust and indiscriminate affection concerned me.

~

Even as I settled into life in Battambang, I couldn't ignore the voice in the back of my head reminding me of the important lesson I'd learned last time: that this wasn't to be an exercise in self-gratification. I needed to make sure those funds we'd raised were spent in a way that had a real, sustainable impact. I had to make sure time didn't slip by without achieving that aim.

But I was still concerned about just handing over our funds to SKO's staff. I couldn't understand why a new dormitory was built and playground equipment installed when there were no water filters, not enough food, and the kids were still dressed in rags. Was it because the German donors insisted on putting the money into buildings and nothing else, or was it some sort of mismanagement of funds? I wasn't sure. I made tactful attempts to ask Jedtha, but he wasn't in charge of the money; Rath was. Jedtha said he'd ask Rath for the last annual report to show me, but it never surfaced.

Rath was always very quiet and aloof with me. As hard as I tried to connect with him, he would hardly even make eye contact. I didn't know what to make of him. I had met quite a few Khmer adults by this time who seemed a bit disengaged and broken by life. Maybe that was the legacy of growing up under the Khmer Rouge.

So I just focused on working with Jedtha, who seemed to genuinely care about the kids. I pushed him for direction on the things that SKO needed. At first he seemed to feel quite powerless, just saying things like, 'I'm not sure, do you have any ideas?'

And I could understand why. With the orphanage on its knees with poverty, there was nothing to do, but there was everything to do.

But I was here to help, with money donated specifically for the kids at SKO. So I started throwing out ideas of my own. Even then I knew it wasn't ideal—an unqualified young foreigner coming up with ways to make over a Cambodian orphanage. But action was needed. So action I took!

I noticed that the kids fell upon any food they were given like starving, ravening wolves. The food they were served was literally just a watery rice gruel and a couple of meagre vegetables. I suspected that the skin conditions I was seeing among the kids were at least partly due to poor nutrition.

SKO's cook was Rath's sister. I generally found her to be a very quiet, unsmiling person, much like Rath. She cooked on the traditional charcoal stove, like Mina did, with very basic utensils. That couldn't have been easy when there were twenty-four kids to feed.

The kids needed better-quality meals; that was undeniable. But food was an ongoing cost, which I couldn't be sure I could continue to provide. I asked Jedtha: 'Is there somewhere that might donate food?'

He shook his head sadly. 'We try. Sometime people give us food, but most give food to monastery. We need more funds every month to buy food.'

So, even though I couldn't commit to providing the funds for this on an ongoing basis, as an interim measure I started giving a daily allowance to the cook to buy more meat, vegetables, eggs and rice for the kids. I also started dropping by the markets every day to buy a big bag of fruit to hand out at my afternoon lessons.

Aside from their nutrition, I was concerned about how poor the orphanage's health and hygiene standards were.

The kids' teeth were in a truly terrible state. Reaksmey told me: 'They never use a toothbrush before.' So I asked Jedtha if it might be a good idea to take them all to a dentist.

'Yes!' he said. 'That is a great idea.'

On a roll, I asked: 'What about vaccinations? Are they up to date on all that?'

'No,' Jedtha replied. 'We not have enough funds to do medical program yet. Only some blood test. Sineit's parent die of HIV so when she got sick Rath take her to get test. That's how we know she has HIV. Also Rath had all older girls tested for HIV. They are okay.'

'Only the older girls? Not all the kids?' I asked.

'No,' he said. 'It would be good to test the other kids, too.'

I was starting to get the impression that the bulk of our funds were going to be spent on health and hygiene issues . . . But I was to find that the health and hygiene issues at the orphanage ran deeper than just a lack of funds.

For instance, there was a dog living at SKO that was the most miserable living creature I'd ever seen. Disease and starvation had turned her into a walking skeleton—just skin wrapped tightly around bone, with only a few hairs left on her cadaverous frame. The poor thing was pathologically timid around people, but she hung around for the sake of the few grains of rice she could occasionally scavenge.

I started buying a bit of cooked chicken for her every few days. I tried to explain to the staff and kids that living with a sick animal could make them sick, too. I don't know how well my message got through, but they were helpful when I called in the local vet (who usually only ever worked with cows and buffalo). Together, we caught the dog, took her into Rath's office and I held her muzzle shut so she could be treated. The vet sprayed her mange-infested skin and then injected her with medicine.

She was so terrified that by the time the vet had finished, there was a pool of dog pee mixed with blood and pus from the broken scabs on her back all over the office floor. No one paid any attention to the pool of filth, so I asked Reaksmey what they had in the way of cleaning products so I could wipe it up.

Reaksmey looked at me for a second with his head cocked, then scooped up an old mat from the doorway, mopped up the mess with it, and put it back in the doorway with a proud grin.

I stood there, blinking.

I'm not a germophobe or a neat freak by any means, but after that, everywhere I looked, I saw germs. There was just such a vast gap between my level of concern about basic hygiene and everyone else's. There was another item for my to-do list: Get kids and staff some education about basic health and hygiene!

~

It was a great day when my friends Fern, Emma, Elise and Chloe arrived at the bus station in Battambang. We piled all their luggage into two tuktuks and set off for the little pink villa. It was wonderful after all these weeks to be able to communicate thoughts, feelings and ideas without having to trawl through a Khmer–English dictionary—and to drop pop-culture references into a conversation without receiving blank stares in return!

The girls settled into makeshift beds in the pale pink villa without complaint, and really, we were very comfortable. It was like being back at boarding school, with Mina as our adopted house mum, making us delicious meals and making us feel at home, and Chan giving us a ride around town when we needed it.

The girls fell instantly in love with the kids and threw themselves into the English teaching at SKO. This meant I was free to go into town with Jedtha to hunt for the things on the list we'd been creating, which now looked like this:

- Support for HIV treatment
- Cleaning products
- Head lice treatment
- Find and cost dentist
- Find clinic for health check-ups
- First-aid kit
- Bicycles x 24 (surprise morale booster for the kids)

Within a few days, we'd sourced everything on the list except the head lice treatment, which no one had ever heard of in Battambang. One shop vendor pulled out a tall spray can of the household insecticide Raid.

'You spray this on hair!' he suggested helpfully. At the look of horror on my face he quickly tried to assure me: 'It definitely kill all!' He looked confused when I agreed wholeheartedly, but still declined the offer.

Jedtha found us a local dentist who had previously treated all the kids at their school, which seemed like a fairly good endorsement. The dentist was very reasonably priced too: US$8.75 for root canal therapy!

The kids had never been vaccinated before, so Jedtha and I tracked down a polyclinic that offered vaccinations. Polyclinics are common in France and some French colonies, and provide emergency and other medical services to outpatients. This one was right next to Battambang's bustling market, Psar Nat. They offered vaccines for hepatitis B for US$10, typhoid for US$10 and tetanus for US$2. The doctor recommended we get a range of blood tests done on all the children first, to check for antibodies. We figured it would be a good way to start a comprehensive medical file on each of the kids.

~

Organising nice surprises for people is one of my favourite things to do—so the best part of the shopping trip was buying the bikes. We got them second-hand at a great price.

Late in the afternoon, when the kids were all home from school, a big truck reversed through the orphanage gates. It was an unusual sight so they looked up from their chores and homework with great curiosity.

Then the truck driver opened up the back of the truck, revealing twenty-four shiny bicycles. The kids climbed to their feet, open-mouthed. Jedtha called them over and they came running, screeching to a halt in front of him.

I often noticed how happy and relaxed they seemed in Jedtha's presence. They called him *Loak Khrew*, the respectful Khmer term for 'teacher'—a habit I fell into myself because it suited him so well. They listened when he spoke, asked questions with confidence and laughed at his jokes. It was a marked contrast to the meek, reluctant way they related to most other Khmer adults.

Their attention was certainly locked onto him now, even the youngest kid, Makara, a cheeky little scamp with a complete inability to focus on anything for more than a few seconds.

I couldn't understand what Jedtha was saying, but I definitely knew when he told the kids I had bought them each their own bike. The younger ones squealed and clapped and jumped up and down. Tears sprang into the eyes of the three eldest girls, Sineit, Sinet and Kolab. What a moment. I would never have guessed that a few bicycles could bring so much happiness.

As soon as the truck unloaded the gleaming bikes, the kids took to them, tracking circles in the dirt of the SKO compound. Most of them could ride already, and those who couldn't threw themselves into the task of learning. I stood and watched them for fifteen minutes or so. It was wonderful to see these kids, who I was coming to really care about, so blissfully happy.

When Chan came to pick me up, I called out goodbye—'*Lee hai!*'—and jumped into the tuktuk.

I looked back over my shoulder to wave and saw twenty-four kids on bikes following us up the dirt road. They were pedalling like crazy and calling out: 'Thank you, Tara!'

I had dissolved into tears by the time we reached the turn-off to the main road. Never in my life had I been on the receiving end of such genuine, wholehearted gratitude. It was a defining moment for me—the moment that I realised what truly special kids I'd met.

~

After the thrill of the bikes, the next few days, unfortunately for the kids, was all about the dentist.

We booked out the surgery for three solid days, and I sat next to the big, green dentist's chair, trying to keep each kid calm as they had their teeth cleaned, scaled, filled and, sadly, sometimes extracted. Some of the kids had teeth that were in an appalling state. Some of them needed root canal surgery to save their adult teeth.

We took 'before' and 'after' photos of the kids—they were all natural hams and loved having their photos taken. They cheered up when they saw the 'after' photos, with the stains that covered their teeth cleaned away. Their smiles, set against their lovely brown skin, looked bright, white and beautiful—even with wads of cotton wool stuffed into the corners of their mouths.

~

Around this time, my friend Lauren Henderson arrived in town to join the other girls in helping us out. I was lucky enough to meet her when I was a volunteer at Oxfam. She was not much older than me, but she was experienced in the NGO sector. It was great to have her support at this time.

Lauren helped me organise hygiene education classes, a head lice eradication program and a basic first-aid box for the orphanage.

The hygiene project was hot, sweaty work but very satisfying. We scrubbed the whole SKO compound clean and gave the kids lessons on washing their hands, brushing their teeth and managing the tropical skin conditions that most of them suffered.

Eradicating the head lice turned out to be an entertaining but ultimately fruitless activity. Since the Raid recommendation, we'd scoured Battambang for treatment to no avail. Desperate, we googled home remedies. The general gist of the advice we found was that suffocating the lice and then picking out the eggs was the way to go.

We tracked down some big tubs of thick, gluggy hair treatment made of clay and some brightly coloured shower caps. The idea was to coat the kids' heads in the stuff, put them in shower caps, and wash it out the next day. At worst, we figured, they would end up with nice soft, shiny hair.

The kids looked ridiculous with their hair slicked down with grey slime and thought the whole thing was hilarious. But then—just to send them into even greater hysterics—they got to wear fluorescent shower caps.

The shy older girls spent most of the afternoon staring at their shower-capped selves in the mirror and giggling behind one hand. Little Makara, who's normally a real boy's boy, decided to go with the whole thing and asked the girls to use some bright pink nail polish I'd given them to paint his nails to match his shower cap. He then demanded to be photographed in a range of effeminate poses, much to everyone's delight. Laugher roared through the orphanage that afternoon.

The next morning, just in time for school, Lauren and the SKO staff helped me wash the kids' hair and pick out the remaining eggs. As expected, they all looked fantastic. They tossed their lice-free, shiny tresses around like little supermodels, and we all felt quite smug about our success.

That afternoon, the kids arrived home from school totally reinfested with lice.

~

Lauren suggested we check with some other local NGOs to see if anyone could help us get the kids' blood tested. Jedtha tracked down an organisation called Reproductive and Child Health Association of Cambodia (RHAC). They offered to do the blood tests and put all the kids aged fourteen and up through a sex education course—for free!

The kids were a little nervous about the needles but they put on a brave face and were very well behaved. We got a full blood count done, as well as tests for HIV and hepatitis. We knew Sineit was HIV positive but Jedtha had never seen any paperwork. So, to be certain and to have a hard copy record, we tested her as well.

Sineit's younger sister, Sinet, was quieter than usual that day. I asked Jedtha to ask her if she was okay.

She said she was worried her results would come back HIV positive. I tried to reassure her—and myself—that there was no reason to think that might be the case. But I assumed Sineit had contracted HIV from her mother ... and Sineit was older than Sinet. So I couldn't help feeling anxious for her.

I had bitten off all my nails by the time the clinic called to ask us to come and pick up the results.

Lauren, Jedtha and I went through the reports with the NGO's clinician, one by one.

Sineit was confirmed as HIV positive. But Sinet was negative. I felt my shoulders relax a little.

All the other kids were HIV negative. But seven of the kids had a big red asterisk next to one of the numbers on the tests.

'Hepatitis B positive,' the clinician muttered, with a furrowed brow.

I looked at her in shock. I suddenly realised I didn't even know what exactly hepatitis B *was*. Was it a death sentence? All I knew was that my doctor told me I needed a shot for it before I travelled.

'It can be they have from they parents,' the clinician explained.

'How serious is this? What does it mean?' I asked. I could feel my shoulders clench again.

'Could be okay, but maybe bad,' she said. We tried to press her for more information, but she didn't seem to know much about hepatitis B either.

We all exchanged worried looks. What were we supposed to do with this information?

The RHAC clinician recommended we take the hepatitis B-positive children to the Battambang public hospital, after the older kids had finished their sex education workshop at RHAC.

Jedtha gave Lauren and me a lift into town on his moto. We each grabbed a cold coconut and a plain baguette (which in Cambodia is often just a hollow, sweet-tasting crust) and headed for an internet cafe. We wanted to do as much research on hepatitis B as we could before we went to the hospital.

The more I read, the more concerned I grew.

Hepatitis B, said Dr Google, is an infectious inflammatory liver disease, which has caused epidemics in parts of Asia and Africa. It is spread through infected blood or body fluids—so yes, it can be spread through unprotected sex and sharing needles—but also during childbirth and by things like sharing toothbrushes and razors. But not by coughs or sneezes or holding hands or sharing drinking glasses or eating utensils . . .

According to Wikipedia: *Chronic hepatitis B may eventually cause cirrhosis and liver cancer—a fatal disease with a very poor response to current treatments. According to the World Health Organization (WHO), an estimated 600,000 people die every year from diseases related to the infection.*

I wondered how on earth the kids had contracted it. Was it during childbirth? If so, how come the twins, Simha and Borey, weren't both positive?

A prickling, paranoid feeling crept up my spine. It was horrible to have to ask myself . . . but was there something awful—appalling— going on at the orphanage?

~

Lauren and I decided to drop in on the older girls' sex ed class at RHAC to see how it was going. When the teacher pulled out an erect, hand-carved wooden penis, I had to immaturely cough back a laugh, but to my surprise, the kids barely reacted. There were a few giggles, though, when each of the kids had to practise putting a condom on it.

Lauren and I couldn't follow what was being said, but the pictures were fairly self-explanatory. They talked to the girls about safe sex, pregnancy and STDs. I studied Sineit's face as they talked, at length, about HIV/AIDS. She didn't react. I wondered what was going on in her head.

Jedtha ferried us all back to the orphanage in three or four trips, with as many of us on the back of his moto as would fit.

I borrowed the Toyota Camry that Chan had bought with the proceeds from the failed cow to take the seven kids with hep B to hospital. Stuffing seven kids into a sedan wasn't ideal, but it would beat squishing three or four of them at a time on the back of a moto.

The kids didn't seem too happy about going to the hospital. In fact, Makara ran and hid behind the kitchen shed and had to be coaxed out with lollies. The other kids marched towards the car like prisoners to the gallows.

'What's wrong with them?' I whispered to Jedtha.

'They see people from they families go there to die,' he murmured. 'They think hospital have many ghosts.'

We pulled into the car park of a sprawling French Colonial building set among patches of green grass. And thus began my first experience of a developing world hospital. The grimy, once-yellow and once-white tiles were identical to the tiles at the Tuol Sleng torture prison. Bloodstains climbed the dirty cream walls. Every surface wore a thick patina of reddish dust.

A woman sitting at an old wooden bureau, which served as a reception desk, gestured us to a long wooden bench to wait to be seen. Just beside the reception space, a deathly thin woman lying on a stretcher bed moaned in pain. Her moans became louder and louder. No receptionist, no nurse, no one answered her cries.

The kids sat grimly with their heads down, and we waited and waited. My level of unease with the place—and the effect it was having on the kids—grew until it was intolerable.

'Jedtha, I think we should come back another time,' I said, my eyes pleading for him to agree. 'Let's come back on our own without the kids, just to ask questions.'

The kids couldn't get out of there fast enough.

~

At dinnertime that evening, I noticed that Sinet looked much brighter, but her sister Sineit was sitting alone. She was playing with her food distractedly.

I assumed the sex education class earlier in the day had upset her. I went and sat next to her to find out. She smiled at me warmly—she was a very kind, gentle girl. But she went back to toying with her food.

'Not hungry?' I asked in Khmer.

She smiled but said nothing. Not being able to speak to her properly was maddening. I got up to find Reaksmey. I had to know what the matter was.

Reaksmey was always happy to help. We sat down next to her, and Reaksmey started chatting away.

'She not feeling well,' Reaksmey relayed to me.

'Is she upset about anything she heard today at RHAC?' I asked.

Reaksmey translated her answer. 'No,' he said. 'She know already she have HIV, she just feel a bit sick today.'

I pressed my hand to her forehead, feeling worried. She laughed off my concern and gave me a big, genuine smile.

'*Ot ay day!*' she assured me. No worries.

'Okay, I need to go home now before it gets dark.' Everyone in Battambang seemed to panic if they heard I drove after sunset, warning me that only drunks and hoodlums, thieves, gangsters and ghosts were out after dark. I gave Sineit a big hug and said to her in Khmer: 'See you tomorrow.' I hated seeing her suffer and was now determined to find out more information about her condition.

~

The next morning, Jedtha, Lauren and I went straight to the hospital. As well as talking to a doctor about getting treatment for the kids with hep B, I hoped we could meet with Sineit's doctor to ask some questions.

We followed Jedtha down the dirty, poorly lit hospital corridors. It took a moment for my eyes to adjust enough to the gloom to catch glimpses of patients lying in their rooms on grass mats over bare wooden slabs. The intravenous drip hangers, holding up bags of bright yellow fluid, were rusted. Some were held high by family members, who sat around the patients, fanning themselves against the heat. Various wretched smells wafted out of each room. I longed for the antiseptic smells of the hospitals in Australia.

In the doctor's office, a bunch of nurses were hanging around chatting. They pulled up a few chairs, invited us to sit down and asked Jedtha endless questions—presumably about Lauren and me, judging by the way they stared at us as they talked. After an uncomfortable half-hour wait, a thin, tired-looking man in long white scrubs arrived. The doctor.

We showed him the blood test results. He stared at them for a long while, saying nothing.

'Do you speak English?' I asked finally.

He smiled and shook his head.

I handed Jedtha the list of questions about hepatitis B that we had prepared for him. They were about further testing, disease management, medication and prognosis. Jedtha kept looking at the list as they talked, but the doctor didn't seem to have much to say.

Finally, Jedtha translated for us. 'He say the children need to take more vitamins.'

'Really?' I was surprised. 'And what about all our questions?'

'I think it's better we check a different hospital,' Jedtha muttered under his breath. 'I think he doesn't know much about this problem.'

Lauren and I exchanged looks of confusion and disbelief as Jedtha stood up. We thanked the doctor in Khmer for his help, then followed Jedtha out.

We didn't know what to think. Was this incompetence? Corruption? Maybe he was expecting a payment from us. Or did he just not care?

Before we left the hospital, we had a meeting with the doctor who was in charge of Battambang's HIV program. This meant walking through the hot, wretched AIDS ward, where four skeletal patients languished on mats, three of them with a single listless, despondent-looking female family member slumped beside them.

The doctor was a grumpy-looking man who seemed unable or unwilling to help. But he did do one surprising thing for us: he gave us a copy of Sineit's medical file. This would later prove to be a lifesaver.

I left the hospital feeling shell-shocked and hoping we wouldn't ever have to bring the kids back there again.

~

We went back to the polyclinic near the markets. They were much more helpful. They set up a vaccination regime for all the kids, and put the seven kids with hep B on a complex multi-drug treatment.

The seven kids were prescribed a 'party mix' of pills to take three times a day, so we showed Reaksmey how to administer the drugs and put him in charge of making sure the kids didn't miss any doses. Jedtha said he'd keep a close eye on Reaksmey to make sure he followed the doctor's orders. Reaksmey was a nice boy, but it was clear that sometimes his head was somewhere else. Hopefully we'd made the job simple enough for him to manage.

I was still concerned about Sineit, and I couldn't seem to get any decent information about HIV from the polyclinic. Jedtha and the staff didn't know what else to do either. But Jedtha agreed that, as the kids' caregivers, they needed to understand more about how to manage their chronic diseases. We decided I should take the copy of Sineit's medical file with me to Siem Reap and see if I could track down an HIV specialist to get some clear information.

6

It was nearly Christmas 2006, and my twenty-first birthday was on 27 December, so I had planned a short, refreshing break to Siem Reap. Lauren, Chloe, Emma and Elise were all heading home before then, but Fern was keen to stay on and celebrate my birthday in Siem Reap with me.

It was sad to see the Aussie girls go. Lauren assured me that she was only an email away, and that she would be happy to help out with administering any extra donations in Australia.

After the farewells at Siem Reap airport, Fern and I caught a tuktuk into town. The next few days were fun—eating at cafes and pubs that served familiar western food, hanging out with interesting travellers, and catching up with some of the kids from Akira's, where my journey had begun.

The night before my birthday, Fern and I went for dinner at the Dead Fish Tower—a multi-level, labyrinthine restaurant with stairs randomly connecting floating wooden platforms, each furnished with cushions and rubber-tyre seats set around low tables. Visiting the toilets involved negotiating a narrow platform built over a crocodile pit. Patrons threw chunks of raw meat to the hungry, bored animals that were kept in a space so small they couldn't move. I felt bad for those poor crocs, but the rest of the place was pretty fun, even if it was an OH&S nightmare.

The food from the kitchen was sent up to our platform on a rope pulley. We watched traditional Khmer Apsara dancers, draped in gold silk, floating hypnotically on a platform in the middle of the restaurant, their long-nailed fingers drawing graceful, double-jointed shapes in the air.

The food wasn't much to write home about. My stir-fried vegetables with cashew nuts was actually just a bowl of fried cashews, with a couple of chunks of onion and pineapple. But the atmosphere was exotic enough to make up for it.

On the way back to the hotel I started feeling a little unwell, but brushed it off as an overdose of cashew nuts.

'I'm such a party animal,' I said to myself as I crawled into bed early—far too early for an (almost) freshly minted twenty-one-year-old. I fell asleep straight away.

About an hour later I woke and sat bolt upright. My dinner really hadn't agreed with me. I made it to the toilet bowl just in time. After an intense bout of vomiting, I realised it wasn't just my dinner. My insides were trying to get out as quickly and violently as possible. I spent the next few hours in various configurations around the toilet bowl, feeling very sorry for myself indeed.

Luckily, Fern, who was in the other bed, slept through it all.

At 4 am, after hours of vomiting and dysentery, I desperately needed water. I tried to stagger downstairs to buy some, but when I got to reception, no one was there. I was so weak I couldn't go any further, so I accepted defeat and headed back to bed. I slept for a few hours and woke shivering into a warm Siem Reap morning. Fern fetched me a bottle of water and, wrapped up in the hotel's fleece blanket, I stumbled down the stairs and into a tuktuk.

Fern instructed the driver to take us to the nearest clinic, but it wasn't due to open for another thirty minutes. So we sat outside the gates and waited. Poor Fern did her best to keep my spirits up while I oscillated between shivering and almost passing out. My field of vision shrank to a pinprick aperture, surrounded by a field of white.

~

I woke up on a slab of padded wood with a drip in my arm. A clinician told me my blood pressure had been dangerously low and a test had revealed I had amoebic dysentery. Amoebas. Ugh. Then he went on reassuringly about how amoebas can enter vital organs. He was quite graphic in his descriptions.

For the next three days, I lay on that slab, completely off my head with fever, obsessing about amoebas. The cook at the clinic was away, so I wasn't given a thing to eat, but that was okay. Food was the last thing on my mind.

The three days of fever, delirium and no food left me in a very sorry state.

Finally, in the late afternoon, a doctor from my travel insurance company arrived. He immediately arranged for me to be evacuated to Thailand.

The next thing I knew, Fern and I were on a little jet plane staffed by medics. 'Isn't this a little excessive?' I asked. 'I think I'll be fine . . .'

I slept the whole flight and barely even woke as I was wheeled into the incredibly fancy Bumrungrad International Hospital in Bangkok.

I spent the next few days in hospital drifting in and out of sleep. When my results came back, the doctor told me the antibiotics given to me at the Siem Reap clinic had cleared up the amoebic dysentery—if I ever had that at all.

What I definitely did have (even though I'd been vaccinated against it) was typhoid fever.

Typhoid fever is entirely treatable in Cambodia with antibiotics. But the Siem Reap clinic had missed the full diagnosis, leaving the typhoid untreated. The whole experience really shook my faith in the Cambodian medical system.

~

Once I recovered enough to be released from hospital, Fern flew home to Australia and I was sent back to Battambang by the insurance company. I was looking forward to going 'home' to my little pink villa, where I could rest without someone waking me in the night to take my temperature, stick needles in my arms and ask about my bowel movements.

My holiday hadn't gone exactly as planned. Instead of returning full of renewed energy and armed with information on HIV, I was weak and easily fatigued and still as clueless on the subject of HIV as when I left.

But it was great to go back to SKO. The kids ran up to greet me when I pulled up at the gates, seemingly just as happy and excited to see me as I was to see them. I doled out some cheap little dog tag necklaces I'd got for them in Bangkok. The tags were each engraved with their names, spelled phonetically in English. They had the exact effect I was hoping for: those beaming smiles I was getting hooked on.

'They say it best present they ever get,' Reaksmey told me with a grin.

There was still one necklace left in the bag. I fished it out and called out the name engraved on it: 'Sineit?'

The younger girls took my hands and led me into the gloom of the girl's dorm. Sineit was lying on her sleeping mat—so motionless that I waited for a moment, my heart in my mouth, until I saw her chest rise and fall. I put my hand on her shoulder and softly called her name. No response. Her skin was burning hot. I called her name again and again but I couldn't get a response.

My blood rushed down from my head to my toes. I'd come to really care about this sweet, quiet girl. I jumped to my feet, my own fatigue swept aside by the surge of adrenaline. I didn't know much about HIV but I knew she needed urgent medical attention.

I phoned Jedtha, who was running an errand in town. 'Please—can you come to SKO?'

He arrived on his moto within just a few minutes.

'How long has Sineit been sick?' I was practically wringing my hands with worry.

'Many days. I take her to hospital this morning,' he told me, his brow furrowed.

'Did they say what's causing the fever?'

'Oh no, they not say, they just give me tablets for her.'

I asked to see the tablets. They were six familiar-looking white pills, loose in a little snap-lock bag.

'Para,' said Jedtha.

'Paracetamol? Has she taken any? Because if she has, they're not working. Her fever is still very high!'

'Yes, she take.' Jedtha shrugged helplessly. It just confirmed my opinion of that horrible public hospital.

'*Loak Khrew*, I think she needs to see a good doctor,' I said. 'I'm so worried about her. She's unconscious now. Maybe we should take her to Phnom Penh to see a western doctor?'

'Okay, if you can take her, that is the best,' Jedtha agreed. 'I can get a taxi for you. Maybe you take her sister, Sinet, too. She can help you to take care of Sineit.'

Similar symptoms had just seen me get airlifted to Bumrungrad Hospital. Looking at that sweet girl lying unconscious with fever, I realised I was face to face with the gross inequality between rich and poor that I'd heard people like Nelson Mandela or Kofi Annan going on about when I was a kid. It had been an abstract, theoretical thing for me until this moment.

Jedtha arranged for the taxi to pick us up from SKO at 2 pm, just enough time for me to jump on my bicycle, get home, throw some clothes in a backpack and rush back.

A grey Toyota Camry taxi was waiting when I rocketed through the SKO gates on my bike. Sinet stood beside the car in a blue trucker hat and a fluoro-green scrunchie. She held two plastic bags stuffed with a few spare clothes for herself and Sineit. I felt slightly embarrassed by my overstuffed backpack.

Jedtha and I helped Sineit into the back of the taxi. She didn't have the strength to sit up, so we put her in the middle so she could lie across Sinet and me. Reaksmey handed me a few plastic bags, in case Sineit was sick on the way down. Jedtha, Reaksmey and the kids all waved solemnly as the taxi reversed out of the gates.

Both girls slept the whole five hours to Phnom Penh. Not me, though. I was quietly freaking out. These two girls had suddenly become entirely my responsibility. It was the biggest responsibility I'd ever been given . . .

Under these dire circumstances, taking Sineit away from SKO was the right thing to have done—she probably would have died if I hadn't acted. However, and this is a big however, this was only necessary because SKO was so seriously discreditable. Social workers, child protection professionals and anyone who has worked for a reputable children's organisation will confirm that, in normal circumstances, having a volunteer take children away from an orphanage or any residential care facility is a serious child protection issue. These matters are best dealt with by professional staff who are qualified to manage such emergencies.

We have learned a lot since then.

~

The trip down to Phnom Penh was wild—like a kamikaze mission. Imagine a single-lane highway, with potholes the size of ponds, with buffalos, cows, people and dogs swarming all over the road. Imagine overtaking with oncoming traffic in plain sight, hurtling towards you, like an insane game of chicken where the rules are that you either swerve back into your own lane just in time, or force the oncoming traffic to make room for three vehicles, even though there are only two lanes. Now imagine doing all that at lightning speeds. Even today, every time I travel from Battambang to the capital on that crazy highway, my heart is in my mouth the whole way.

While both the girls slept, I kept my eyes off the road and my thoughts away from our impending death by reading through all the information I'd printed out from the most reputable websites I could find about HIV/AIDS. I compared it with the few notes in Sineit's file from the public hospital.

There wasn't much in her file, just a few sheets of paper with percentages recorded on them and a medication book with about six entries in it. It did give me the name of the antiretroviral (ARV) she was on. The printouts said that ARV therapy requires strict, near-perfect adherence. The medication needs to be taken at the exact same time, every single day. The implications of poor adherence to ARV regimes were very serious.

I wondered if Sineit had ever been told any of this. I thought back to all the times the kids had looked at my watch to find out the time, because SKO didn't have a clock. With no clock, how could Sineit possibly have known when she needed to take her medication? I started to worry that her sudden decline was because she had built up a resistance to the drugs.

Lauren had emailed me from Australia to say that one of her Oxfam colleagues had recommended the MSF (Doctors Without Borders) office in Phnom Penh, so I asked the driver to take us there. After a hot and exhausting journey, we pulled up outside a big villa in Phnom Penh with the MSF logo over the door. I rang the bell and a tall Khmer man opened it.

'I have a young girl with HIV who is very sick,' I said, feeling terribly out of my depth. 'We've travelled all the way from Battambang—please, can you look at her?'

'We don't have a clinic in Phnom Penh—this is just an office,' he said in perfect English, in a rehearsed kind of way . . . but then he looked past me, to where Sineit leaned heavily on Sinet's shoulder, and his eyes softened. 'Bring her in and I'll check her out.'

Sineit sagged in her seat as he checked her pulse, blood pressure and temperature. He spoke to her kindly in Khmer. He wrote down some addresses and handed them to me, saying in English: 'She's running a very high fever and she's exhausted. The only good clinics in town are closed now, so please check into a hotel, let her get lots of sleep, and then take her to either of these clinics in the morning.'

I swallowed the lump of fear in my throat and nodded. I'd really hoped I could get her into a clinic that night.

I was just grateful that I'd brought Sinet with me. All the little things that make negotiating Cambodia so frustrating for a foreigner—getting around, finding the MSF office and securing food and lodging—was easier with her there. I was impressed with her confidence and general street smarts.

That evening, while Sineit was sleeping, Sinet and I tried our best to communicate via my Khmer–English phonetic dictionary. We started with small talk but eventually the conversation turned to the more serious matters at hand.

'Will she be okay?' Sinet asked cautiously.

I didn't know. And I didn't want to lie. 'I hope she okay,' I said in Khmer, after trawling the dictionary for the word 'hope'. 'Sineit have HIV how many year?'

Sinet took the dictionary and flicked through. 'Long year,' she replied eventually.

I had to ask. 'Sinet, Sineit have HIV how?'

Sinet spent a small eternity leafing through the dictionary, head bowed in concentration. Eventually, she made a pencil mark in the dictionary and passed it back to me. The word 'rape' was underlined.

Fucking hell, I thought to myself. That information totally floored me. I wanted to cry. I could feel that big ball of emotion rising up from the pit of my stomach, but there was no way I was going to let myself cry in front of Sinet. She had enough worries on her plate without feeling like she had to look after me as well. A million questions were running through my head but I didn't want to question her further without some professional support around. So I gave her a hug and we said goodnight.

~

The next morning, Sineit's fever was still raging and she was nauseous. She was little more than skin and bone, so I was longing to see her eat something. I tried to encourage her to eat a bit of rice porridge, but she was too nauseous to swallow much more than a few mouthfuls.

The three of us set off in a tuktuk to the Naga Clinic, the first of the two clinics MSF had recommended. Poor Sineit vomited over the edge of the tuktuk all the way there. I held back her hair and tried to soothe her as best I could. I was desperately hoping this clinic was going to come through. A French doctor who was standing at the front desk took one look at Sineit and put her straight in a bed. Relief washed over me. At least she was in the hands of a doctor now.

After running a few tests, they told me she had pneumonia and oral candidiasis—both of which, I learned, are opportunistic infections common to HIV patients. They kept her in overnight.

The next day was a school day, so I reluctantly put Sinet in a taxi back to Battambang. I wasn't looking forward to navigating this situation without her.

I packed up our things and moved to a guesthouse near the Naga Clinic. I was in and out of the clinic constantly over the next few days.

After day three, the doctor, Cecile, told me that Sineit would be okay. Her fever had come down and she was responding to intravenous treatment. 'But you must get her HIV treatment regime checked by a specialist,' she cautioned. I told her of our frustrations with the doctors in Battambang. She nodded, empathising. 'I will get you the address of someone you can talk to here in Phnom Penh.'

She discharged Sineit as an outpatient with a prescription for oral antibiotics, and made an appointment to see her again the following day.

It was such a boost to see Sineit feeling a bit better. I had high hopes that soon I'd be talking to a competent HIV specialist. But the doctor Cecile sent me to turned out not to be an HIV specialist after all—in fact, he didn't have that much knowledge of HIV. But he knew just the guy to help me. He gave me a name and address, and I made another appointment, still feeling hopeful . . . and it happened again.

Over the next two weeks my hope drained away, and Sineit suffered nausea, vomiting and fevers. As instructed by the doctors at Naga Clinic, I spent long hours through the night covering her in wet towels and feeling utterly desperate. Whenever the fevers got too high, above forty, I'd take her back to the clinic again. The clinic was trying to keep costs down, letting her recover in a hotel, but part of me wished she could have just stayed at the clinic where she was in knowledgeable hands.

She suffered monstrous headaches, and begged me to massage her temples with tiger balm, which seemed to soothe her. By the end of the fortnight we were so closely bonded I was ready to kick down doors for her.

After what felt like an endless stream of false leads, we ended up in the consultation room of one of Cambodia's most esteemed HIV doctors.

Sineit rested on the examination bed while the doctor looked through her files, his brow furrowed.

'There are tests missing,' he grunted. 'She start this program many year ago, so why there only three pages filled out here?'

Yep. More evidence confirming my misgivings about the Battambang public hospital . . .

He carefully examined Sineit, took some blood samples and asked us to come back in a few days' time. This was the first time since we'd arrived in Phnom Penh that I felt we were actually making progress.

Thankfully, over the next few days, Sineit picked up a bit and some colour returned to her cheeks. I grabbed the chance to take her somewhere fun to boost her morale. As she was a teenage girl, the Soya Shopping Centre seemed like the smartest option! Even though she was quite frail, she was soon smiling from ear to ear over her first ride on an escalator, all dressed up in a brand-new outfit.

We went back to the clinic the next day to find out the results of Sineit's blood tests. Dr Sergey's brow furrowed again when he told me her results were 'very bad'.

'Her CD4 count is only forty-nine,' he said. 'For a healthy person like you and me the CD4 count is from five hundred to twelve hundred. Under two hundred mean it progress to stage-three infection, which we call AIDS.'

I felt the blood drain from my face. 'AIDS?' I squeaked.

'It's okay,' he said. 'She is looking strong enough now and her other results are not so bad. We can give her treatment. But if patient has CD4 go below two hundred, normally we prescribe prophylactic treatment so they don't contract opportunistic infection like the pneumonia she had. I don't understand why they don't follow correct treatment in Battambang.' He shook his head.

He prescribed a course of prophylactic treatment for her and told us she had to adhere strictly to her antiretroviral regime. 'I know some doctors who are working in Battambang hospital,' he said. 'They used to be my students. I will call them to follow up for you.'

'Oh . . . but can't she be treated by you here, in Phnom Penh?' I asked, following up quickly with: 'I don't mind paying for her treatment.' We had come so far. I didn't want to just end up where we started, back in that godforsaken hospital.

'Oh, no, in Cambodia it's not so easy,' he said. 'The patient must be treated in province that they live. If she lives in Battambang she must be treated in Battambang. But don't worry, I will ask my old students to follow up this case and make sure they keep better records. It is very important for her to follow the regime and take care of her health.

She must take her medication at the same time every day—should not be even ten minutes late. She should be eating a lot of meat and vegetables. You can buy her some Ensure—it is a high-energy milk drink that is very good for patients with HIV.'

I was madly scribbling everything down as he spoke, when something he said suddenly struck me. 'Several more years?" I echoed. 'What happens then?'

He gave me a sympathetic look. 'HIV is serious illness,' he said. 'The ARV only can work for about ten years and she already in stage three. In Battambang we don't have any more options for treatment available.'

'But—' I glanced at Sineit, relieved for once that she couldn't speak English '—she's been on it for five or six years already ... what will happen then?'

The doctor explained, gently and kindly, that HIV patients will inevitably become resistant to the treatment, develop AIDS and die of opportunistic infections such as pneumonia, candidiasis, lymphoma or tuberculosis.

'In Battambang HIV program, not have other options for treatment yet like in your country,' he explained.

'Can I bring in the medicine for her from Australia?' I wondered aloud.

'It's possible,' he agreed. 'But not easy and very expensive.'

I felt that ball of emotion well up inside me again. It was partly relief that we had found the doctor, partly grief and anger that Sineit's treatment had been compromised for so long, but mostly just terrible sadness. Because this lovely girl, not much younger than me, only had a life expectancy of about five years ...

~

When we arrived back at SKO, Sinet and the other kids greeted us at the gate and admired Sineit's new outfit and smothered her in hugs. I caught Sinet's eye and we both exchanged a very happy, relieved smile. At least Sineit was better for now.

I brought Jedtha up to speed on everything the doctor had said. He listened intently, and said: 'Thank you, Tara! We need to know this—nobody on the staff knows any of this information. Nobody told us.'

We went straight to the markets to buy a good-quality watch for each sister, so Sinet could help Sineit remember to take her medication on time. I set the alarm on the watches for six in the morning and six in the evening, to make it even easier to remember.

I was seething over the incompetence of the Battambang HIV doctors. According to the records the doctor in Phnom Penh had shown me, they knew her CD4 count was below 200 and still didn't put her on prophylactic treatment.

Jedtha and I decided to talk to them the following day.

I was feeling just a tiny bit obstreperous when we arrived. As soon as we were called into the doctor's office, I started laying down all the information given to me by the doctor in Phnom Penh.

'So why wasn't she on treatment?' I finished.

The doctor clearly didn't like my tone. He waved his hand to dismiss us from the office, telling Jedtha: 'No, we didn't do anything wrong.'

But I sat tight in my chair, punching the numbers for the Phnom Penh doctor into my phone. When he answered, I handed him the phone.

He gave me a death stare. 'Hello?' His voice rose and things got a bit heated, then he calmed down, saying, '*Bat, bat, bat, ba, ba, bababaaba,*' — 'Bat' being the masculine word for 'yes' in Khmer. He handed the phone back to me.

'It's okay, Tara,' said the doctor in Phnom Penh. 'He understands and will do what I ask now.'

'Thank you so much!' I said.

As we spoke, I could hear the Battambang doctor muttering angrily, getting quite worked up.

When I hung up, he said in an icy tone: 'If you take patient to Phnom Penh again, cannot bring her here again. We not treat her.'

The full meaning was clear in his livid face. It was a death sentence for Sineit.

Jedtha and I took our leave.

I realised that I'd made a cultural blunder by being so overtly angry with him. It's not the way to do things in Cambodia. But at least Sineit would get the treatment she needed now.

7

By early February 2007—after the stress of the last few weeks—I was worn out and a bit lonely for a familiar face. So it was wonderful to hear that Sally Power was flying over to visit and meet everyone she'd been hearing about by email.

The day she was due to arrive, I waited impatiently in the yard of the pink villa with Chan's wife, Mina, and their little daughter Chea. Finally, a taxi pulled up outside the front gate and Sally hopped out, petite and elegant in long flowing pants and a headscarf.

I squealed, tumbled out of the hammock I was lying in, and ran to the gate.

'I can't believe I'm finally here!' she said, giving me a big hug.

As soon as she'd had a shower and settled in, we sat on the day bed in the yard eating one of Mina's delicious curries, catching up on all things CCT.

Sally is a big-picture thinker, and she had all kinds of new ideas for raising funds when we were both back in Australia again. It was important to us to be completely transparent with our donors. We both felt strongly that donors and supporters had a right to know exactly where their funds were going—and they should know about the failures as well as the successes. Sally suggested we start documenting operations at SKO so that, in the future, we could provide detailed reports to prospective donors.

We also thought it would be a good idea to buy the orphanage a vehicle. A moto seemed like the best choice—it would be affordable to buy and run, and it was the most culturally appropriate vehicle for the staff to use.

Talking to Sally gave me an extra surge of energy and optimism. I was so happy to have her there.

~

The following morning Sally and I cycled out to SKO. I had discovered earlier that there were no case files for the kids, so the first job Sally and I got started on together was helping Jedtha, Reaksmey and Rath put them together. After a hard morning's work sorting through piles of confusing government documents, we took a break and headed out with Jedtha to buy a reliable moto for SKO.

Sally was all fired up about getting corporate sponsorship, and kept asking Rath if she could see the latest financial reports for SKO. He kept saying, 'Okay, okay,' but, once again, the reports never materialised.

Given the lack of financial transparency at SKO, we just didn't feel comfortable donating the funds directly. We were aware that there were administration costs, but apparently the German NGO was covering most of those already. Jedtha didn't have access to an SKO bank account, so he couldn't tell us anything about SKO's current financial situation. Until we could see some financial documents, we decided to tread very cautiously.

Sally felt that the problems were deeper than just poverty and incompetence. She thought that the bare offices, the lack of any clear systems or policies and Rath's steadfast refusal to produce financial records was not right. She didn't trust him. And, though he would never have said this directly, it was clear that Jedtha didn't either.

We decided to trust Jedtha—we felt we had to trust *someone* at SKO. In hindsight we should have considered consulting with other NGOs, but Jedtha didn't seem to have a bad bone in his body. We liked him, the kids adored him, and whenever we gave him money he was scrupulous about keeping detailed documentation and receipts. Between us, Jedtha and I accounted for every cent raised at that first fundraiser.

~

While Sally was visiting it became apparent that, just as I'd feared, Reaksmey was not coping with the task of keeping on top of the kids' medication schedules.

'Yes, it not good,' Jedtha agreed. 'SKO need more staff. Usually SKO's social worker, Savenh, she take care of these kind of job, but now she away. She come back soon but I think one thing SKO really need is a nurse to help take care of the children health. Maybe you can help us pay for salary for one nurse?'

Sally and I agreed that sounded like a great idea, so Jedtha put the word out that SKO was looking for a nurse.

The best application for the role of SKO nurse came from a woman named Davi, who also happened to be the sister of SKO's social worker, Savenh. She seemed lovely and we were impressed with all her answers in the interview, so we unanimously agreed to give her the job.

~

Sally fell madly in love with Battambang. I think if she was as free of responsibilities as I was, she'd have moved over immediately. She loved the people, the food, the beauty of the landscape and, of course, the kids.

One day while we were riding down a dirt road on the very edge of town, when the sky was a sharp shining blue and the breeze was making ripples through rice fields, I was rambling whimsically about how often I found myself rapt with awe at the rough, unbridled beauty of Cambodia.

Sally suddenly asked me: 'Do you think you could live here?'

'Ah, I dunno,' I said. I was definitely committed to SKO, and planned to continue supporting the kids into the future. But I hadn't yet worked out a plan for how I was going to do that. I had been thinking I was going to try to build a career in something that either paid incredibly well, or gave me time to keep fundraising. I wasn't quite sure . . .

Contemplating the next steps made me feel a bit depressed for a moment. I'd already been away for two of the three months I'd budgeted for this trip and I knew that in just four short weeks I'd be faced with the harsh realities of going back to life in Australia. The last month or so had seen me almost completely forget about the life I'd left behind.

That's how it often is, though, when moving between such profoundly different places as Australia and Cambodia. 'Mutually unimaginable' is the only way I can describe it. Even these days, when I spend time in Australia—the other side of the rabbit hole—Cambodia seems like some kind of crazy dream.

~

One afternoon, I arrived at SKO to find Sineit sitting on the moto, tears streaming down her face, desperately trying to start the engine. A few of the older kids knew how to ride—but they were forbidden to ride the moto and Sineit knew it.

I raced up to her and yelled in Khmer: 'Sineit! Stop. What wrong?'

She shook her head, got the moto running and steered it out of the gates.

'*Stop! Stop!*' I cried. Then, giving up, I yelled: '*I go too!*' and jumped on the back.

We travelled about forty metres before we had to make a left turn onto a bigger dirt road. Sineit, who was upset and shaky and not as experienced as she, or I, had thought, overshot the turn. Sinet and some of the other kids happened to be on their way home from school, heading towards us. They got to enjoy the dignified sight of us careering into the deep water-filled channel running alongside the road.

We were both a bit shocked at first, but by the time we climbed to our feet we were laughing. The kids, relieved, helped pull us and the bike out of the filthy water. We were lucky enough to get away with just a slight fracture in poor Sineit's ankle, and a whopping great purple bruise on my arse.

Sineit had more reason than most to have a fit of teenage angst but I was intent on finding out what had upset her. Sinet filled me in. It turned out Sineit had been badly upset by her boyfriend. She was a romantic soul despite all she'd been through, and dreamed of falling in love, getting married and having beautiful babies. Hearing this made me feel very sad. Being HIV positive with just a five-year life expectancy ... it was heartbreaking.

~

After we got Sineit patched up, I decided my bruised butt needed a rest, so I took the afternoon off and headed into town to write a few emails and catch up with friends and family. I went to an internet cafe and signed into MSN messenger. To my delight, Fiona Reynolds was online.

> **Tara**: Hey! Fee! How are you?
>
> **Fiona**: Hi Tara, great to hear from you. How are the kids?
>
> **Tara**: They're really good. How are YOU?
>
> **Fiona**: I've had some bad news. The tumours have come back but they're inoperable this time. The doctors say they can make the end as comfortable as possible.
>
> **Tara**: What?
>
> **Tara**: Fuck.

Tara: No! Oh god. Fee!

Fiona: I'm sorry, the doctor's here. I gotta go. Talk soon. Love
you x

Tara: Love you too. So much. I'll call x

I cried and cried until I couldn't breathe through my nose. People in the cafe started to look at me curiously.

I sent an email off to Sal Reynolds, Fee's little sister, asking for more information. Was it true? Was there any hope? If I flew back early, could I see her?

Sal was in the year below Fee and me at NEGS but she was also a horsey girl who I'd come to know very well. Sal was a lot like Fee—a high achiever and a born leader. She and Fee were extremely close. It made me think of how I'd feel if I was ever faced with losing Noni. The thought was utterly unfathomable. I was always so impressed with how well Sal managed. She had been such an incredible support to Fee throughout the three years of operations and treatment.

Sal wrote back the next day to confirm that Fee didn't have long. It could be just a matter of days. 'Don't come back for her sake, Tara. She's not really herself anymore. Only come back if you think it will help *you*,' she said.

My heart sank, but I knew I had to keep it together. I had to call Fee in case I didn't get another chance to say goodbye.

I bought a phone card and shut myself in the cafe's phone booth, hands shaking as I dialled her number. Her mother answered.

'Hi Binny, it's Tara.' I started to cry.

'I'm so glad you called,' she whispered gently.

'I'm so sorry, Binny.' I couldn't imagine how she must be suffering right now.

'Thanks, Tara,' she said. There was a long, painful silence. 'I'll see if Fiona's awake.'

A few moments later, my friend came on the line.

'Tara?' Fee's voice still sounded exactly the same.

I had a lump in my throat the size of a bowling ball. 'Yeah, Fee, it's me . . . I've missed you so much.'

'I've missed you too!' She sounded surprisingly normal. 'How are the kids?'

The kids?! For an instant, I'd forgotten where I was.

'The kids are good, Fee. They're doing much better now. But I'm leaving as soon as I can to come home and see you.'

'That'd be really nice,' she replied, a little fainter this time.

There was a long silence on the line. The bowling ball grew in my throat.

'How are the kids?' Fiona said again, clearly forgetting she'd asked already.

I cried as quietly as I could into the phone, thinking about what Sal had said.

'The kids are good. They're doing much better now,' I said again.

She must be so scared, I thought to myself. I wondered if she knew I was calling to say goodbye. I thought about what a traumatic experience that would be—a horrifying reminder of your imminent demise.

I scrambled to find the right words. 'Fee, you know you're one of the most exceptional human beings I've ever met? I really mean that. You've been such a wonderful friend to me. You know, you always made every single person in our grade at NEGS feel like they were important and they mattered. I'm sure you've made every person you've ever met feel that way. I can't tell you what an inspiration you are to me—the way you set your mind to things and then actually achieved them. I feel so incredibly lucky to know you and call you my friend.'

'Wow, Tara. Thanks. That means a lot. I can't wait to see you.'

'I'll be home to see you really soon. I love you, Fee.'

'I love you too, Tara.'

'Bye,' I whispered.

'Bye, Tara.'

The phone went dead. I held it to my ear and cried hard. There was so much more I wanted to say, but what words could ever be enough in the last conversation you have with someone you love?

Sally and I decided to leave immediately, a few weeks earlier than we'd planned. I was twenty-one and had never lost a close friend before.

Sally helped me arrange everything. We handed the pink villa back to the landlord and set up an account for CCT at the ANZ Royal Bank where Jedtha could receive funds from us. I had a couple of friends who were coming soon to volunteer, so I'd hear how things were going.

I bade a sad farewell to Chan and Mina, promising to stay in touch and continue to help them if I could.

I also said a really wrenching goodbye to the kids, promising to come back one day soon. They got very emotional, which meant I got emotional, too. It was awful.

Sinet seemed to be particularly devastated that I was going so much sooner than expected. I felt terrible, like I was abandoning her. So I gave her my Cambodian phone, with some credit on it and my Australian number programmed into it. I hoped this would show her that the connection between us wasn't being cut for good.

Sally helped me pack and we both left Battambang late in the evening. Chan drove us through the night to Phnom Penh airport.

~

My ex-boyfriend, Altiyan, picked me up from the airport in Sydney.

My conversation with Fee was the last she ever had. She went to sleep after we spoke and never woke up again.

Altiyan drove me to Orange, about three and a half hours west of Sydney, for the funeral. Fiona had asked if I could play a song I'd written for her at the service.

The church hall was full of familiar faces from NEGS—girls from all different grades, boys from our brother school and many of the NEGS teachers.

I couldn't handle it when Fee's mum, Binny, got up to speak. All the tears I'd been holding back came gushing out at once. And every time I looked over at Sal, I lost it again.

Holding it together enough to perform that song was one of the hardest things I'd ever had to do in my life. Luckily, Altiyan is a talented musician, and he supported me by playing guitar and singing a beautiful harmony line. I probably couldn't have done it if it wasn't for him. He was a rock for me to lean on that day.

Fee's illness and death brought Sal Reynolds and me closer together and I'm thankful for the role she continues to play in my life.

I still think of Fiona Reynolds all the time and try to imagine what amazing things she would have done with her life. I have no doubt that, whatever she chose to do, the world would have been a better place with her in it.

~

For the next few months, I tried to reconnect with friends and family and work out what to do next. But I was in another downward spiral.

It was partly the grief, of course. It put me in a bad place, made everyday life just bloody hard going. And when life is hard going, my eating disorder tends to take over. The unhealthy thoughts and feelings win.

I did bits and pieces of work, none of which I particularly enjoyed. I worked at the racetrack, testing racehorses for drugs, which basically involved shoving saucepans under the horses when they're taking a piss, after each race, to collect their urine. I taught horseriding and I did some voiceover work for my dad, Peter.

But the dark clouds continued to engulf me.

Through all of this, though, one thing that never wavered was my enthusiasm for SKO. I spent a lot of time talking with Sally Power about all things Cambodia.

I'd never want to imply that running off to work in a 'third world' country is a solution to 'first world' problems. I generally find every part of that particular narrative reductive and potentially quite dangerous.

But nevertheless, thoughts of going back to Cambodia did kind of keep me going.

~

Sally and I spent hours trying to think up more ways to raise funds for CCT, so we could keep paying SKO's nurse and keep supplementing the orphanage's food budget. We managed to get CCT's logos designed, business cards printed, and a website up and running, mostly with pro bono assistance.

I occasionally received very short basic messages from Sinet—things like *Hello sister!* or *I miss so mach*. I missed her and the other kids too, and I found myself worrying about them a lot.

I just hoped I could earn myself enough money to justify going back sometime in the not-too-distant future.

~

Several weeks into this dark patch a family friend, Dave Hibbard, invited me out to a gig at Tatler, a bar in Darlinghurst. Dave is a well-known drummer in Sydney and had been one of the volunteers to visit SKO after Sally and I left. I really had to push myself to go, but I knew it would be nice to see him, and I looked forward to talking with him about SKO and Cambodia.

It turned out to be a good night—the music was great and it was fun to catch up with Dave and other friends who turned up. Towards the end of the night another familiar face dropped in: Carolyn Shine, the keyboard player who had given me piano lessons the year before.

There was something very different about meeting her out at night. I was all dressed up, being a twenty-something girl in Sydney, but she was dressed more casually. With her long, dark wavy hair and piercing blue eyes, she could get away with anything. I suddenly felt self-conscious and overdressed.

But she seemed surprised and happy to see me, and we were soon chatting easily. She'd spent a few years living in Hanoi, and could speak quite fluent Vietnamese. With an interest in South-East Asia in common, we had a lot to talk about.

After the night ended and I'd made my way home, I couldn't stop thinking how cool it was to bump into Carolyn. She seemed like a lot of fun and genuinely interested in my stories from Cambodia. I texted Dave and asked him for her number.

~

In time, the grief and the bad feelings started to ease a bit. I decided to be proactive—I bought a bicycle and started riding around the streets of Sydney in an effort to make my life feel more South-East Asian. I longed for the flat Cambodian roads but still enjoyed the pace of life and the inadvertent exercise that comes from getting around on a bike.

Then, one afternoon, I was going way too fast around a bend like an idiot, had a crash and fractured both my wrists. Which is actually exactly what life in South-East Asia can be like sometimes!

So I was in a cast the next time I caught up with Carolyn.

We went for a walk around Centennial Park together, chatting about our travels at first, then skipping on to linguistics, music, science and scepticism. She was a bit older than me, but it didn't seem that way when we were together. She was such a fun, passionate and free-spirited person. We seemed to meet in the middle and I was over the moon about our wonderful new friendship.

~

By early May 2007, I was feeling good enough to get back to focusing on my career. Maybe I should go and study something IT-related— computer science or graphic design or maybe even a science degree?

I was still pondering this and talking over options with Sue and Peter when my grandmother Joan sat me down with the most exciting, unexpected news. She had decided to donate an unbelievable $25,000 to CCT!

'I'm impressed with the work you're doing in Cambodia, Tara,' she said. 'I'm very proud of you and I'm looking forward to coming over to Cambodia to see what you do with this money.'

'Oh my goodness, Joan!' I gasped. 'Really? Are you serious?! Oh my god! Thank you so much!' I flung my arms around her and gave her a huge hug. It was probably the greatest gift I'd ever received.

The money was for the kids, of course, but I was thrilled to have been given the opportunity to continue what I had started. But the real gift to me was knowing how much Joan believed in me.

It took a while for the enormity of what she'd done to sink in. This was even more money than we'd raised last time! I wrote to Jedtha immediately to let him know the good news and tell him that I'd be back in Cambodia before the end of the year.

~

It turned out the donation came not a moment too soon. A couple of weeks later, I got the following email from Jedtha:

Dear Tara,

I would like to inform you about news from sko.

Yesterday, Rath warned to fire Reaksmey and social worker from sko.

Could we start new organisation soon? I think if we delay longer, the staff will receive more and more pressures, especially the nurse from Rath! And the big problems could come out.

I look forward to hearing your reply soon.

What the hell? Start a new NGO! Where on earth had this come from?

I wasn't even sure what he meant, let alone what to make of it. It sounded very worrying though.

I'd spent enough time in Cambodia by now to know that getting to the bottom of all this by email was going to be pretty much impossible, so I booked my flight for early August.

I let Jedtha know that I would be back in Cambodia soon, so we could discuss this all in person. I tried to offer the only real reassurance I could by adding: *Don't worry, we will all sit down together and work out why Rath is upset and work to resolve the problem.*

Then, just a few weeks before I was due to leave, I received a very strange text message from Sinet.

Hello Tara. Don't worry me. I be brave.

Here was another cryptic message that I didn't quite know how to interpret. I knew she must have trawled the dictionary to find those words. Why did she need to be brave? What was going on over there? I replied, asking her what she meant, but didn't hear from her again. There was no point in calling—neither of us had the language skills to have a proper conversation. I crossed my fingers, hoping it was nothing serious.

But getting back to Cambodia felt all the more urgent now.

~

'The big problems could come out . . .' Those words of Jedtha's kept rolling around in my head. At the time, I had no idea what Jedtha meant. I came to learn just how cautiously he chose those words, which is no surprise given his history.

In 1976, the Khmer Rouge was in power and Year Zero had ticked over to Year One. Thousands of Cambodians had been murdered. Money was outlawed, along with religion, music, private ownership, family relationships, western medicine and personal freedom. Cambodia was renamed Democratic Kampuchea and was ruled by the Angkar, the anonymous leadership.

Into this state of chaos, a boy was born in a field. His mother was working the land for the Khmer Rouge, far from her village. She named her baby Jedtha: Pon Jedtha.

When the Vietnamese invaded Cambodia and the Khmer Rouge were ousted in 1979, three-year-old Jedtha and his family returned to their old village in Prey Veng province. They began rebuilding their lives, doing the job that had allowed them to survive the regime—working the land.

In the years that followed, when most of Cambodia was in the grip of a terrible famine, the Pon family's farming skills stood them in good stead. They grew rice on their five hectares of land. This meant they could expand their business into breeding livestock such as cattle, buffalos, chickens and ducks. They were well off compared to most of their countryfolk in the early eighties.

The eldest child of four, Jedtha soon had responsibilities well beyond his years. By the time he was six, his mother and father already relied heavily on him to help with farm work and look after his younger siblings. There was no time for games, or rest, or fun. Working meant the difference between eating and going hungry, between life and death. Jedtha knew of other kids his age who didn't have work to do, who had died of hunger.

In 1989, when the Vietnamese troops finally withdrew, the country was renamed the State of Cambodia and Buddhism was re-established as the country's official religion. Cambodian people were hopeful that there were good times to come. But for the Pon family, 1989 was the year everything started to go wrong.

Jedtha's father started having an affair and abandoned his family. The night before he left, he beat Jedtha badly and threatened to kill him with a knife. Jedtha's parents couldn't legally divorce because at that time Cambodia had no laws, but Jedtha's father never spoke to his wife or children again.

Jedtha's mother struggled to recover emotionally, work the farm on her own and look after her four children. One by one, she had to sell off the animals, and soon the rice fields were bare for lack of sowing. She fell into a deep depression and started drinking. All responsibility for the family fell on the shoulders of Jedtha, now thirteen.

Jedtha and his siblings bore the brunt of their mother's rages. Jedtha once kept aside a little of the family's rice to give to his aunt, who was starving. When his mother found out, she flew into a rage and accused him of stealing. Jedtha was often nursing wounds and bruises from her beatings while he worked to carry water, gather fire-wood and cook.

Despite his responsibilities, Jedtha did do his best to attend school, which was six kilometres from home. Even though he only managed to attend one or two days a week, he made above-average grades.

In 1991, when Jedtha turned fifteen, a peace agreement was signed in Paris, and Prince Sihanouk was again crowned king of Cambodia in 1993.

Jedtha's paternal grandmother, Toing, loved her kind and sensitive grandson fiercely. She could see how smart he was, and often told him so. She knew times were changing in Cambodia and that Jedtha had to seize the chance to make something of himself. She suggested he join the local pagoda as a novice monk so he could continue his studies. There is a long tradition in Cambodia of 'temporary ordination'. Young men like Jedtha spend months or years as monks, learning Buddhist teachings before disrobing, marrying and making a life out in the world.

Jedtha recoiled at the thought of leaving his mother and siblings, who were so reliant on him, but his grandmother assured him they would survive and reminded him that he could support the family much better once he got himself an education and a job. So he went.

Jedtha's mother and siblings did struggle while he was away. They rarely had enough to eat, and at times his mother would take off, leaving the little ones at home alone. They were subject to violence from their neighbours, who looked down on them for being in such a destitute state. On some nights, hearing that his mother had wandered again, Jedtha would leave the pagoda to stay with his younger siblings.

At the pagoda, Jedtha studied every chance he had. He learned the Pali language, Sanskrit, English and other subjects. He also studied at a private school. The head teacher there let him pay only what he could afford.

Jedtha worked hard and learned enough English to start teaching his own students. That was his 'big break'. He was finally able to earn some money to help support his family. He also did what he could to help the Khmeng Wat 'temple boys' (poor kids from the villages) who lived at the pagoda, working for the monks. He spent his own money making sure they had enough food.

After fifteen years he became one of the most highly respected monks in the Battambang community—renowned for his kindness, intelligence and incorruptibility. He worked with well over one hundred temple boys, who still visit him to this day in gratitude for the support he provided them. He even trained three keen foreigners to become Buddhist monks.

In 2003, Jedtha's mother, Sarom, fell seriously ill. Jedtha took her to the public hospital in Phnom Penh, where she was diagnosed with advanced lung cancer. She died one month later.

This left Jedtha with even more responsibility for his younger brothers and sister, who had never really learned how to take care of themselves. His sister had, in desperation, taken a job as a 'beer girl'—a young woman who promotes beer in local pubs, which can be a step away from becoming a sex worker. She was now walking a dangerous path for a Cambodian girl. Jedtha decided to disrobe, leave the monastery and get a full-time job to support her and his two brothers.

It wasn't an easy transition for Jedtha. Cambodia had only recently opened its doors to tourism, the new economy was in its infancy, and there just weren't a lot of jobs around. Jedtha moved into a weatherbeaten shack in the slum that fringes Battambang's railway station and continued to teach English while he looked for work.

A friend of Jedtha's who was working for an NGO in Battambang told him about a small orphanage called SKO. The orphanage was looking for someone to help with their administration, but they had no funding—meaning there was no salary on offer. Jedtha politely told his friend he wasn't interested. His main goal was to earn money to support his family.

When the director of SKO, a fellow ex-monk named Rath, heard that the position had been put to one of Battambang's most respected monks, he approached Jedtha himself. He explained that the orphanage urgently needed his help—they needed someone who could speak English to write proposals to get funding. And when funding came in, there would be a salary for him. Jedtha allowed himself to be persuaded. He cared about Cambodia's youth and reasoned that gaining experience in an NGO made sense. He could fulfil his passion for helping others while keeping a roof over his siblings' heads.

Jedtha worked at SKO as an administrator for many months without receiving a dollar. Finally, Rath stepped down as director, giving himself the role of administrator as well as accountant, and invited Jedtha to take over the role of director. Shortly after, Jedtha managed to secure some funding from the International Organisation for Migration and the German organisation, GIZ. Finally, there was some more funding for SKO's operational costs.

Jedtha rented a small house in town and invited his sister to live with him. He continued saving money from his work at SKO as well as English teaching, until he had enough to buy a cheap block of land with a rough wooden shack on it.

But something was bothering Jedtha. The more time he spent at SKO, the more he began to worry about Rath's agenda. Rath was very secretive about a lot of things, including the unrestricted funds that were coming into SKO from individual private donors. Jedtha heard more stories from other staff and neighbours and his suspicions and concerns for the kids grew.

Jedtha wasn't good at confrontation—he'd grown up in a world where you earn respect by being a good, kind person, not by being a strong, forceful leader. And he was a pacifist at heart. He was at a loss as to how to deal with Rath. He could only hope that his suspicions were wrong, that everything would somehow turn out okay.

8

Jedtha picked me up from the bus station in Battambang on 8 August 2007 and took me straight to a meeting at his house with Davi (the nurse), Savenh (the social worker) and Reaksmey.

The four of them sat around the table and grimly told me their story. Jedtha and Reaksmey helped to translate. They were now jobless, and absolutely outraged.

Rath had denied Davi access to SKO, meaning the kids couldn't get their medications.

'Wait—' I struggled to comprehend. 'What? Why would he do that?'

Davi and Savenh started talking rapidly in Khmer. I only understood an odd word here and there.

Jedtha translated, but it was still hard to understand—not because of Jedtha's English skills, but because Cambodians have this way of talking around issues that can be rather confusing for a foreigner.

'He said she was not staff of SKO because he never agreed to hire her,' Jedtha said. He was visibly upset. 'So many things to tell you!' He shook his head. 'Rath, he not good. He put his family into SKO. Ten of the children at SKO are his niece and nephew. He always make the other kid wait to eat—his family always eat first! So there is not much food left for the other kids. Rath is always hitting the kids. I see Rath whipping them—with my own eye! The kids they very scared so much. Sacha, Sinet's younger brother, he run away already after Rath whip him too hard! Oh, it is so bad at SKO!'

I was shocked. I had been expecting a problem, but nothing like this. I didn't have a chance to say much more than 'Oh no . . .' before Jedtha launched into the next bit.

'Rath, he fire me, Savenh and Reaksmey from SKO and cannot come back again. Now he hire his relative to work at SKO. This is not correct way for NGO to work in Cambodia. And Rath, he say very bad thing to Sinet. He say she can't go to anywhere or talk to anyone, only stay at SKO and go to school. She is like prisoner! He take the phone you give to her and tell her and all the children they cannot talk with you, me, Reaksmey, Davi or Savenh.'

Reaksmey added: 'All the girls crying a lot. They're very scared.'

They all warned me that I shouldn't go back to SKO and see the kids.

'Rath, he really angry that you give your money to me, not to SKO bank account,' Jedtha said.

'Oh . . .' I felt terrible as I realised I may have inadvertently caused some of this problem. 'Did I make a mistake, Jedtha? I know Rath is the SKO accountant, but Sally and I felt we just couldn't trust him.'

'No, it is not your mistake,' Jedtha responded. 'Normal way is for donors to give money to NGO bank account and NGO have good management and finance staff who spend the money carefully. But I not trust Rath also, so I think you make clever decision, so he not take your money.' He placed a reassuring hand on my shoulder.

~

I staggered home to the guesthouse I was staying in that night, reeling from everything I'd been told.

I had some big questions about some of the very serious accusations Jedtha, Reaksmey, Savenh and Davi were making. It all sounded very convincing, but I couldn't quite fit all the pieces of the various stories together into one clear picture.

I also couldn't help feeling a bit suspicious. I was aware I was only hearing one side of the story. How much of what Jedtha and the others had told me was true and how much was exaggerated? I'd really only known these people for a couple of months. How sure was I that I could trust them at all? And what was I to do about all this anyway?

That led me back to thoughts of the kids. It killed me to think they were scared, and hungry, with no idea that I was just up the road.

To clear my head, I decided to have dinner at a local expat hang, the Balcony Bar. It's a lovely, open-air, traditional wooden Cambodian house nestled in the treetops overlooking the river.

I got chatting to an older Australian guy I'd met on my last trip who was working for an agricultural NGO in Battambang, Needing someone to vent to, and hoping he could give me some advice, I told him about some of the things I'd heard about Rath and SKO.

'Just pay this guy Rath more money,' he scoffed, chugging down his Angkor beer. 'That's how it works over here. Just pay them more money and there'll be no trouble.'

This spun me for a six. *That's ridiculous!* I thought. Then: *But, actually, it makes sense. But no, hang on, Rath's abusing the kids . . .*

A little later, Stephan Bognar, the CEO of the Maddox Jolie-Pitt Foundation (MJP), arrived. MJP is a well-respected NGO working to preserve the habitat and wildlife in the Samlout District of Battambang Province while also providing support to the surrounding community.

Stephan sat down next to me at the bar and ordered dinner. If anyone could give me good advice, it would be him.

He listened patiently to my story and then said kindly: 'It's an awful situation. I really feel for those kids, but I'd just stay away from orphanages if I were you.'

I didn't want to admit that I had no idea why he was saying that. It was the first time I'd heard anyone say anything negative about orphanages.

I went home feeling even more confused. Cambodia just seemed so hard to navigate.

But those words certainly did stay with me . . .

~

The next morning I woke early, determined to get some solid answers. I called Jedtha and explained, as respectfully as I could, that I'd like to check with other sources to confirm their stories of Rath and SKO.

He agreed without hesitation and came straight over to pick me up. First, he took me to meet some of SKO's neighbours.

The first woman we spoke to lived in a small shack just around the corner from SKO. She seemed to know Jedtha well. She leaped out of her chair to greet us and rushed around to find another couple of chairs for us.

Jedtha didn't take long to get straight to the point. He asked her something about Rath but she shut down immediately. 'Oh oh, I don't know,' she said in Khmer, shaking her head. When pressed, she said: 'I don't like to gossip.'

Feeling a little like a Jehovah's Witness, I followed Jedtha to the shack next door, where another woman was placing burning incense in the gleaming Hindu shrine that seemed to adorn the front of every household in Battambang.

She welcomed us warmly, insisting we sit down on the plastic chairs in front of her small home.

'Sister, can we ask you some question about Rath?' Jedtha asked in Khmer.

'Oh, yes—okay . . .' she said, furrowing her brow and pursing her lips.

As they talked, I listened intently and picked up some words here and there, but not enough to follow a complex conversation. There was anger and frustration in her voice. Often when Rath's name was mentioned she'd close her eyes, shake her head and hiss. Jedtha did his best to translate. It was clear from her body language that she disliked Rath, but I needed to hear it for myself, in English.

Jedtha then took me to talk to the head monk at the Buddhist pagoda near SKO. He was a very serious, dignified older man with a very shiny bald head, dressed in a saffron robe. We sat down together in an open and airy room, covered in murals.

'Oh, Tara! You cannot sit with crossed legs in front of a monk,' Jedtha told me quietly. 'We must sit like this,' he said, tucking both legs to one side. Pointing the soles of your feet at another person is the height of rudeness in Cambodia. I quickly tucked my feet away, hoping I hadn't offended.

The monk spoke English very well. He looked at me dead in the eye and told me what he knew of Mr Rath.

He said that Rath came from Prey Veng Province, where he had gone by a different name. When he came to Battambang he became a monk and caused many problems in different pagodas in Battambang. He used money raised by his pagoda to buy some land that was meant to be used as a cremation site, but instead he put the land title in his own name and used it to start the SKO orphanage.

Jedtha interrupted to point out to me that because Rath owned SKO, it would be almost impossible to fire him because there was no funds to set up SKO somewhere else, so the children would have nowhere to live.

'He cheat us many times,' the monk said, shaking his head. 'Corruption is very big problem in Cambodia!' I sensed a low, simmering anger in his voice.

I thanked him for the information.

'You be careful of Mr Rath,' he warned.

I walked back to Jedtha's moto feeling shaken. What had I got myself into?

~

Jedtha suggested that next we should visit the kids' school, just a stone's throw away from SKO. The school was run by a French NGO to provide education and other assistance to disadvantaged kids in Battambang. It was a performing arts school, and seemed like a happy, positive place, with an art gallery, sports field, playground, theatre and circus tent.

We met with a very smart, sympathetic middle-aged Khmer woman named Darlin who was a social worker at the school. She spoke just enough English to get her message across, with some assistance from Jedtha.

She told us the school had recently ceased all support of SKO, and would no longer be collaborating or communicating with Rath in the future. She said she could see how badly neglected the SKO kids were. They were coming to school without shoes, and lately they'd lost weight and were always asking for food. Apparently one of the kids told her that Rath would discipline him by whipping him with palm leaves. She'd seen the marks on his back, bleeding. Jedtha interrupted to emphasise that he'd witnessed it happening. Darlin shook her head and continued, saying that the children often told her they were scared to go home. Most days Sinet would hide in the school library for hours after school to avoid going back to SKO. She said she was very concerned, but felt powerless to help the children.

It confirmed almost everything the staff had told me.

After our meeting, as we walked back to the gate, we passed a class of older kids sitting in a circle outside with their teacher. A young girl jumped to her feet and called out to Jedtha: '*Loak Khrew!*'

It was Sinet! She nearly died when she recognised me.

'Tara!' She ran straight for me, fell into my arms and burst into tears.

'*Sok sobai!* How are you? I'm so happy to see you!' I said, giving her a big hug. I wasn't sure whether her tears were happy tears or traumatised tears. 'Sinet, are you okay?' I asked her gently.

She clung to me, but didn't stop crying, and wouldn't—or couldn't—answer.

'Let's go somewhere,' Jedtha said quietly. Sinet nodded meekly and I understood—when Cambodian kids feel threatened, they tend to shut down. The school felt too open to the whole world for Sinet to feel safe speaking.

Jedtha got permission from the school's social worker to leave with Sinet, and we all went back to Jedtha's tiny house where we could talk properly. Jedtha laid out some rice cakes and fruit for Sinet to eat. She'd lost a lot of weight and ate everything hungrily.

Jedtha asked her a few questions in Khmer, and after a few minutes, she gathered her confidence and answered through her tears.

Rath was hitting and threatening the kids, she told us. The new staff were almost as cruel, and the kids were terrified of them. After sacking the nurse, none of the kids got any medicine. Rath was making them work on his farm before and after school, like slaves. He let his relatives eat first and the rest of the kids only got to eat whatever was left over, assuming anything was left at all. The starving kids were catching tiny fish in the nearby rice fields and picking wild morning glory—a vegetable similar to spinach—from around the nearby waterways. Sometimes, they managed to catch mice or rats to eat.

Rath had taken Sinet's phone and told her never to contact me again. He took away some of the clothes and bikes and things I'd bought for them and sold them at the market. Apparently he used to do that whenever donors bought things for the kids. A group from Japan had visited recently and bought new shoes for all the kids. As soon as they left, Rath took them from the kids and sold them back to the market.

Her story was so horrifying, I wanted to sweep her away immediately so that she never had to go back. But Jedtha pointed out that we didn't have the right to take her from SKO. And if she wasn't back soon, Rath would suspect something was up.

So we drove her back to school, from where she could walk home to SKO.

I hugged her fiercely at the gates. 'Don't worry. It will be okay,' I promised.

She nodded, meek and subdued, dried her eyes and walked towards SKO. Seeing her like that was devastating.

~

The course of action *seemed* obvious—report the corruption, abuse and neglect at SKO to the government, so they could get the kids removed and placed somewhere safer. I kind of hoped the Cambodian equivalent of Australia's child protection system would leap into action like a well-oiled machine.

But even *I* knew what a naïve hope that was.

Jedtha arranged for us to meet at a Khmer eatery in town with four very official-looking men from the Department of Social Affairs, Veterans and Youth, known more commonly by the acronym DoSVY (pronounced 'doh-sa-vee'). They listened sympathetically and were rather amused at my attempts to communicate in Khmer.

They explained that getting SKO shut down would be a very complicated process, but they could help facilitate a transfer of the kids to another registered orphanage. But until we found another orphanage that was willing to accept the kids (and risk making an enemy of Rath), there was nothing we could do.

I was badly disappointed by this response. After they left, I turned to Jedtha. 'Wasn't that the craziest thing you ever heard? Removing the victims instead of the perpetrator! How can they let a person like Rath look after children?'

'Cambodia is different to your country,' he said, his tone placating.

I stared gloomily at the bowl of curry I'd barely touched. Cambodia seemed to be so hard to navigate. Leaving the kids in a dangerous situation until another NGO agreed to step in just didn't make sense to me.

As it happens, the Cambodian government did (and still does) have a sound policy in place on alternative care for children. It was developed with the support of UNICEF and adopted in 2006. But even today, the government still says it feels powerless to implement its policies at the local level. They don't have sufficient resources or training to ensure even mediocre governance.

Jedtha was unfazed by all the obstacles raised at our meeting with DoSVY.

'We can start a new organisation,' he said. 'We can give the kids a safe home by ourselves. We not need other NGO!'

I thought: *Are you serious? Where were we going to find the money and staff and knowhow to set up an NGO? This is all so crazy!*

'*Loak Khrew*, we can't do that,' I objected. The past few months had given me a reality check about how hard fundraising is, let alone how much it costs to look after a group of kids in Cambodia. And that was in an existing organisation, with grounds and buildings and staff already in place . . . The prospect of setting up something on our own seemed ludicrous.

Jedtha nodded and looked at the table glumly. I could see he'd been clinging to the hope that I could somehow put him and the kids into a new organisation. Now he was jobless, with family who were depending on him, and he would have to find a way to move on and accept the horrible injustice of it all.

I excused myself to the bathroom to get some fresh air. A voice inside me was screaming: *THIS IS NOT* RIGHT!

I have a very particular reaction to injustice. It begins with a small ball of heat in the pit of my stomach. Like an infection, it grows and the heat enters my chest and begins pulsing through my veins. While infected with this rage, I feel no fear; I feel calm and focused, strong and totally unstoppable. Symptoms can last for days . . .

I have a tattoo across my torso that reads *Fiat justitia ruat caelum*, a Latin phrase meaning 'May justice be done, though the sky may fall.'

Standing outside the bathroom, staring up at the night sky, I realised there was no way I was going to be able to move on and go back to my life and forget about the suffering of those kids.

I sat back down at the table opposite Jedtha.

'We're not going to give up!' I told him. 'I know you want to start a new orphanage but that would take a lot more money than we have. So as a first step, let's just see if we can find another orphanage who would be willing to help us.'

'Okay,' Jedtha nodded. 'We will try!'

~

Jedtha picked me up on his moto the next morning, both of us determined to persevere until we found a solution. The kids' school had some boarding options for poorer children, so we headed back there to discuss this with them. On the way, Jedtha warned me that proposing that the school take the kids would be a big ask.

And sure enough, he was right. The head of the school didn't even entertain the notion for a moment before apologetically explaining that they were at capacity and wishing us the best. We met with two other orphanage directors in Battambang and the response was the same—it was all too hard, too risky and they didn't have the funds to take on so many children at once.

It was disappointing but also understandable. If Rath had acted as badly as people were saying, then getting involved would pose too big a risk to their organisation and the kids they already had in their care.

'What now?' I asked, hoping Jedtha had started thinking about a plan B.

'Let's find a powerful friend to help us,' he suggested.

He dropped me off at an internet cafe and told me he would go and meet some friends who he thought might be able to help. I sent a long email to Sally Power, letting her know what was happening. Half an hour later Jedtha burst into my booth at the internet cafe. 'We have a meeting with the assistant governor of Battambang! Quick, we have to go now!'

We met the assistant governor at his office in the Battambang Provincial Hall. He was a lovely man and very sympathetic to our plight. He told us he had no power to close SKO or to make another NGO accept the kids, but he could help us with the application to set up a new local NGO. He said he thought this would be the fastest way to help the children, because he could help speed up the application process.

'See, Tara?' Jedtha said after the meeting. 'I told you before, it is the best way.' His face was alight with hope.

By now, I didn't really need much more convincing. It seemed that the assistant governor was offering us the only way forward and I couldn't shake that sense of urgency to get the kids away from Rath.

'I only have twenty-five thousand dollars from my grandmother. How far will that get us?' I asked Jedtha. In that moment, I took my first step down the path marked 'no return'.

'Twenty-five thousand is enough. We can start a new NGO and support the kids for a few months. And we will find more donor to support us, the same like I do for SKO.' He was so sure, so totally convinced that we could succeed that his certainty was infectious.

'Okay,' I said. 'Let's do it!'

STEP 2

Start an orphanage.
Find out that's a bad idea

9

Jedtha was now a man on a mission. He arranged for us to meet with the assistant governor again the following morning. We came away with a long list of things to do.

Having a registered orphanage meant we had to apply for registration as a local NGO with the Ministry of Interior in Phnom Penh and sign an MOU (Memorandum of Understanding) with the Cambodian Ministry of Social Affairs, Veterans and Youth Rehabilitation, known as MoSVY (pronounced 'moh-sa-vee'), the governing body that oversees DoSVY. This involved an unbelievable mountain of paperwork.

We had a big job ahead of us. As well as drafting the registration application and all the supporting documentation, we had to find an appropriate and affordable new house for the kids, fit it out with everything necessary to turn it into a home, hire new staff, open a bank account and so much more.

And I was going to have to let my family know that I probably wasn't coming home for a while . . .

~

I emailed Peter, Sue and Noni and told them our plans. Their reply was fairly supportive—they all said Jedtha and I had made a good and brave decision, but Peter and Sue pointed out, as kindly as they could, that they couldn't afford to financially support me or the kids. They told me later that they were worried that if they did, they could end up being CCT's sole supporters, which wasn't an unreasonable fear at the time. They said they would do what they could to help, but I would need to find a way to raise enough funds to support the kids.

I couldn't help but wonder what else was being said around the dinner table that night. I can only imagine how they must have really felt about it all.

~

One of the first things we had to do was find a home for our new orphanage. There were no real estate agents in Battambang, so the only way to find a house to rent was to jump on the moto and trawl the streets in search of 'for rent' signs, all written in Khmer, of course.

After what felt like days, we found the perfect place. It was a typical Cambodian house with a wooden upstairs, a tiled brick downstairs and cute blue window shutters. It had a room on the upper floor for the boys, a room on the lower floor for the girls, a big yard for the kids to play in and a public school just around the corner. It was clean and tidy with lots of natural light and cost only US$80 a month. We put down a deposit and signed the contract immediately.

When we told Savenh, Reaksmey and Davi about our plans, they were over the moon. They immediately offered their support and allegiance, even offering to work for free to help us fill out all the paperwork needed to register CCT as a Cambodian NGO.

It was a wonderful feeling to be surrounded by such a great team of enthusiastic people all working towards a common goal. In Khmer they call it *Sammaki*—solidarity.

~

A day or two later, we met with the two men from DoSVY at their office. The assistant governor also joined us. They seemed pleased to hear that plans were in motion to register our own NGO. At the suggestion of the assistant governor, the men from DoSVY agreed to help us by expediting the rescue process. Even though the signed registration papers and MOU wouldn't come through for another few weeks, as long as they had proof they had been submitted and accepted by the Ministry of Interior and MoSVY, they would facilitate an offer to the children to leave SKO if they wanted to.

In hindsight, this plan was probably pretty dodgy. But as far as we knew, we were following the advice of the local authorities. In Cambodia, it's often hard to know if you're going by the book, or by the dodgy book.

~

Two days later Jedtha, Savenh, Reaksmey, Davi and I were sitting around the table at Jedtha's house, tearing through all the paperwork.

I got stuck on the part of the application that required us to submit our 'vision' and 'mission'. I put down my pen and pondered. A mission, yeah, we were on a mission all right—to rescue the kids! But a vision, that was another story . . . I hadn't thought that far ahead yet! All this NGO lingo was doing my head in.

Suddenly I heard someone call my name from outside. 'Tara?'

I looked up. Vibol, one of SKO's older boys, was standing at the gate.

The sight of him paralysed me for a moment. The kids weren't supposed to know I was back. He hung there, a ghost of his former self, so gaunt and frail I barely recognised him. His clothes hung off his skeletal frame.

He looked at me, wide-eyed. 'Tara?' he called again softly.

And then I was at the gate, hugging him. His rib bones jutted from his back. He managed to muster a faint smile.

'*Sok sabai te?*' I asked. 'How are you?' Before he had a chance to answer, a shady-looking guy called him back to his moto. He was watching Vibol intently. Vibol pressed a piece of paper into my hand before they drove off down the road.

I took the message back to Jedtha. It was from Rath—just something about Jedtha's severance. The four of us sat looking at each other with forlorn expressions. So Rath would now definitely know I was back in Battambang. The others started speculating on what Rath was going to do next in intense, dramatic tones.

I broke down in tears. *Vibol is so frail! How could anyone let this happen? I can't believe this is really happening. It's so surreal . . .*

I tried to dry my tears and get back to work but I couldn't concentrate. I looked at Jedtha with pleading eyes. 'I need to see the kids,' I said.

His expression softened as he looked at me. 'Okay,' he agreed. 'Rath, he will know you're back now anyway. So we can go now.'

We jumped on his moto, just as thick sheets of rain started falling. SKO was only a short trip from Jedtha's place, but we were drenched by the time we pulled up at the orphanage gates.

'*Tara mow veng hai!*' I heard young Khmer voices calling out from inside their dorms. *Tara's come back!*

Kanya and Maly, two of the pre-teen girls, ran to me. We hugged in the rain for a minute, all of us sodden to the bone. They didn't have an ounce of fat on them and looked just as frail and unwell as Vibol.

Then Rath's relatives, the new SKO staff, came out. They said nothing, but they were looking daggers at us. The girls pulled back and took a step away from me, eyes darting towards the new staff nervously.

'I'll see you soon,' I told the kids. 'Don't worry.'

We left, without speaking a single word to Rath's relatives.

~

We had several more meetings with the assistant governor and the men from DoSVY to discuss the logistics of rescuing the kids. These men moved mountains for us. On 16 August 2007, we had our last meeting to sign off on the final plan.

We would hire a bus and meet the DoSVY officers out the front of the new CCT house at eight o'clock the next morning. The officers would escort us in the bus to SKO. They would then present a list of names to whichever staff member was on duty. Unfortunately, we could only offer the opportunity to fifteen of the twenty-four children. Rath and his family had legal custody of the rest. The fifteen kids would then be informed that, if they wanted to leave SKO and come with us to CCT, it was now or never . . .

My biggest fear was that the fifteen kids would be too intimidated to speak up and say they wanted to leave. So when Jedtha and I happened to see Sineit, Vibol and Veasna hanging around the Psar Nat market later that night, I practically bounced off the back of the bike. I had to talk to them.

Jedtha was shocked to see them out on their own so late and tried to tell them to go back to SKO. But Sineit just fell into my arms, sobbing.

I stroked her hair, just about ready to break down and cry myself.

'What happening?' I pleaded in my clunky Khmer, looking at Veasna and Vibol. 'What's happening at SKO?'

But the boys just shook their heads and looked at their bare feet.

Jedtha told them gently that we had a new *onga* (NGO) for them to live in, if they wanted to leave SKO.

Hearing this, the kids just shrugged and murmured in Khmer: 'I dunno . . .' They looked upset and scared.

Jedtha spoke to them very gently in soft, reassuring tones. In moments like these, he goes into 'social worker/counsellor mode' and it's a remarkable thing to see. I have always been impressed by how good he is with kids.

I found out later that Rath had caught wind of the plan (of course) and had sat all the kids down and said: 'Put your hand up if you're planning to go with Jedtha and the *barang*?' (Barang literally translates to 'French' but in this context just means foreigner.)

In an act of defiance, Sinet put up her hand. At this, a sea of hands shot up.

This enraged Rath. He threatened them with terrifying repercussions if anyone tried to leave SKO. And he played on the kids' insecurities, telling them I planned to traffic them.

But Jedtha managed to reassure them a little. We didn't want to try to persuade or convince them to leave SKO—that was ultimately their choice—but we wanted them to know that if they did decide to leave, they would be safe and everything would be okay.

'Want to come see new *onga*?' I asked the kids. Some instinct told me this might help.

They agreed and followed us on their bicycles to the new house. It was just a few blocks from the markets.

In the light of the moto's headlamp, the three kids looked into the pleasant yard, filled with palms and coconut trees. They could see the quaint little house, with its blue window shutters and red-tiled roof.

They smiled faintly, but they were still not saying much.

Eventually, we said goodbye. Jedtha insisted we escort them on the moto. 'It's so bad SKO allow them out so late. It's too dangerous,' he said.

In that moment, I felt much more certain of the trust I'd put in Jedtha and the decision we'd made together. He genuinely did care about those kids.

'Jedtha, do you think they will come with us tomorrow?' I asked.

'I think they want to, but they really scared,' he told me. 'I not sure they will come or not.'

~

That night I lay awake. This must be exactly how Alice felt as she tumbled down, down, down the rabbit hole into a strange and unknown world.

~

The next morning Jedtha and I stood outside the wrought-iron gates of the new CCT house, waiting for the government officials who had promised to escort us to SKO. I kept looking back at the house, wondering if it really would become home to fifteen kids.

Soon I would know. My heart thudded in my chest.

A cream-coloured twenty-seater bus pulled up. I climbed aboard. Jedtha waited at the bus doors and made a call to see how far away the convoy of officials were. He hung up the phone, jumped on the bus and sat opposite me.

'*Mow hai,*' he told me. *Coming now.* It was the first time he'd ever communicated with me solely in Khmer. He was probably nervous, too.

Soon enough, the police truck appeared. The bus driver started the engine, and we were lumbering down the narrow bumpy roads that led to SKO. We certainly weren't going to be able to make a quick getaway. I kept looking over my shoulder to make sure the officials were still behind us.

After an incredibly tense fifteen-minute journey, we pulled up at the SKO gates. Jedtha and the officials weren't mucking around. They jumped out immediately and strode into the orphanage compound. I stayed on the bus, biting my nails and watching through the window as they spoke to a staff member, one of Rath's relatives. Documents were produced along with some fairly assertive body language.

I stood up and moved down to the open door of the bus where I had a better view of the action. The staff member was now on the phone. Rath's sister, the cook, appeared in the yard, her normally impassive eyes now darting around the compound.

One of the officials headed off towards the kid's dorms with the list in his hand. He stood at the doorway and called out each of the fifteen names.

A bunch of kids burst out through the door, clutching a few belongings to their chests. Rath's relatives stepped aside, powerless, as the kids bolted past.

Makara and Nimol, the littlest boys, reached the bus first and flung their skinny arms around me. Their pre-teenage cousin Rithy called, 'Tara!' and, without pausing, crashed up the bus stairs like he was running from a stampede.

I was nearly buried by kids, but out of the corner of my eye I saw Rath pull up on his moto. His face was swollen with fury.

My heart missed a beat. He looked much scarier than I remembered.

Until that moment, I'd never experienced such hatred towards another human being. I felt that small ball of heat form in the pit of my stomach. As the heat pulsed through my veins, my fear was replaced with a familiar rage. The rage that makes me brave and totally unstoppable . . .

I marched through the gates, past Rath and his relatives and Jedtha and the officials. I had to be sure that everyone who *wanted* to come understood that they *could*. A couple of stragglers, grasping swollen plastic bags full of their belongings, were on their way to the bus. They stopped quickly to give me a hug.

Then I saw what was causing the delay. The rest of the kids, Rath's nieces and nephews, were sitting on the steps, and they were crying.

For a moment my rage melted into horrible sadness. I sat on the tiles beside Sopheap and Dara, who had tears running down their faces, and gave them a hug. They were very sweet girls, but there was just no way they could come with us. Of course, they didn't understand that. All they knew was that their friends were going and they were being left behind.

'*Knyom somtoh,*' I whispered to the girls. *I'm sorry.*

Perhaps even sadder was the sight of Vibol—one of SKO's brightest kids—who had first seen me at Jedtha's house last week, and had come to the new house with us the night before. He was sitting tight, his expression resolute. He wasn't going to leave.

I was completely blindsided. Why was he taking this stance? Was he scared of Rath? He couldn't look at me, blinking away tears. I didn't know it then, but there was a little romance going on between him

Sue, 1977

Learning to ride, 1986

Peter, 1978

With grandma Nagy, 1988

CORAL TAYLOR

Champion girl rider, 1999

Holiday in Vanuatu, 1987

At Ta Prohm temple Siem Reap, on my first trip to Cambodia, 2005

Dusty Battambang

The treehouse at Akira's Landmine Museum, 2005

The statue that greets all new arrivals to Battambang

Battambang in 2005

Battambang countryside

Children from SKO orphanage catching their own food in nearby rice fields

CCT gates, a few months after we rescued the kids from SKO orphanage, 2008

Jedtha

Savenh

Sinet and me, 2008

In Mondulkiri, with a rescued elephant, 2009

Downtown Battambang

Farming in Battambang

Stung Sangker riverside

Battambang's green oranges

Pagoda in Battambang

Rush hour, Battambang

and one of Rath's nieces and he was too loyal to leave her. I touched him on the shoulder, so sorry to have to leave him there.

'Tara!' Jedtha called. '*Dho!* Let's go!' He strode off towards the bus.

I gave Dara a kiss on her forehead and told her: 'I will help.'

I knew exactly what had to be done. I would do whatever it took to have SKO shut down.

Back on the bus, the doors creaked shut behind me and we started to make a very slow getaway. I stood in the aisle at the front, looking down the two rows of seats. Fourteen pairs of wide eyes stared back at me.

Jedtha was in the front seat to my left, sitting beside a little girl I hadn't met before. The churning of the bus's engine was deafening. No one said a word. No one moved a muscle. I held on to the rail numbly, not knowing what to do or think.

A moment later I locked eyes with Sinet, sitting dead centre in the back row. Tears sparkled in her eyes. And then the hint of a smile appeared at the corner of her mouth, and I realised—they were tears of deliverance, of relief, of hope.

We did it. We really did it! I thought to myself, smiling.

Sinet smiled back, causing the tears in her eyes to roll down her cheeks. She laughed a bit as she wiped her face. The other kids were all smiling now too, every one of them.

'You want to go to your new home?' I shouted in English.

'*Yes!*' they erupted.

~

I will never forget 17 August 2007, the day we rescued fourteen kids from SKO.

From the moment the kids poured off the bus into the quiet, shady yard, CCT felt like home. The kids' ecstasy was contagious and everyone was smiling again.

My gaze drifted from the happy kids to our new team: Jedtha—now officially CCT's director; Savenh, our social worker; Davi, our nurse; Mina's sister Heng who was to be our new cook; and Noit, a very sweet girl in her twenties, who would be Heng's assistant.

Savenh, Noit, Davi and I would work shifts to ensure there were always at least two carers on duty, and at least one other staff member present at CCT.

We put Jedtha's cousin, Reaksmey, on a small assistant's salary. He was to live upstairs, supervising the boys. When he was off duty, he would be busy with his university studies.

The party atmosphere on that first day continued into the night and evolved into a slumber party. We had no beds yet, just mattresses laid out on the floor of the biggest room in the house. So we laid out platefuls of the kids' favourite fruits and for hours they ate, played games and told stories (which I did my best to follow).

I met three new kids: Tula, Mao and Chanlina. Chanlina was Maly and Amara's sister, and Tula and Mao were their cousins. They had arrived at SKO while I was back in Sydney.

They were bright, sweet kids and had heard a lot about me and were just as comfortable around me as the others. I looked at their happy faces, wondering how on earth they'd ended up at SKO. Whatever the reason, I felt so glad they'd been brave enough to leave.

~

The next morning the kids woke early to the smell of hot *bor bor* porridge on the stove, and immediately bounced out of bed like all their Christmases had come at once. I, on the other hand, woke up in my little downstairs room in a cold sweat: reality had set in. I lay there listening to fourteen young voices, all talking and giggling at once. Fourteen kids. I was now responsible for fourteen kids.

I'd made some big promises to these kids, promises that were a lot easier to make than they would be to keep. Raising fourteen children to adulthood was going to cost a lot of money, even in Cambodia. How was I going to do it?

I'd never been responsible for anyone else before. I was just a city girl who had trouble keeping her room tidy. I still felt like a kid myself. And until now, any failures in my life had affected only me, and had resulted in a bruised ego at worst.

Now the stakes were incredibly high. I had fourteen lives in my hands. My life was not just about me anymore.

I rolled over on my mattress, booted up my laptop and opened the spreadsheet I was using to keep track of the money we had spent, how fast we were spending it, and how much we had left over from Joan's donation.

We needed to cover the monthly fixed costs of food, rent, utilities, and staff salaries; we also needed to replace everything I had donated to SKO, because none of it had been recoverable in the rescue. This included all the medical supplies and medications, school uniforms, casual clothes, textbooks and school supplies, beds, bedding, cupboards, shelves, desks, kitchen equipment, cups, plates, cutlery . . . the list was terrifying. We even needed to reapply for the children's birth certificates—the SKO staff had told the officers at DoSVY they'd misplaced them. Though it's quite possible they never had them to start with.

I had to find more money quickly. I got dressed lightning fast and went outside to face the *bor bor*. My spirits lifted as soon as I saw the kids, all sitting cross-legged around a long bamboo mat at the side of the house, thoroughly enjoying their breakfast.

'Tara!' they roared.

I squeezed in beside them. Life can't just be about work, after all. I allowed myself a few hours to enjoy their company and shower them with love.

But at midday, I prised myself away and asked Jedtha to give me a lift into town.

As soon as we pulled clear of the gates, Jedtha blurted: 'Tara, Rath might try payback at us!' His eyes, meeting mine briefly in the rear-view mirror, were clouded with worry.

I thought of Rath's face the day before, and felt the hairs on the back of my neck rise. 'I hope not.' What else could I say?

I set up my laptop in the corner of my favourite internet cafe and wrote down the whole story, right from the beginning. I finished by making it clear how badly we needed financial help—and not just financial help for today or tomorrow, but enough to keep us going until the kids were all grown up. Writing those words in black and white filled me with fear. I had taken on mission impossible.

One step at a time, I thought to myself. And then I sent the story to everyone I'd ever known.

10

Here's what an average day looked like in 2007.

Wake up. (God, it's hot.) Listen to the sounds of fourteen ravenous kids eating breakfast. Stagger groggily to the bathroom. Close eyes and grit teeth while throwing buckets of cold water over head.

Call out Khmer phrases. Get ready for school! Brush your teeth!

Help the littler ones get ready for school. Plait the girls' hair. Check all the kids in the morning class are in uniform. Look around for Sinet. Ask her to remind you how to say: 'I'm sorry, but I must insist that you wear your shoes to school.'

Help Reaksmey to get the other kids to wash their clothes and do their chores. Remind Davi, the nurse, to give Sineit her medication. Wonder why you have to keep reminding a qualified nurse to do her job, but smile and be nice . . . be nice . . .

Notice that Jedtha is looking stressed out. Savenh is too. Cross your fingers and hope they've got things under control. Leave them to it.

Roam around the building tidying up, hoping you'll find Makara and Amara's shoes. Why is there rubbish everywhere? Damn. Where are Makara's and Amara's shoes? They've lost two pairs in the last fortnight. We'll go broke just buying shoes! Why do the kids prefer to go barefoot? Worry about foot worms. Greet the morning-school kids coming home from their lessons. More of them have lost their shoes. Great.

Sit down with everyone for lunch. Damn. There's so much meat. You just have rice and soy sauce, which you quite like anyway . . . Tell kids to change out of school uniforms; they need to be kept stain-free as we can't afford new ones. Get afternoon-school kids out the door. Oh, let's just forget about shoes today.

Cycle into town. Buy some supplies from your list. Curse the fact that family-sized bottles of shampoo are so heavy. Go to an internet cafe. Spend the afternoon sending emails begging for money. Friends and family are pulling out all stops to help, but it's still stressful. Try to remember that you're not asking for yourself; you're not even being paid. Update the website. Cycle back to CCT with shopping bags dangling from bike handles, getting in the way of pedalling. Ouch. Bruised knees.

Everyone is home from school. Tell them to change out of their uniforms. Watch them play. Aw, they're so cute! Okay, homework time. We seriously need to get some chairs and tables. They're on the list. Can't afford them now, though. The kids are asking for tutors. Add that to the list, too. What is this crap they're learning? You can't read their textbooks, but it seems to be all rote learning. You don't have time to think too much about that.

Shower time. Fill up kids' containers with shampoo. Far out, they go through a lot of shampoo. At least the hygiene lessons are working.

Have dinner. It's nice eating with all the kids and staff. Damn, more meat. Oh! Heng has made fried morning glory. Yum!

Tell kids to brush their teeth. Get the little ones to bed. Let the big ones do some reading. Wish them goodnight. No, I promise there are no ghosts. Turn out the lights. Thank goodness they're safe.

Go back to your own room. Brave another cold bucket of water over the head. Feel content but exhausted. Try not to think about money problems. Read a bit. God, it's hot. Read a few more pages. Fall asleep.

~

Every afternoon for that first week I rode my bike to the internet cafe in town, hoping desperately for good news.

And thankfully, just a couple of weeks after the rescue, the good news came.

An email from the journalist Caroline Marcus appeared in my inbox titled: 'Interview'. It said something like:

> Hi Tara, I'm a journalist from the *Sydney Morning Herald*, and I heard from a friend of yours about the work you're doing with CCT. I'd love to write an article about you and the kids! I think it's an amazing story.

I could hardly believe my eyes. A journalist! And from a big Aussie newspaper! I promptly wrote back, 'Yes, definitely!' (or words to that effect), gave her my Cambodian number and pedalled home frantically to wait (nervously) for the phone to ring.

Caroline was lovely and I couldn't believe how well the interview went. I've never been comfortable with public speaking or performing, but talking to Caroline was easy. I just told her everything I'd been writing over and over again in all those emails.

Sally was jubilant when I told her. 'This is just the break we need!' she said.

Caroline told me the story was going to be a double-page spread in the Sunday paper, so she'd need a few photos. I got Jedtha to help me take them. As usual, I hated all of them, but I gritted my teeth and sent them off anyway.

The response that rolled in that Sunday was even better than Sally and I had hoped. We were soon inundated with emails from people wanting to donate, to fundraise, to volunteer and to extend their good wishes.

We were both frantic, spending almost every waking hour trying to keep up with the influx of correspondence, saying 'yes, please,' and 'not yet, but please stay in touch,' and above all 'thank you,' 'thank you,' 'thank you' . . .

The donations that resulted from the article were enough to keep us going for several more months. Sally and I were blown away by the power of the press. Suddenly it felt like everything would be alright.

~

For our next fundraising effort, we launched a monthly donation program. After all, it was what all the big charities were doing to keep funds coming in and it would hopefully provide us with a sustainable flow of income. Securing cashflow—regular, reliable funds on which we could depend—was a really important step. We needed to be able to plan more than just a few weeks ahead.

People started to sign up as regular donors immediately. It was a fantastic start for our fledgling organisation.

~

Not long after the rescue, just as I was drifting off to sleep, I woke to a blood-curdling shriek.

I slipped out of bed to see who it was.

All the kids had bedding and designated bedrooms, but most of them felt safer sleeping together on the cool tiles of the downstairs common room, right outside my tiny ground-floor bedroom.

Getting up to check on the kids was becoming a nightly ritual of mine. There was always at least one other staff member on duty at night, but I wasn't sleeping all that well and woke at the slightest peep. Most of the kids suffered nightmares or night terrors or some other legacy of a lifetime of trauma, hidden behind those happy smiles.

As I stepped into the common room I strained my eyes in the golden glow of the night-light. I could barely make out the silhouettes of the sleeping kids, who looked like they'd been flung randomly around the room and had fallen asleep on the tiles exactly as they'd landed: upside down, slumped up against a wall, or flopped over a piece of furniture.

A whimper drew my eye across the room. In the flickering light, I saw that it was Rithy, moving restlessly in his sleep. I tiptoed around the sleeping bodies to sit next to him. He was asleep, but crying. I stroked his hair for a few minutes until he settled into a more peaceful sleep.

And then, as was my habit at this time, I counted the sleeping bodies one by one. If you've ever looked after multiple kids you'll understand that compulsion, I'm sure.

My eyes—and my heart—stopped when I spotted someone sitting alone, shoulders slumped but wide awake, in a dark corner of the room. It was Sinet.

Why was she awake? I grabbed my Khmer–English dictionary, crept around the other kids, and sat next to her.

'What wrong, Sinet?' I said softly in Khmer. 'You can tell me.'

'Tara,' she breathed, wiping away tears.

And so began the first of many late night talks between Sinet and me.

We had to work together to converse, relying heavily on the dictionary. It took an incredible amount of concentration to follow what she was saying. But every evening, I managed to learn a little more of Sinet's life story.

~

Sinet was born at home in a small, Khmer-style house on stilts.

The house was made of thatched palm leaf, but the thatching was old and riddled with holes, which were mostly patched up with old rags, plastic bags, scraps of cardboard and whatever else came to hand. Some of these holes were so big they were difficult to patch, so at night, as Sinet was falling asleep on the wooden floor, she could look up and see the stars. And in the monsoon season, she slept in the rain.

During the rains, the swollen waterways would overflow into the low-lying land around her home, carrying with them sewage and rubbish from the surrounding area. A swamp of filth engulfed the long legs of her rickety old home, providing a haven for mosquito larvae, parasites and water snakes.

For the first six years of Sinet's life, both her parents worked selling lanterns made out of empty condensed milk cans. On a good day they made about a dollar.

A dollar was not enough to feed all six kids, so the family were often forced to pick wild morning glory and hunt tiny pest fish in the rice fields nearby. Covered from head to toe in mud from the paddy, they'd catch the fish with their hands.

On rainy nights, Sinet went out into the fields to catch bullfrogs with her dad. Once caught, the bullfrog's skin would release a noxious sticky fluid that stained their hands black. Sinet didn't mind, though, because if they were successful she'd wake up the next morning to the mouth-watering smell of bullfrog frying over hot coals.

Most days, however, there was no breakfast. And what the kids got, they had to fight for.

Sinet's family was the poorest in the village and most of their neighbours looked down on them and thought they were savages. Their mother was violent with the kids and had a gambling addiction, and she and Sinet's father constantly fought with each other.

Sinet wet the bed often and, because she had no fresh clothes to change into, her ragged shorts smelt of urine. Her hair was never washed or brushed. She had lice and skin infections all over her head, which left bald patches in her hair. She was out in the sun a lot so her skin was very dark, which is seen as the height of ugliness in Khmer culture, and her skin was always covered in mosquito bites. Her baby teeth were stained brown and some had rotted almost to the gum line, and she was bullied by the village kids.

When Sinet was six years old, her mother had another baby girl. Her name was Srey Noit. She was very small and underweight. But she was smiley and sweet and, in Sinet's eyes, she was the most beautiful baby ever.

Srey Noit was never fed enough and was always crying from hunger. She looked like a little skeleton covered in skin, but with a very swollen belly. Sinet would often take Srey Noit in her arms and go and find her Ma—who was usually off gambling away the little money she had—and beg her to breastfeed Srey Noit. She ached for her little sister.

One night during the wet season, Srey Noit developed a very high fever. Ma bought some medicine from the local pharmacy, but Srey Noit couldn't hold it down. She started vomiting, had a seizure and died. She wasn't even a year old. There are no photos or record of her existence—a fact that haunts Sinet to this day.

Srey Noit's death had a big impact on Sinet's parents. Ma stopped gambling and stopped being quite so violent with her children. Sinet's father borrowed money to buy a few chickens and started selling the barbecued meat at the market.

They were also fortunate enough to be given a small piece of land by a French NGO. They pulled down the old house (which was squatting on someone else's land), took the materials to the new block and built a small but more sturdy home.

The house still leaked a little but it was more comfortable than anything they'd lived in before. They even made enough to buy their own television. Thanks to the barbecued chicken business, for the first time ever the family had enough to eat every day.

For the next couple of years, Sinet's parents worked hard. Their health seemed to suffer, but they took no notice of that. The two oldest boys left home to work in Thailand.

But then, one day, their father was struck down with a bad cough, high fever and diarrhoea. Over the next ten days, his condition grew worse. So Sinet went with him to the provincial hospital and stayed there, nursing him for several weeks.

The weight fell off him. The drugs the hospital gave him were expensive, and weren't working anyway, so he decided to stop taking them and come home.

Sinet and her family stayed by his side, and continued to look after him as best they could.

He was in terrible agony for several months. And without his income, the family's financial situation was soon desperate. Ma sold everything they owned; the TV, their clothes and all the chickens. They couldn't even afford paracetamol to ease his suffering.

Sinet was just nine years old when she lost the second member of her family. Her father's frail body was carried to the nearest temple and cremated. After the cremation, the nuns at the temple took his bones, put them in a bowl full of water and made the children drink from the bowl to stop them from missing their dad.

Sinet was numb. And Ma fell apart. After the cremation, she told her children she was going to find work in Poipet, a town near the Thai border. Sinet, her ten-year-old sister Sineit, and their two younger brothers, Phala and Sacha, were left at home alone with only a little money and no adults.

Fortunately, the four children already had well-honed survival skills. They caught fish and frogs and picked the edible wild morning glory that grew along the sides of neighbouring streams, just as they used to do with their parents. The nearby French NGO saw what was happening and gave them rice almost every day. And every few months, Ma would return and give a few dollars to a neighbour to buy the children some food.

Still, living alone was scary for the kids. Almost every night during this period, little Phala had night terrors and would run out the door in his sleep, calling for Ma and Pa to wait for him. Sinet would run after him in the dark, catch him, and bring him back to bed.

After many months of living this way, Ma came home with some news. She had a new husband in Poipet and the whole family was moving there.

And so they followed Ma to an unfamiliar town to meet their new father and move into a tiny rented house in a dodgy neighbourhood. Ma got a job selling fruit at a market across the Thai border. Their new stepfather had some work as a labourer. Sinet and her siblings helped to make money by working as rag pickers in the local rubbish dump.

After about a year of living in Poipet, Ma fell ill. She had a cough, fever and diarrhoea, just like Sinet's father.

Sinet went with her to the provincial hospital in Banteay Meanchey Province and looked after her there, while Sineit and her younger brothers stayed with their stepfather, working in Poipet. After several months in hospital, even though Ma wasn't at all well, she took Sinet back to Poipet to check on her sister and brothers.

On their return, Ma had a terrible argument with her husband, and the couple split. Sinet had no idea what caused the breakup, only that it had something to do with her older sister, Sineit.

Ma moved the kids back to Battambang. Her health was deteriorating fast. She spent several weeks at the Battambang hospital, but eventually decided that there was nothing more the doctors could do for her. She kept Sineit at home to look after her, and sent Sinet and the other children to live at the local pagoda.

So now Sinet and her siblings were temple children—the impoverished or orphaned kids who help the monks in return for food and accommodation.

A few months later, Ma died, and Sineit came to join them at the pagoda.

Sinet was ten by this time. She didn't cry the day her mother died. In fact, she didn't shed a single tear for many years after. She says that pieces of her heart died on the day she lost her Ma and that's why she lost the ability to cry for so many years.

Life was tough for the temple kids. Each morning they were woken at four o'clock for chanting and then were assigned cleaning duties for the rest of the day.

Rath was the head monk at the pagoda. He disciplined the temple children by beating them with sticks, often hard enough to break skin. The children, and even the other monks, lived in fear of Rath.

But there was one thing to be glad about. Sinet was allowed to join the monks' classes. She finally had the chance to learn to read and write. Reading became her greatest escape. She was never happier than when she had her nose buried in a book.

Sinet and her siblings lived at the pagoda for two years. Then Rath decided to leave the pagoda and form an orphanage. He took the temple children with him. He called the orphanage Sprouting Knowledge Orphans (SKO).

It wasn't until much later that Sinet and her siblings learned that their parents had died from AIDS, and Sineit had contracted HIV.

~

'Tara, I try so hard to forget about my old life,' Sinet confided one night. 'But I can't. When I close my eyes I see it and when I sleep I dream of it. I can't escape. I'm so happy I have a new life now, here with you, but still I always think about my life before. Why do I think so much about it?'

Some instinct told me that, considering I didn't yet have the Khmer words to comfort her, the most helpful thing I could do was listen. So I let her do most of the talking.

As her story unfolded, I was more and more stunned that this beautiful, intelligent girl who I saw smiling every day could be the survivor of a life so incomprehensibly cruel.

These talks became a time in which she could grieve for everything she had lost. Sometimes she cried on my shoulder until my shirt was damp. But how do you console someone who's lived through horrors that you can barely imagine? Her life experience had been almost the polar opposite to my own.

One night she told me: 'At SKO we worked so hard in the fields, before and after school. We never had time off. When we harvested the rice and vegetables Rath would take them and sell them for his family. Our lives were very hard, but we were too scared to tell anyone about it—and about the other things Rath was doing . . .'

'What things?' I asked.

After a long, painful pause, her words came out in a rush. 'We were all so scared of him, especially me. I think I was the most scared out of everyone. I really am a coward, Tara. You know, Rath, he did something . . .' Her voice trailed off.

'What?' I pressed. 'What he do?' A chill scuttled down my spine.

'Never mind,' she said, trying to fake a smile.

'Sinet, please trust me. What you were going to say? What did Rath do?'

She put her hand to her face and let out a little sob. I immediately regretted asking.

Finally, she took a deep breath and looked around the room to see if any of the kids had woken. She looked back at me, and with tears splashing off her quivering bottom lip, she whispered: 'He raped me.'

~

In the days that followed, Sinet told me more. When she first moved to the pagoda, Rath seemed to notice her. He'd often say scary, seedy things about how pretty she was, how one day he'd like to take her for his wife.

She was sixteen when he first acted. It wasn't every day, but it was often.

Life became a game of cat and mouse as she desperately tried to avoid him, and he orchestrated ways to get her alone. Like making her clean his office. Or look after him when he was sick. Or the time she stayed behind while everyone went to the water festival so she could avoid him, but then he came home early on his own . . .

He threatened to kill her if she told anyone. She was terrified.

When I arrived to volunteer in 2006, the abuse stopped for those two months until I went back to Australia. Then it started again.

Thus Sinet came to associate me with safety.

After Sinet's revelation, my deep hatred of Rath intensified. I dreaded to think what he might have done to the other girls—and what he might continue to do to the girls we'd left behind. Sinet said she couldn't be sure but she had seen him acting in similar ways towards Sopheap, his niece.

I wanted to put him behind bars. I wanted to see him rot in jail for years and years. But Sinet swore me to secrecy, for all the obvious reasons, and I didn't want to betray her trust.

~

Meanwhile, Sinet's upset stomach and lethargy grew so bad she started to miss school. I asked Davi, the nurse, to look into it, but she kept putting it off, saying she'd get to it soon.

Davi was always nice enough to me and the kids, so I couldn't work out what the problem was. Surely if a kid was so sick she was missing school, she should see a doctor?

It sometimes felt like quite a struggle to get all the staff to act on their own initiative, without me having to ask them to do things all the time. Sometimes it just seemed like they lacked basic common sense.

In the end I took Sinet to the local polyclinic myself. Naturally, I wondered if her illness was some kind of psychological fallout from what Rath had done to her, but I wanted to rule out any physical problem first.

They ran some tests and told me she had *Helicobacter pylori*, a bacterial infection. This was not great news. If left untreated, it could lead to stomach ulcers and, possibly even to stomach cancer. They told me it was fairly common in Cambodia, and gave me a 'stomach ulcer pack' with all the medicines needed to clear it up. But as the weeks passed, Sinet just got worse. Eventually, we set off on the local bus to Phnom Penh to see Cecile, the French doctor at the Naga Clinic who had helped us when Sineit was sick.

Cecile ran some tests and asked us to come back for the results. She was outraged by what she found. 'She doesn't have helicobacter, she has four different parasites!' the doctor cried. 'One of these, giardia, okay, it's hard to catch. Sometimes you do a stool test and you miss things. But to miss *all* of these—it's criminal!' She gave a despairing sigh. 'Maybe you should come to us from now on.'

Great, I thought. *So all the medical staff in Battambang are incompetent, and I'm supposed to travel for eight hours by bus any time one of the kids is sick—that bus ride takes almost as long as a flight back to Sydney!*

It was extremely disheartening.

The good news was that Sinet improved quickly once she'd started on the treatment prescribed by Cecile. The bad news was that a lot of the kids had also started to have very similar symptoms. Cecile recommended we get them all tested.

The pathology lab in Phnom Penh, the Institut Pasteur, offered to help me. They gave me a discount on their services and provided test tubes and containers for our nurse, Davi, to collect blood and stool samples. The staff at the lab showed me how to choose which tests to order and the test tubes required for each test.

It was an epic process—at five in the morning, Davi would take blood samples and get the kids to poo into the pre-labelled containers. We'd pack them into a cooler full of ice, and I'd take the coolers all the way to Phnom Penh, drop them off at the lab and order the tests. Then I'd take all the results to a clinic with a western doctor and sneakily ask them to review all the results and prescribe the required medication. I was often told I should really have a separate appointment for each patient and the patients should be present at the appointment, but I always managed to talk my way around it.

I learned a lot more about medicine in this time than I ever thought I would.

~

One morning, a few months after rescuing the kids, I woke up and realised, *Hey! I can speak Khmer!*

Okay—so it didn't happen quite like that, but it's not far off.

I never thought to myself: *You know what? I have to learn Khmer.* I just picked it up because I was immersed in Cambodian life and no one around me spoke much, if any, English. So it was either speak Khmer or don't speak to anyone at all.

Sinet was one of my greatest supports as I learned her language. She was always able to get the gist of what I was trying to say and translate it into something everyone else could understand. Hearing her reshuffle my words back to the kids and staff definitely helped a lot.

At first I learned to speak in phrases and sentences, knowing that 'all these sounds strung together means this', rather than learning the individual words. For example, I knew how to ask *What time is it now?* or *Can I get a receipt for that?* Only gradually did the meanings of individual words begin to emerge.

Acquiring the language without much translation meant that I learned to think in Khmer from the very start. As a result, even today, translating from Khmer back to English isn't as easy for me as you might think. I may know what certain words mean in Khmer, but translation is such an inexact science that it's not always easy to find a word to convey the same meaning in English.

In some ways, colloquial Khmer is an easy language to learn. The real challenge is the pronunciation. The phonemes—the sounds that make up the words—are very subtle in variation and many of them simply don't exist in English. If you get it even a tiny bit wrong, you just won't be understood. Khmer is not a tonal language though, so I suspect that Cambodian people are just not accustomed to hearing their language spoken with an accent.

At the market, I once stood in front of a pile of coconuts, pointed directly at them and said '*dong*' instead of '*daung*'. The two older women who ran the store looked at me blankly and shrugged, with absolutely no idea what I was on about. I pointed again, repeating '*Dong! Dong!*' (thinking: *Come on! It's gotta be pretty close!*). They shrugged again and hurried into the back of their stalls, leaving me frustrated and thirsty. There's no mean-spiritedness behind this. Often, when Cambodians see a foreigner coming, they'll start getting nervous that they aren't going to understand what the foreigner wants—so no matter how close the attempt is, their standard response is 'no, sorry, I don't speak English and can't understand what you're saying'.

I got around this obstacle by subconsciously mimicking Sinet. She would always pay out on me for making mistakes, but the joke was on her. For a while there, people said they couldn't tell our voices apart when we were both speaking in Khmer.

I have my own badass style now, so that no longer happens. But Sinet still relishes any opportunity to point out my mistakes.

11

A very good friend of mine, Vicky Baron, who is now one of Australia's most esteemed makeup artists, once told me that the key to success when you're first starting out in something is to say yes to everything. Every opportunity to come your way—no matter if the pay is shit, or the hours are inconvenient, or you think it's too easy, or you're terrified and think you're way out of your depth . . . you say yes.

So when I got a phone call in September 2007 from a well-known Australian current affairs TV show asking to film a piece on my story, I said yes.

And then I shat myself.

~

As I tell you this story, I'm going to refer to the Australian TV show involved as 'the current affairs show' and I'm going to change the names of the major players. It doesn't seem fair to name and shame people who were, after all, just doing their job.

The producer, who we'll call Fred Nerk, confirmed the offer with an incredibly friendly email, describing my 'remarkable work' and 'infectious spirit' and offering CCT a primetime spot on the network, as well as magazine opportunities. He pointed out that the story would be viewed by close to 2 million people, which would help us raise the funds he knew we badly needed. And he guaranteed that he would treat me, and CCT and the kids, with 'a great deal of heart at all times'.

Ho. Ly. Crap.

The thought of being on primetime television may have been utterly terrifying, but what an amazing opportunity for CCT—with nearly 2 million viewers this opportunity could set the kids up for life.

This was no time to let fear get in the way. It just had to be done.

I forwarded the email to Sally and my family, saying: *How amazing is THIS?! :)*

Their replies were far less enthusiastic. The show was notorious for its sensationalist reporting, and Sally was worried enough to call a contact of hers who worked at the same network.

The contact told her that the current affairs show was planning to do a negative story about some high-profile Australians who were involved in a Cambodian orphanage and hadn't come good on their promises.

As I read this, my heart started racing and my palms turned clammy. A negative story on CCT could destroy us. No one would ever trust us again. We'd lose what little support we had. *Fuck. Why does everything have to be so complicated!*

So Sally sent an email to Fred explaining that we weren't ready for a major news story yet, but thanked him for thinking of us.

Later that day, I had a call from Sally. I answered in surprise—it was expensive to call from Australia, so we usually emailed.

'Fred Nerk just called me and he was absolutely revolting!' she said, her voice tight with shock. 'He told me he'd heard we'd accepted another media deal with a different network, and when I told him that wasn't true, he accused me of lying! Then he accused me of with-holding funds from you and the kids! I can't believe this!'

'What?' I exclaimed. 'Bloody hell! Why would he do that? Why would he say that? This is not what we need right now.' Sally told me to try not to worry. But I was worrying. I was worrying a lot!

About a half an hour later, my phone lit up with a strange number. I answered, heart pumping.

Yep, it was Fred. His demeanour was that of a deeply concerned friend. 'I'm sorry to have to tell you, Tara, but we've found out that your friend Sally has some other agenda for working with you. She's not focused on helping the kids, like you are. Why else wouldn't she want you to take part in our story?'

'Oh no, it's not that,' I squeaked. 'It's just the kids have been through so much and we don't think it's in their best interest to be filmed.' Then I blurted, 'I'm sorry, but I have to go now.'

I talked to Sally, and Peter, and Jedtha, and we decided to get some advice from Oliver Shtein, a contact of Peter's who was an expert in charity law.

On Oliver's advice, we issued an official press statement, explaining that as a fledgling organisation with the best interests of the children in mind, we did not feel ready for such high-profile media coverage.

But Fred wasn't going to take this lying down. He sent another email, saying he meant every word he said in his previous email, and that it was a shame we had been 'dishonest' about signing up with another media outlet. All he ever wanted, he said, was honesty. And so, once again, we were falsely accused of having another media deal. I rolled my eyes at this, but inside I felt like a helpless mouse that had just managed to escape the clutches of a lion.

Forty-eight hours later, Jedtha came to me with some chilling news: a foreign reporter had turned up at SKO and interviewed Rath.

I don't know exactly how Jedtha found this out, but news travels fast in Battambang, in that gossipy small-town way. Someone also told him they'd overheard Rath tell the reporters that we'd stolen the children and were planning to traffic them.

By now I was a nervous wreck. This was more serious than a threatening phone call. Reporters were here! In Battambang! And they were out to get us.

Rath's story was absurd—fancy a rapist accusing us of being the criminals. But the last thing we needed was for these reporters, who were just after a 'good story', to fan the flames and enrage Rath any further. They were aiding the abuser and putting his victims at risk. These were real lives they were messing with. How could they be so reckless, so heartless? I couldn't understand it.

Then I got another call on my mobile phone from an unfamiliar number.

'Hello, Tara?' It was a male voice with an Aussie accent. 'This is John Smith—I emailed you a few weeks ago about wanting to film a story about CCT?'

Ah—I remembered that name. John Smith (again, I've changed the name) was a documentary maker or something. I'd had an email from him about a week earlier, wanting to talk about filming a story. But when I got back to him asking for more info, he hadn't followed up.

How on earth had he got my mobile phone number, though? We'd only communicated by email and no one knew my number outside of my small circle of friends and family—except, of course, the current affairs show . . .

'Hi John,' I said, my mind racing with all these thoughts. 'I'm so sorry, but I'm in the middle of things right now—do you mind if I call you back?' I got off the phone as quickly as I could. Had John got my number from Fred Nerk? Was he working undercover for him?

I started imagining cameras everywhere, all pointed at me: *This is the girl who stole children and planned to traffic them.*

When I told Peter and Sally there was now an Australian film crew working in Battambang, they pulled out all the stops. They got in touch with a second lawyer and a friend who worked for the ABC. The advice was unanimous: lie low, don't do anything, just wait them out because they can't stay in Battambang forever and if they don't catch you on camera, they don't have a story.

~

So now I was under house arrest at CCT. And because my room was right beside the main entrance to the house, which was always open during the day, I was pretty much confined to my hot little room.

Holding it together isn't easy when you find yourself trapped in a room that resembles a solitary confinement unit that's hot enough to practise Bikram yoga. Especially when the cook keeps coming in and saying things like: 'There's a foreigner with a big camera at the gate, filming into the compound.'

It didn't help that my phone kept buzzing with phone calls that I wasn't foolish enough to answer. I was trying to read a book on Khmer history when a lovely text message came through from John Smith. Why, he demanded, was it so difficult to get a response from myself or CCT? He said he had a number of recorded interviews making 'very damaging' accusations about me and CCT. He was offering me a chance to put forward my side of the story. And he would have thought we'd appreciate the media interest and its power as a vehicle for raising funds! He warned that if we didn't address the accusations he had documented, there may be 'serious consequences'.

Now all my fears were confirmed. We were being set up to create a bullshit, sensationalist 'news story'. All for the sake of ratings!

I'd never felt so powerless.

If CCT's first introduction to the Australian public was a big black mark against our name then we'd probably never recover, no matter how much good publicity followed. Australians can be suspicious and untrusting of overseas charities as it is.

What was I going to do? I locked the door to my sweatbox and flopped down onto my mattress, head pounding, feeling utterly helpless.

The temperatures climbed and the mattress started to feel like a roasting pan. I was so hot I couldn't think straight. I grabbed a pillow and flopped onto the tiles, Khmer-style. That's how I found out that Cambodians are smart to sleep on the floor. The heat and pressure that had built up in my head seemed to drain away into the cold tiles.

For the next several days I worked from the floor of the sweatbox, putting together reports, holding meetings with staff—everything happened on the floor. Heng very kindly tried to make food for me but couldn't quite grasp the vegetarian thing, so she resorted to supplying me with endless bags of grilled bananas and green mangos.

The phone kept ringing and I kept ignoring it. Following Oliver's Shtein's advice, I kept detailed records of each call and message, noting the date, time and phone number of each call.

Carolyn Shine, who was fast becoming my closest friend at this time, put me in touch with a friend with PR experience, who confirmed that we should just keep doing what we were doing.

About four days later, the calls and messages finally stopped. But I still had to stay in my room until we knew for sure that John Smith had left Battambang.

Twenty-four hours after the last message from John, another call came through from a different number.

I *had* to know if the coast was clear or not. So I answered: 'Hello?'

'Hi Tara. It's Fred Nerk from the current affairs show. I'm in Cambodia.'

I said nothing, feeling the blood drain from my head.

'My colleague Jane Doe and I will be in Battambang tomorrow and would love to catch up with you for dinner, without the cameras.'

'Thanks for the offer, Fred,' I blurted. 'I'mverybusyatthemoment butI'llgetbacktoyousoon.' I couldn't hang up the phone quickly enough.

Frantic, I called Peter. He said he'd call the lawyer and Sally and get right back to me.

Half an hour later, Peter called with the verdict. The bottom line was, we didn't trust them, so no matter what, we weren't doing the story. That being the case, there was no point in listening to them sweet-talk me over dinner. I should send a message back thanking them for their offer but restating that I stood by the press statement we'd released.

Of course, they still weren't taking no for an answer. They persisted with phone calls and messages.

Fred picked up where John left off, bombarding me with unfriendly text messages. A colleague of his we'll call 'Jane Doe' seemed to take on the role of 'good cop'. She would send messages like:

> Hi Tara! [Jane Doe] here from [large TV network] . . . Trying to reach you and would love to meet—no cameras—over a meal to check information I have about your orphanage. Please reply :0)

And then Fred would write:

> I'd still love for you to give me a call. We are doing a story and were hoping to do it with your help. There's some serious questions that need answering about your organisation. Questions I hoped could be cleared up by you. We've interviewed a number of experienced NGO-related people here in Cambodia and Australia who've raised questions about your organisation. Your refusal to even meet raises more questions. We need your help to respond.

Which would result in me sending things like this to Peter:

> They keep calling and calling. I'm just not picking up. Wish they'd go away! I'm scared.

This went on for ten days. I was dying to go outside, check my emails, do a few hundred stretching exercises and eat something—anything— besides grilled banana and green mango. But I had to wait until we could confirm that Fred and his crew had left Battambang.

Back in Sydney, Peter was furious at how I was being treated. He hated seeing me scared and miserable. When Sally told him the current affairs show team had gone digging for dirt on us, he was even angrier.

Things went quiet for a few days, but we couldn't be sure if the crew had left Battambang and I was safe to leave my room or not. So Peter came up with a brilliant idea . . .

With the chutzpah he's famous for, he called Jane Doe on her mobile number, trying to sound happy and upbeat, like an old friend.

'Hey, Jane!' he chirped. 'Are you back in Sydney yet?'

'Yeah, we just got back yesterday,' she said. 'Sorry, who is this?'

'Thank you. Goodbye!' And he hung up.

Then, on a roll, he decided to call John Smith, the mysterious filmmaker.

'Hi, John!' he said cheerily. 'Just a quick question. Are you still with the current affairs show?'

'Yeah, I am. Sorry, who's speaking?'

'FUCK YOU!'

~

Peter let me know I was now free to emerge, blinking, into the bright Cambodian sunshine again.

Fucking hell, that was unbelievable, I thought. *What next?*

It didn't take long to find out . . .

Because it seemed that when the current affairs show went digging for dirt on us . . . they'd found some! It turned out there was something very wrong with CCT's official registration in Australia.

That was a horrible shock to all of us—we'd tried so hard from the start to be squeaky clean and do everything by the book. But it turned out we actually didn't have tax-exemption status in Australia, or even a licence to fundraise. This meant that, technically, the fundraiser we'd held at the art gallery was illegal and we owed tax on every dollar we'd raised.

We tried to contact the 'charity consultant' Caz and I had hired to set up CCT to take this up with him. But guess what? He'd skipped the country. It turned out he was a complete fraud and a con man.

Oliver Shtein put his hand up again to help sort things out. (Oliver's law firm, Bartier Perry, has continued to provide free legal services to CCT in Australia. Thanks, Oliver!)

Oliver found out that our trust deed had also not been set up properly. Getting this news from Sally and Peter over the next few days was like receiving multiple blows to the head, one after another after another.

Fortunately, Sally and Peter found that the staff at the tax department had already heard about our dodgy consultant. There were a number of other people who were in the same situation. So they knew the fault didn't lie with us and were gracious and understanding about it all. They told us there were lots of unofficial small fundraisers like ours happening around Australia without proper licences and mostly they don't bother policing them. But as this was brought to their attention by the current affairs show, they were required to take action. They wouldn't fine us, but they needed us to close down CCT in Australia. This meant pulling down the website, closing the bank account and starting the registration process all over again.

In the meantime, all the cheques we'd received after the *Sydney Morning Herald* piece had to be returned, and the only way people could donate was via a laborious and costly international transfer or international money order to our bank account in Cambodia.

It was a devastating blow.

~

Registering an Australian charity to support an overseas project wasn't simple.

For the next few months, three little letters came to dominate our conversations—DGR.

'DGR' stands for 'Deductible Gift Recipient' status. Any new Australian-based charity we formed would require DGR status so donors could claim a tax deduction on their donations. Getting that tax deduction on charitable donations is a big part of Australian culture—everyone knows about it and expects to get it (as you would, really). Without it, our credibility as a professional organisation and our ability to secure funding from Australia would take a major hit.

We were up shit creek and in desperate need of a paddle. So when I saw one floating by, I grabbed it.

It came in the form of an email from a man named Terry, who was working at a local NGO that we'll call New Dawn Orphanage. New Dawn had been the primary target of the current affairs show witch-hunt. They were filming an exposé on a couple of Australian celebrities who were supporting New Dawn. So, as it turned out, CCT had become a casualty in this story—a case of 'why not kill two birds with one stone?' In an act of solidarity, he wrote to introduce himself and suggest we catch up to share war stories.

So one afternoon, Jedtha and I rode out to New Dawn to meet him.

It was about a ten-minute ride from town—further than I'd been for a while. We crossed the river and headed down a dirt road into rice fields that extended, green and flat, all the way to the horizon. But as we came round a bend, a large white 'castle' seemed to loom up out of the flat rural landscape.

Holy shit! I thought to myself. CCT's quaint little home seemed so humble compared with the massive white-walled fortress that New Dawn had set up for their kids.

But as we drove through the impressive, wrought-iron gates, I realised just how new this orphanage was. It was still very much a building site—noisy, dusty and full of construction workers and unfinished structures. Not exactly kid-friendly, I thought. We followed the internal road towards a small group of kids hanging out in front of one of eight white bungalows.

The kids all turned and watched curiously as we pulled to a halt. A tall, kind-looking man in his fifties came out of one of the buildings to greet us.

'Tara, Jedtha, Hi! I'm Terry.' He shook my hand warmly. 'Let's go and talk in my office.' A few of the littler kids dangled off his arms as he walked.

It wasn't long before Terry and I were chatting like old friends. It was great to have a chance to talk to another Aussie about everything we'd been through.

Then Terry told me his story, which was, in a way, chillingly similar.

New Dawn had been started by a group of Australians to help a monk called Samlain who was running a small, struggling orphanage at his pagoda. These Aussies were connected with a large AIDS charity in Australia. With help from the AIDS charity and the two Australian celebrities (who were subsequently targeted by the current affairs show), they raised the funds to buy the block of land we were standing on and build a shiny new orphanage.

Shortly after the monk and his children moved into the new premises, the Australians discovered Samlain had defrauded them. Terry said he had deceived the local community into donating the land to build a school, but nobody told the Australians about that. Samlain then sold it to the Australians at a hefty price and pocketed the cash. On top of that, for many years, Samlain had inflicted terrible abuse on the children.

Terry and another board member had managed to get the corrupt monk removed from the organisation and now Terry was trying to juggle multiple management and administrative roles just to keep things going.

Meanwhile, the disgruntled Samlain launched a campaign of terror on the orphanage. He and his gang of thugs would wait near the orphanage in the evening and then, as the orphanage staff drove out the gates and down the dark, unlit road back into town, the thugs would drive up beside them and try to kick them off their motos.

Terry's story got even darker.

He found out that nearly a third of the kids were somehow 'related' to Samlain. He had organised these kids into a group who acted as his henchmen. Terry said he'd found balaclavas, machetes and other weapons hidden in one of the kids' dormitories.

And then, just when things were settling down a little, Terry and another board member were contacted by my favourite current affairs show!

The journalists twisted their words around to make a story that defamed the orphanage's celebrity supporters, blaming them for the orphanage's lack of funding.

Hearing all this made me comfortable enough to relate everything the current affairs show had put us through, too. I'd been trapped in my room! They tried to set Sally and me against each other! They turned up at the gates and scared us all half to death and now we had to give back all our donations . . .

Terry shook his head sympathetically. 'Let's try to find some way to help each other,' he said.

I wasn't sure how I could help New Dawn . . . but, boy, could I think of a way New Dawn could help me! 'So, Terry, tell me . . .' I said. 'How did you guys get DGR status in Australia?'

'Yeah, they make it difficult, don't they?' said Terry. 'My involvement in the AIDS charity has been a big help. The AIDS charity acts as a conduit for New Dawn, accepting donations under their umbrella in Australia and issuing the tax receipts for us.'

Suddenly I spied a glimmer of hope. Maybe we could convince New Dawn and the AIDS charity to help process CCT's donations too. Then we'd have a way of accepting donations from Australia again.

~

Sally called me a few days later. 'I just had an email from Jake, the chairman of New Dawn's board,' she told me. 'He's coming back to Battambang and wants to meet you. He's a member of the AIDS charity too, like Terry. This is our chance to see if we can partner with them!'

So one of CCT's first-ever visitors was Jake, a flamboyant blond man who turned up in shorts and a tank top, exuding easygoing Aussie charm.

I showed him around and the kids peeked shyly at him from behind their homework. He was very generous with praise about how clean and tidy and organised the place was and how polite and happy the kids were.

After showing him around our facility, I invited Jake to sit down with me at the stone table in the open area downstairs. It was time to ask him for help.

But before I could open my mouth, he said: 'Tara, I'm completely blown away by what I've seen here today. You and Jedtha are doing a fantastic job at managing this place. You'd think the kids had been here for years!'

I'm as vulnerable to flattery as the next person, so I broke into a smile.

'Look what you've done here!' he continued. 'You've got all the parts working together like a well-oiled machine. I tell you, we need a good operations manager like you at New Dawn. So what do you say? Want the job? We'll put you on a monthly salary—and you can bring your kids over to us too!'

My jaw dropped. I hadn't been expecting this! But it was a fantastic idea, one that would solve all my problems.

Once I'd regained the ability to speak, I replied, 'Wow, what an amazing offer! I've got to talk to Jedtha, Sally and the team first, but I think it sounds like a great plan.'

~

Over the next few days, I talked at length to Jedtha and Sally about the details—and logistics—of merging our two organisations.

Jedtha was a little wary about trusting another organisation, and the stories about the disgruntled monk really worried him. They worried me too. But we both felt that we had to grab this chance while we had it. We urgently needed a way to accept funds. We'd just have to work out a plan to manage the risks.

Sally and Jedtha and I decided that, first of all, we needed the AIDS charity to approve CCT as a partner. In time, provided we all worked well together, we'd merge the two centres into one. But we didn't want to move CCT's kids before we were certain it was going to work. The last thing the kids needed was more instability.

Jake understood this and promised to talk to the AIDS charity about accepting CCT as a partner for the interim. He told me that Terry was delighted with the plan because he was swamped by his fundraising role. Jake assured me I had the full support of Terry and the board in my upcoming role.

~

Although we were serious about merging with New Dawn and the AIDS charity, Sally and I decided we'd set the wheels in motion to register our own Australian charity too, just in case.

It would be a huge job, but Sally was on to it. We decided to call the new Australian foundation Green Kids Global (GKG), inspired by Sally's vision for building a self-sustaining eco-village.

~

Jake, who was now back in Australia, asked me to write a proposal outlining my aims and objectives in bringing the two centres together, and my requirements for bringing New Dawn up to standard. So I started visiting New Dawn to scope out the project.

I was a bit surprised by what I found . . .

It was clear New Dawn was seriously understaffed. The few staff they did have mostly looked bored and uninterested. The minimum standards set by MoSVY stipulated that residential care centres should have at least one staff member per twenty kids. From what I saw, New Dawn didn't come close to reaching that ratio.

Whenever I arrived I found large groups of toddlers and young kids playing unsupervised without an adult in sight. Sometimes it'd take me over half an hour to find a staff member on duty. And when I made visits two or three days apart, I'd notice that some of the kids were dressed in the same dirty clothes and smelt of urine.

Many of the kids were suffering from serious illnesses and

disabilities like tuberculosis, HIV and cerebral palsy and it didn't seem like they were being treated or managed properly—if at all.

The general level of hygiene at the centre was worrying, too. A putrid stench from the toilets filled the halls of the large dormitories and there were food scraps and rubbish everywhere.

Given the poor level of supervision, I couldn't help feeling somewhat alarmed to see kids regularly playing and swimming in a creek that ran through the back of the property.

One day I had a little chat in Khmer with a boy who was sitting alone looking very glum. He looked like he was about ten years old.

'*Sok sabai?*' I asked him in Khmer. *How are you?*

'*Ot Sok sabai,*' he replied. *Not good.*

'What's up?' I asked him gently.

'I want to call my mum and dad. I miss them.'

'Huh?' That couldn't be right. 'Where are your mum and dad?'

'They're in Battambang, not so far from here,' he told me, gesturing towards town.

'Why are you living here if you still have a mum and dad?' I asked, confused.

'I don't know,' he said with a shrug.

Why was this kid was living in an orphanage when his mum and dad were still alive? I resolved to ask Jedtha to help me get to the bottom of it.

I added that conversation to the growing list of action items I was writing in my diary. Working for New Dawn was clearly going to be a hard slog, but I was champing at the bit to get started. I was sure I could bring good things to the organisation, and I couldn't wait to put a long-term solution to CCT's administrative woes into place.

~

After I finished the proposal and submitted it to the New Dawn board, I received some very warm emails from people on the board, saying things like: 'This proposal is exactly what we need.' Buoyed by this, I started checking my email more often than usual, hoping the official job offer would arrive soon. I was desperate to sign it and get started.

But then one of the board members (let's call her Julie) wrote to ask if she could meet me before the job offer was made.

Uh-oh—this didn't sound good. I knew Julie and Terry were good friends. I hoped Terry wasn't feeling threatened by my appointment, despite what Jake, the New Dawn chairman, had told me. But over the past few weeks, Terry had never been anything but amiable, professional and welcoming. He'd even invited me and some other expats to his place to watch Australia's best-loved horserace, the Melbourne Cup.

Still, some instinct told me that Julie's request was cause for concern.

~

The morning after Julie arrived in Battambang, we went to a cafe to have lunch and a long chat.

Julie, a retired social worker, seemed to be a down-to-earth type. She put my mind at ease by stressing that she was absolutely supportive of my appointment as operations manager. However, she wanted my starting date to be postponed because New Dawn was dangerously low on funds. So low, in fact, that Terry had been forced to use his own funds to keep the orphanage going, and they didn't even have enough to pay for next month's operating costs.

'Terry's in a very tough spot,' she said. 'These kids have nowhere else to go. He's doing all he can to keep the doors open.'

Terry was supporting New Dawn himself? I was still reeling from this awful news when Julie continued: 'It's very important that you, Terry and Chum, New Dawn's country director, can all work together as a team. Sometimes Jake can be a bit too hasty when making decisions with New Dawn. Things will be much smoother if you start in mid-January instead, when Terry will be in Battambang. That way, he can assist with your induction.'

Something about the intense way she said this made me ask: 'Julie, I'm sorry, but is there some kind of conflict happening on the board?'

She admitted that yes, there was some friction on the board. Jake hadn't consulted with the other board members at all before offering me the role when he first met me in Battambang. 'We have a meeting scheduled for December at which all the issues of funding and new appointments will be discussed.'

It all sounded terribly messy and complicated. I agreed that my starting date should be postponed until after the board meeting. I was glad I'd been given a chance to digest all this information before I jumped in at the deep end.

~

That night I wrote to Jake, telling him that I was now aware of the friction on the board and that I was going to sit back and wait for the committee to make a unanimous decision about how and when we would proceed.

His reply came back the following morning:

> Tara, please don't worry about anything Julie said. She and
> Terry are best mates. But please don't be put off by either of
> them—everyone else on the board wants you to start ASAP.

A few hours later, Jake sent me—and all the members of the New Dawn board—an email with my official job offer, and told me he'd informed Chum that Jedtha and I were to start work the following Monday. A few emails came in from other board members welcoming me to the team.

I wasn't nearly as happy to see the offer as I would have been before I met Julie. Now it was just confusing.

Should I follow Julie's advice and wait? Or follow Jake's, and jump in? I really didn't want this plan to fail. Eventually, after a chat with Sally, Jedtha and I decided that as Jake was the chairman of the board and Chum was now expecting us, the best thing to do was to follow his direction.

~

Jedtha and I arrived at New Dawn on Monday at nine on the dot. We said a quick 'hi' to some of the kids and made our way to the main office to meet the orphanage director, Chum.

Chum was slouched in his chair, drumming the long talon of his pinkie finger on the desk. He did not look one bit pleased to see us. When I saw him, his demeanour reminded me of Rath.

Jedtha and I bowed politely and sat down opposite him. But before we even had a chance to introduce ourselves properly, he launched into a full-blown rant in English.

'New Dawn not need foreigner!' he informed us. 'We no need foreigner to work in Cambodia. All staff should only be Khmer. New Dawn not need to hire more people because I can do all myself. I have enough ability!'

I looked at Jedtha, wide-eyed. Jedtha looked horrified. We sat in silence for a minute with the shock from that outburst still hanging in the air.

'Why you don't want to work with foreigners, Chum?' Jedtha asked in English.

'Foreigner hire staff with no ability! Foreigner can't understand how to do in Cambodia. If board in Australia want to stop Terry, that is good too. I can do all myself!'

I was shocked again (and secretly quite impressed) when Jedtha, in his calm and polite way, accused Chum of racism.

'You don't know Tara,' he added. But he didn't push it any further. Clearly, Chum was not going to make us welcome. So we wound up the conversation and left.

On the way home, Jedtha told me in Khmer: 'I know Chum. He is the long-time assistant of Samlain, the monk who was the director of New Dawn. I knew Samlain when I was at the pagoda. He is Rath's brother.'

I nearly fell off the back of Jedtha's moto. All this time, I had been gearing up to work alongside the assistant of Rath's brother!

I was to learn with time that 'brother' doesn't always mean 'biological sibling' in Cambodia. But whether Jedtha meant 'brother' or 'relative or close friend' the meaning was the same—Rath, Chum and Samlain were tight. I wrote to Jake as soon as I could to tell him all about the meeting. I also told him that I was not prepared to work with Chum, putting CCT in the direct spotlight of further resentment from Chum, Samlain and Rath.

Jake wrote back. Then Terry wrote back. Then Julie wrote back, and the rest of the board weighed in, and the complications multiplied like wildfire. It seemed I'd walked into the middle of a small war.

I contacted Geraldine Cox, another Aussie who runs an NGO in Cambodia—Sunrise Children's Villages—and asked for her advice. Geraldine was in a tearing hurry when I spoke to her, but she listened to my story and her advice was succinct: 'Whatever you do, don't merge with New Dawn. They're a sinking ship and will take you down too.'

Jedtha, Sally and I agreed with Geraldine. We couldn't afford to get involved with such a dysfunctional organisation.

~

The whole saga left us with a horrible legacy. By now, several thousand dollars in donations to CCT had gone to the AIDS charity in Australia. The plan was that the money would be transferred to New Dawn, and then on to us.

But very shortly afterwards, New Dawn's relationship with the AIDS charity completely collapsed. It took us months to get our money back—at a time when we were in urgent need of funds.

I believe that everyone involved in New Dawn had good intentions. They just wanted to help the kids. But it was a valuable lesson for me: good intentions just aren't good enough. Without knowledge and expertise and a deep insight into the culture it was too easy to inadvertently make bad choices and end up doing more harm than good.

It's unfortunate that New Dawn's problems continued into the future. Terry resigned soon after I stepped away. He still lives in Battambang and continues to be a great support to CCT and me.

New Dawn was investigated multiple times by DoSVY. Unfortunately, they didn't have the wherewithal to take any meaningful action.

Several Australian volunteers came and went, dismayed and sometimes outraged by the hopelessness of the organisation.

A little later, some of the older kids protested publicly after they were turned out of the orphanage with nowhere else to go. It hit the national papers in Cambodia. CCT helped to arrange temporary shelter for them until they found somewhere permanent to stay.

While I continue to hope that New Dawn will adopt better practices, and worry about the wellbeing of the kids in their care, I'm extremely relieved our involvement with New Dawn ended when it did.

12

Thanks to a small but steady trickle of funds coming into our Cambodian bank account from new supporters, there was a period of time after the New Dawn saga when life settled into a pleasant routine. I started having dinner almost every evening with my adopted Cambodian family: Chan and Mina and their three kids.

One afternoon Ponlok, Bopha and I wandered down the dirt lane from their house to pick up a few groceries for dinner from a street stall. On the way, a little old lady with short white hair and a toothless mouth full of betel nut stopped us to try to sell us some sweet Cambodian rice cakes.

As always, I listened to the conversation with ears pricked, paying attention to the subtleties in tone and the way my Khmer friends' mouths effortlessly wrapped around the complex phonemes. I could understand spoken Khmer quite well by now. It was great fun to listen to the conversations happening around me.

But my attention kept getting pulled to the palm tree beside us, where a wretched-looking dog was slumped in the shade.

God, she's almost completely bald. I thought to myself. *Is it mange?*

Or maybe it's just old age? I'd be surprised if many dogs here reached old age though . . .

Usually, I found the dogs in Cambodia endearing. To my eyes, they were quirky little creatures of all kinds of funny shapes and sizes. But this one was beyond quirky . . . Besides being bald almost all over, her other defining feature was a very conspicuous set of nipples.

She could have fed a Brahman bull calf with teats that big! She must've had a thousand litters, the poor thing.

And sure enough, a couple of metres away a litter of eight guinea pig-sized puppies were lying in the sun, emitting tiny squeaking cries for their mum.

I watched as eventually the mother dog heaved herself up to respond to their soft yelps. One by one, she picked them up and moved them to a safe spot under a stone chair in the shade. She carefully lowered herself down next to them to let them feed.

'*Yiyay*,' I said, using the Khmer word for 'grandmother', 'can I look at the puppies?'

She showed me an expanse of red-black gums, and waved me over.

The old mama dog saw me coming, raised her head for a moment but then flopped back down in the dust, unfazed. The puppies' eyes were still shut so I guessed they couldn't have been more than a week old.

As a great fan of all things canine, I usually react to puppies of all breeds with cries of adoration. But now that I was up close, I was taken aback by how . . . well . . . ugly they were. They looked kind of like hyenas, with their mottled coats. Their dark brown muzzles were alive with fleas that wove under, over and between their eyes and nose.

In Cambodia, the idea of dog ownership is very different from the one I'd grown up with, because when people do it tough, animals tend to do it tougher. For most Khmer families, the dog lives a loveless life as a guard dog. Sometimes dogs even wind up on a spit, sold as a snack at roadside beer stalls.

Ponlok and Bopha and the old woman wandered over to see the

white girl fussing over a pack of flea-bitten mutts. The old woman chuckled and then asked me if I wanted one.

It was a tempting offer—a part of me desperately wanted to rescue the poor little things. *I'm going to be living in Cambodia for a fair while*, I thought to myself. *Maybe I could get a dog . . .*

But I resisted, knowing I was already up to my eyeballs in commitment. And the pups were way too young to be taken from their mother anyway. So I pushed aside all thoughts of adopting a dog, smiled at the old woman and shook my head.

'Let's go,' I said to the kids, before I had a chance to change my mind. Ponlok scooped up the cakes he'd bought and we continued on down the road.

~

All thought of the puppies fled my mind in the weeks that followed, because Peter came to visit. It was great to see him. He loved the kids and staff and Chan's family, too. He said: 'I feel like I suddenly have fourteen grandkids!'

So it wasn't till about four weeks later, when Ponlok, Bopha and I were taking the same route to the grocery stalls, that I decided to make a quick stop to see how the puppies were getting on. The old woman was there as usual, sitting on the stone chair.

'Hello, Grandma,' I said pressing my hands together politely. 'How are the puppies?'

'They are all dead—including the mother dog,' she informed me. 'There's just one left.' She pointed in the direction of some big cement pots. The sole survivor was cowering behind them. I reached around and picked her up.

'All of them? What happened?' I asked.

'They were all run over by a car,' the old lady said.

It was rather a strange story, but I didn't see much point in questioning her further. I put down the struggling orphaned pup, who immediately scampered behind the pots again.

The old lady picked up a stick and whacked the pots repeatedly to scare her out again for me. After three or four good whacks the pup came bolting out and froze, tail between her legs. Then, to my horror, the old lady delivered a final whack directly to the puppy's behind and cackled gleefully.

In an instant, the terrified pup was in my arms and I couldn't stop my mouth from saying: 'Please can I keep the puppy?' The old lady cheerfully agreed, squeezing my arm affectionately and flashing me a scary smile.

Oh well, I thought. Jedtha was always telling me: 'Do something good for yourself!' And for me, there's almost nothing that brings me as much joy as a puppy.

I took the puppy back to my room at CCT. The kids looked up from what they were doing, said, 'Oh, Tara's got a puppy,' and went about their business. I was relieved that they weren't interested. They weren't very nice to animals, I'd found, having never been taught to treat them with any kind of respect.

After the puppy was washed, wormed and tucked into a nice soft bed in the corner of my room, I decided she was actually a pretty cute little thing. She still looked like a hyena, but she was a very cute-looking hyena. And she had big, bright, hazel eyes that begged to be loved. I called her Ruby.

Ruby became my shadow, never letting me out of her sight. She'd pad around behind me while I was on duty at CCT, ride around town with me on my bike, hang out with me at the internet cafes, and sit loyally at my feet through every meeting. Ruby was a great morale booster for me.

We became a familiar sight at the markets, where I'd swing by regularly to pick up 'chicken tails' for Ruby's dinner—a 25-cent stick of chicken meat. One evening, on the way home from running some errands in Chan's car, I stopped by the bustling Psar Nat market to get Ruby some dinner. It was peak hour and there was nowhere to park, so I pulled up by the stall that sold the chicken tails and sang out over the crowds of people: 'Sister, can I get some chicken tails?' The ladies at the stall froze. Then they—and practically the whole marketplace—exploded with laughter.

As soon as the words came out of my mouth I knew I'd made a grievous error. In Khmer, the word for 'tail' and the rude slang word for 'female genitalia' are almost identical. So what had I just had shouted out across the busy market? 'Sister, can I get some chicken pussy?'

For weeks after, whenever I pulled up to buy Ruby dinner, the ladies at the barbecued meat stall would cry out: 'Ah! It's the chicken pussy girl!'

Over time, Ruby grew glossy on her diet of leftovers and chicken tails. And she grew to love the kids as much as I did. Despite how much they tormented her, she'd yodel with happiness when they got home from school in the afternoons and she was as gentle as could be with them.

In some ways I think Ruby helped crystallise a new feeling that was growing inside me. A feeling that Cambodia was now home.

~

It wasn't long before one dog turned into three dogs—Ruby, Rosie and Franky (short for Frankenstein).

The second addition was Rosie. Chan's next-door neighbours had found her wandering around the market, alone and afraid. They'd heard that I'd taken in one orphaned dog and so thought that perhaps I'd like this one too.

I was hesitant at first, but I couldn't turn her away and thought it would be nice to have a friend for Ruby.

Rosie is cute as a button—a red ball of fluff who's very protective of me and almost never lets me out of her sight. Franky was in such a state when I first met him that we named him 'Frankenstein'. Ironically, he grew up to be a very handsome fellow.

~

Early one evening at CCT, the kids and I were sitting around the pink stone table in the front yard chatting away waiting for dinner, watching the sky begin to turn pretty colours. The kids were getting very excited about the smell of pork cooking on the hot coals. I told them that back home some people keep pigs as pets.

'No way!' they said, cracking up in fits of laughter. 'That's so crazy!'

'I'd like to have a pet pig,' I told them.

'Okay, Tara, you can get a pet pig!' they replied, still laughing.

'No, I couldn't do that. I'd come home one day to find you had turned it into pork chops!' I said.

This quip was greeted with a chorus of laughter. I was stoked. It was my first successful joke in Khmer.

When the laughter died down, cheeky little Amara piped up. 'You already have a pet pig.' He paused for effect, then said: 'Her name is Rosie.'

This caused another round of great hilarity. Rosie was famous for her insatiable appetite. In fact, the kids had nicknamed her Si-Daik, literally 'eat-sleep', after her favourite pastimes. Some days she'd sleep in till around midday, until she smelled the scraps from the kids' lunches hitting the deck and smouldering on the hot slabs of concrete.

I reached underneath the stone bench to give Rosie a comforting pat, but she wasn't there. Ruby and Franky were still sitting at my feet but Rosie was nowhere in sight. I called. And called again. But she didn't come.

Finding Rosie had disappeared made that pork chops joke suddenly seem a lot less funny. In Cambodia, a wandering dog could indeed end up on someone's dinner plate.

We searched every inch of CCT, and then trawled the streets calling her name and asking the neighbours if they'd seen her. When it started to get too dark, I took the kids home and went straight to Chan's house.

Seeing my distress, Chan and Mina sprang into action.

'It's okay, *P'oun srey*,' Chan assured me. 'We can put news you lost Rowsee on Battambang Radio. We can also get tuktuk with big phone to try to find for you.'

I wasn't sure what exactly he meant by a 'big phone', but I was getting more desperate by the minute, and it sounded better than wandering around in the dark on my own.

Chan pulled out his mobile and started talking at such a fast clip I couldn't follow. Next thing I knew, we were on the way to the local radio station with a message written out in Khmer. It only cost $10 to get an announcement made on the radio. It would be broadcast several times that night and the following day.

When we got back to CCT there was a tuktuk waiting with an enormous, rusty megaphone tied to the front. The 'big phone'!

What an understatement.

I set off in the tuktuk with Chan, Sinet, Ponlok and the tuktuk's owner, who doubled as our broadcaster for the evening. We drove all over the neighbourhood, blasting the same message over and over again.

'*Lost dog. Red colour. It has a collar with a tag and the owner's phone number. If you find the dog we will give you a twenty-dollar reward!*'

Soon, a dozen or so guys on motos were charging off in all directions to try to find Rosie and earn the reward.

As the hours ticked by, the reward went up and up. By eleven o'clock, it was $50.

Soon it was so late we had to admit defeat and go home. But I couldn't see how I could sleep. I was already haunted by images of my poor Rosie being killed, skinned and butchered.

'Don't cry, *P'oun srey*,' Chan said. 'You give Rowsee a good life.'

~

The next morning there was still no sign of her. I forced myself to eat a little breakfast, threw a bucket of water over my head and tried to focus on responding to some emails from potential donors. It was hard to concentrate on anything.

Suddenly Mina burst in, shouting breathlessly in Khmer: 'I think we've found Rowsee! Chan is waiting for us.' My chair fell over backwards as we both raced to the gates and jumped in Chan's tuktuk.

We pulled up at a small house just a few blocks away. I could hear dogs barking.

A rough-looking Khmer man in his forties led me out the back of his small brick home. Two dogs, both barking wildly, were tied up near the back door. My heart sank. No Rosie.

But then the guy pointed to the back corner of his yard where a hunched, trembling dog crouched. Rosie! She took a few steps towards me as I hurried over and knelt in front of her, but she was sort of tucked over, dragging her back legs. Something was terribly wrong. A broken back? Broken legs? Then I realised she was pissing herself, she was so relieved to see me.

I hated to think what must have happened to her in the hours that she'd been missing. Chan reckoned the guy had planned to sell her and the other dogs there as meat, but the $50 reward was probably more than he would have received for selling off her parts.

I was so overwhelmed with relief that I didn't spare a single thought for the other dogs left tied up there. Thinking back now, I wish I'd paid for their release too . . .

For months afterwards, strangers would come up and ask if I ever found my red dog. They had never heard of anyone giving a reward for a lost dog, much less driving around at night blasting it from a megaphone.

~

I look back now at those golden weeks as my 'honeymoon phase'.

But there was still something that kept me awake at night. Rath had raped Sinet and got away with it. He was still running SKO and there were still kids in his care.

Sinet had made me promise not to tell anyone but it was a hard secret to keep when I knew he was still running an orphanage, still in charge of young girls.

Also, I worried that if we pretended nothing had ever happened, Sinet wouldn't get the counselling and support that she needed. She was terrified of Rath and came home a trembling, teary mess whenever she saw him or one of his relatives around town. What long-term effect would the trauma have on her?

So one evening, after all the little kids had been put to bed and the older kids were busy doing homework or reading, I sat down next to Sinet.

'Sinet, we need to talk about what you told me about Rath,' I said in Khmer. 'I worry about you.'

Sinet looked confused for a moment and I wondered if I'd used the wrong words.

I pressed on. 'I think you need to talk to a doctor who can help you feel better.'

She didn't say anything.

'Do you understand?' I asked.

'Yes,' she said. 'I understand, but I don't want counselling.' She was pretty emphatic about it.

I explained to her that I thought it was important for Jedtha and Savenh, our social worker, to know what happened. I reminded her that they also cared about her and, if she didn't want to see a counsellor, at least she could talk about it with people who spoke Khmer better than me. I also reminded her she had done nothing wrong, that she had nothing to feel ashamed about.

'So can we tell Jedtha and Savenh?' I asked.

She nodded. 'Okay, I don't mind telling them.'

~

Jedtha and Savenh were both shocked to learn what had happened to Sinet. Then their shock turned to outrage. They started talking about pressing charges.

We worried that Rath may have hurt other kids as well. So as well as counselling Sinet, Savenh also conducted counselling sessions with the rest of the kids.

Thankfully, after Savenh met with each one of the kids, she reported that while the other kids had suffered violence and neglect at Rath's hands, none of them reported any sexual assault.

~

One of SKO's older girls, Kolab, left SKO before the rescue took place. Kolab was mature for her age, and managed to get into a hairdressing school in Battambang. She hadn't been able to start school till her pre-teens, and she was bright and keen to get out and start her life, so this seemed like a good fit for her.

Her younger sister Kanya—a sweet, quiet little girl—had come with us to CCT. Kolab would come to visit Kanya occasionally, and after she finished training, she asked if she could come and stay with us, too.

Life in the outside world after leaving the orphanage was tough—Kolab was working full time, but the pay of $40 per month was so meagre she barely had enough to feed herself, let alone cover rent. It had all turned out to be much harder than she thought it would be. But Kolab was almost twenty; coming back to live at CCT's orphanage wasn't a step in the right direction.

Still, we couldn't leave her struggling to get by on $40 a month, sentenced to a life of poverty, while we educated her younger sister. Not only did it seem unfair—and being fair is a pretty big deal, really—but with the better education we were providing Kanya, when she grew up, finished school and got a job, she would probably end up having to provide ongoing support to her older sister, who hadn't had the same opportunities.

This is how it works in Cambodia—without the welfare safety net we have in the west, almost every working Khmer adult I knew was caring for extended family members. This would keep Kanya from escaping a life of poverty, too.

We eventually managed to get Kolab a place at a beauty school in Phnom Penh where she could board and get more formal qualifications as a hairdresser and beautician. Securing the funds to put Kolab though college wasn't easy, but eventually we found a donor who was happy to increase their monthly donation to help cover her costs. Jedtha and I hoped we might be able to help Kolab set up a little hairdressing stall at the markets after she graduated so she could support herself. We'd just have to wait and see how she went.

~

Sinet continued to be a huge help to me in those early days of CCT. I came to really rely on her to navigate the complicated world that is Cambodia. In time, she became my substitute little sister and a very dear friend.

I was so impressed with what a bright, inquisitive and free-thinking young girl she was. For someone who had grown up in such abject, isolating poverty, she was passionately interested in worldly matters. I'd talk to her about science, politics, religion and world history and she'd soak it up like a sponge. She seemed able to see horizons far beyond the scope of her life experience. She was a natural leader and so wonderful with the other kids.

But she was also very fragile. When the subject of Rath came up there'd be lots of tears. She would often say she felt like his actions must have somehow been her fault, that she'd done something to bring it on herself. She said thinking about it made her feel dirty, like she needed to shower and scrub herself clean. I told her constantly: 'You did nothing wrong! The wrong is all his! He is a disgusting, bad man who did something very illegal. How you feel is normal and understandable. Many other girls in Cambodia, and around the world, have suffered the same. You are a brave, strong girl. Remember that, okay?'

One day, Jedtha and Savenh had a meeting with Sinet at the pink stone table in the yard to talk to her about prosecuting Rath. Jedtha was absolutely convinced that pressing charges was the right thing to do. It was also the only way to stop Rath from hurting anyone else.

'You have the right to prosecute him,' he told her. 'We can take him to court if you want.'

To my great surprise, she said: 'Yes. We should.'

'Good! I'm happy to see you being strong,' Jedtha said. 'We can go and talk to LICADHO to get their advice.' LICADHO is the French acronym for the Cambodian League for the Promotion and Defence of Human Rights.

I looked across the yard to where some of our girls were giggling together over a game of jump rope, looking so happy, and so vulnerable.

There was still so much about Cambodia that I didn't understand. I worried about how we were going to navigate through this situation, while not putting Sinet, ourselves or any of the other kids in harm's way. But I completely agreed with Jedtha—justice is important and Rath shouldn't be allowed to get away with what he had done.

We all agreed to give it our best shot.

~

Knowing the cold hard reality hidden behind some of the kids' bright happy faces was an ongoing worry for me. They had suffered violence and gross neglect at SKO, and many of the kids had been abused long before they'd fallen into Rath's hands.

The signs were there, all the time, that terrible things had happened to these kids. A lot of them suffered traumatic nightmares. We sometimes saw inexplicable crying jags, mood swings, angry outbursts and behaviours that seemed obsessive. This was more than just the normal ups and downs of childhood—it was clear to me that we needed to do more to help them.

If the kids felt sad or had problems, the only adult they could really talk to was Savenh, our social worker. She had a lot of field experience and had done some specialised training workshops, but she had no formal training. Social work wasn't even available to study at any university in Cambodia until 2008. Savenh herself often said she was at a loss as to how best to address these behaviours.

Another issue we had was that the kids tended to come to me, not the staff, with their problems. Sinet, in particular, would only talk to me. They just didn't trust Savenh and the rest of the staff in the same way. I was painfully aware that I wasn't qualified to properly help them—I just knew the kids needed to feel safe and secure, and loved. But I didn't know what to do to make sure they all grew up feeling that way. We needed help, an expert we could call on, something . . .

One unseasonably hot afternoon, I had this reality brought home to me more strongly than ever.

I was working on the cool tiles in my room when an unholy racket, like feuding tigers, blasted in at me from the play area outside.

I stumbled out to find seven-year-old Nimol clutching his forehead, crying bitterly. Sinet, Kanya and Maly cuddled him, trying to calm him down. Meanwhile, someone was emitting primal screams from the back of the building. Savenh, her face grim, was striding across the yard towards the noise. I rushed over to join her, my eyes full of questions. We both pulled up short in shock at what we saw.

Little Makara, the baby of the CCT kids, was holding on to the fence. He lapsed into silence as we approached.

'Makara!' I called out reflexively. Makara had a special place in my heart. He was melt-your-heart cute, with a big cheeky smile and a gravelly little voice, a bit like the Cookie Monster. He was very easy to love and he adored me, too. But when he turned his head to look at me, my heart froze. His eyes were completely wrong; they were black pools of hate. He screamed in a voice like a chainsaw: 'Go away!'

Savenh gently pulled me away. 'Let him calm down,' she advised.

We went to check on Nimol and ask the other kids what had happened. The news was troubling. Nimol and Makara, who were brothers, had been playing together when something set Makara off.

The smaller boy had picked up a rock and smacked Nimol across the side of his head.

Within an hour, Makara had calmed down and was playing with the other kids again like nothing had happened. Jedtha, Savenh and I sat together watching them and talking things over.

'Makara has a very bad temper,' Savenh said. 'He hits the other kids all the time. He'll be fine and then suddenly he just snaps. Nothing seems to bring him out of it except time—just leave it and he gets over it.'

Jedtha and I nodded—we'd seen it too. Makara's temper was a problem, and it wasn't his only problem. He was kind of hyper a lot of the time. At school, he couldn't concentrate. He'd just run out of the classroom and play outside.

Sometimes he'd be fine for several days but inevitably something would set him off and BOOM. A lot of the time it wasn't even clear what the trigger was.

Jedtha's eyes were deeply troubled—he had a soft spot for Makara, too. 'I think maybe we should send him to another organisation. He's a risk to the other children. Maybe it's best if he goes somewhere else.'

'I can't see how that would help him,' I said. 'And we can't separate him from his brother. But we definitely need to do something.'

There were no services in Battambang providing mental health support for children, but an NGO that provided psychological health services to adults gave us a lead to an organisation in Phnom Penh that might help.

Makara's mental and emotional health was important enough to warrant a trip to Phnom Penh. We decided I should be the one to take him.

~

Navigating around the edgy, bustling streets of Phnom Penh as a foreigner can be challenging. Navigating with a five-year-old boy who was all smiles and sunshine one moment and a cartoon Tasmanian devil the next . . . that was an education.

Getting Makara from one place to another was a complete night-mare—he had his own ideas about what he wanted to do. I was terrified he was going to run off and get lost. At one point he had a temper tantrum and I ended up towing him grimly down the street, with him hitting my hand the whole way.

Another time we disagreed over where we were going, and he tried to fling himself out of the tuktuk we were travelling in. '*Makara! Please!*' There was no reasoning with him when his mind was made up. I held on to his fierce little fists like my life depended on it. Thank goodness he was only five.

The counselling session that I took him to did not go well. I don't suppose any counselling session *could* go well when the patient has to be dragged there kicking and screaming.

It took place in a hot little room, with a fan turning slowly over-head. Makara was supposed to sit on a wooden chair opposite the counsellor's desk, like a suspect in a police interrogation room. But he wouldn't even sit down. Instead, he stood in the furthest corner, refusing to speak, his face a closed mask of defiance.

The counsellor asked questions like: 'Tell me, why are you upset? Why won't you talk?'

So ... no. Not a very successful session.

We eventually walked back to the hotel, my heart in my toes. That was not what I'd been hoping for. I wasn't sure how child psychology actually worked—wasn't it a long process where you played games and drew pictures and slowly built trust? It was pretty obvious that what-ever child psychology was, the organisation we'd just left didn't do it.

I had no idea what to do next.

By the time we got back to the hotel, Makara had already completely forgotten about the tantrum earlier. That evening, when I was putting him to bed, he told me he was scared to have the lights turned off. 'There are ghosts here, Tara!' he announced dramatically.

I knew enough about Cambodian culture to know that telling him there's no such thing as ghosts wasn't going to cut it. Even many adults live in terror of ghosts. But I had to say something to calm his fears, so I turned a night-light on and told him: 'We don't have to worry about ghosts, Makara. We're good people. Ghosts don't hurt good people.'

Makara shook his head glumly and said the saddest words I've ever heard a five-year-old utter. 'I'm not a good person, Tara. I'm bad. I'm a bad boy. And stupid.'

'No you're not!' I cried, stroking his hair. 'You're a good boy. And a very smart boy, too!'

'No.' His voice wobbled a little. 'I'm not.'

'You are, Makara. You are a very good person. Remember that time I spilled that big bottle of soap on the floor at CCT? Do you remember that?'

'Yes . . .' he answered, his puppy-dog eyes brimming with sadness.

'No one helped me clean it up but you. You are very kind and thoughtful.'

A big wide grin spread across his face and a solitary tear rolled down his cheek.

'And you know what else? I think you speak English more clearly than all the kids at CCT. It's true! You're a very clever boy.'

By this stage he was beaming. He wrapped his little arms around me to give me a hug. It was true, Makara had an uncanny ability to pronounce English words. And he could sing along almost perfectly to English songs, even though he had no idea what he was saying.

'I speak English good!' he boasted in English.

'You sure do. Now don't worry about ghosts. You are a very good boy so they can't hurt you.'

He nodded, rolled over and fell asleep. I lay awake on my rock-hard bed, with my pillow that felt like a brick, thinking over what had just happened.

I'd never heard a child express such a low opinion of themselves before. I wondered if anyone had ever told him he was a good kid. It was quite possible that he had gone through his life only ever hearing what a bad, naughty and stupid boy he was. I'd heard the kids and even the staff yell those words at him, in a fit of exasperation. So why would he believe any different?

When I thought about it, I wasn't sure if I'd ever taken the time to single him out and let him know how much he mattered, what a special little boy he was. In an orphanage filled with kids, with so many needs, there just wasn't the time to spend on each child's individual needs. We were always too busy getting food on the table, or getting everyone out the door to school, or just generally putting out fires. The only time Makara would ever hear feedback about himself was when he'd done something wrong . . .

I resolved to try to do better. The next few days seemed like the perfect time to start.

~

Over the next week I continued the hunt for a counsellor. But every time I was told there was a child psychologist I could try, it turned out to be dead end.

Makara came everywhere with me, and every time he did anything even mildly good I told him he was a good boy, or a clever boy, or a kind boy.

He blossomed under all this positive, individual attention. His behaviour improved so much I could take him anywhere. I even took him horseriding as a reward, and he was so brave and proud of himself . . . it was adorable. He still remembers it as one of the highlights of his childhood.

'I want to be a vegetarian,' he told me one day over lunch. I told him it wasn't a great idea for kids. 'Okay,' he conceded. 'But when I grow up I want to help people like you do. Tara, can we give some money to that old woman begging over there?' He had somehow, miraculously, turned into the perfect child.

He asked endless questions about my life in Australia. 'Tara, are there people begging in Australia, too? How many times have you ridden in an aeroplane? When I get older, I'll learn to drive an aeroplane and I can take you everywhere you want to go! Tara, do you have brothers and sisters in Australia? Did you know I have two brothers and one sister?'

'What?' I was surprised. 'Who? I thought you only had Nimol?'

'No, I also have one younger brother and one older sister.'

'Where are they?'

'I don't know.'

'Oh, okay.' I made a mental note to ask Jedtha if this was true. If Makara and Nimol really had siblings, shouldn't we know about this?

Makara's behaviour improved so much that I was able to take him into the bustling, crowded Central Market. The market is housed in a gorgeous Art Deco building constructed in the 1930s. It has everything from food to flowers to antiques to luggage to clothes and electronics. Makara loved it—the sights, the food, the smells. But he was very good and stuck with me.

I stopped at a clothing stall to pick out some new things for him. Like all the kids, he didn't exactly have a wardrobe full of options. While I was browsing, I looked down reflexively to check that he was still beside me. He was there, waiting patiently, but he was clearly mesmerised by a stall opposite us. I followed his gaze. He was looking at a child's black tuxedo.

He looked up at me and took my hand.

'Look! Tara!' he growled. 'Like *Men in Black*!'

How could I say no to that little face? I checked the price tag and, thankfully, it wasn't too much.

While he changed into the tux at the back of the stall, I grabbed him a pair of cheap black sunnies. Just the thing for a five-year-old MIB. He was soon strutting around like the coolest thing on the planet.

'That's for being such a good boy,' I told him.

~

Hanging out with Makara in Phnom Penh turned out to be one of the highlights of my time in Cambodia up to this point. It was all fart jokes and wisecracks and games of hide-and-seek. The night before we left to go back to Battambang, he was hiding behind the chairs in the hotel room, and jumped out at me growling: 'Rah! I'm a ghost, Tara!'

'I can't see any ghosts, Makara,' I informed him.

'You can't see ghosts because you're a big person and I'm a little person,' he replied. 'But we don't have to be scared because we're good people.'

'That's right,' I said. 'We're good people.'

I never did find a decent child psychologist in Phnom Penh. But by the time we headed back to Battambang, Makara was behaving so beautifully I wasn't sure if it was even necessary anymore. A bit of extra attention and TLC, combined with some positive reinforcement, seemed to be the answer. The trick was going to be to get everybody at CCT on board with that.

~

Makara bounced out of the car when we got back to CCT, all dressed up in his little tuxedo, and started recounting everything he'd seen in the big city to all the other kids.

'Horses! Escalators! Ice-cream!'

When I got a chance, I called a staff meeting to talk about Makara. I said: 'With Makara it is simple: if you want him to be bad, tell him he is bad. And if you want him to be good, tell him he is good. And he will be.'

I got Jedtha to help me to explain my theory more thoroughly, to make sure they definitely understood the concept.

They all agreed to try it.

The change in Makara was like an overnight flip—a turnaround so dramatic that everyone was motivated to keep working at it. Even the kids took it on board and stopped calling Makara 'stupid'.

In the months that followed, Makara blossomed into one of CCT's biggest charmers.

Jedtha was incredibly excited about it: 'Do you know what Makara did? Did you see Makara today?' he would say, like a proud parent. 'He is just a different boy!' He couldn't believe that we could shape a child's behaviour like that. To this day he says it gave him a confidence he'd never had before that he could actually make a real difference for these kids.

Seeing such a profound change in Makara planted the seed of an idea in my head. If I hadn't spent that one-on-one time with him, I never would have realised that what Makara really needed was . . . a mum.

~

It was so obvious, I was embarrassed that I hadn't seen it earlier. Of *course* Makara needed a mum . . . or a dad, or some other parental figure. Someone to nurture him, give him that special love and attention.

And he needed a family—a core group of people who were tightly bonded to him, who had his back for the rest of his life, just as my family had mine . . . No amount of good nutrition, good education or healthcare would make up for the fact that he didn't have that. No matter how good an orphanage is, it's never going to take the place of a family. And a family was what every single one of these kids needed.

Realising this made me feel quite sad. How could any orphanage give them that?

I didn't know, but I had to try.

~

I sat down with Jedtha and tried to explain all this to him. It was too complicated a concept for my Khmer, so I resorted to Khmenglish— a mix of Khmer and English.

'We can't give them a mum and dad,' I concluded, 'but perhaps we can make CCT feel more like a family.'

Jedtha looked a little confused. 'But the kids have a good life here with us, Tara! They are so happy!'

'But, Jedtha, when the kids have problems, the staff don't notice them because it's a big group,' I said. 'I think we need to spend more time with each of them like I did with Makara, so we don't miss these problems and the kids get the care they need.'

Jedtha nodded—it seemed he got the idea. 'Okay, but how do we do that?'

'Maybe we could start by including more art and physical activities in their schedules? That would give us a chance to spend more one-on-one time with each of them.'

So we decided to bring in a Khmer arts teacher on Saturdays; we'd heard of other orphanages doing that. I put my hand up to run little 'physical education' classes with them on Saturdays. And we'd run excursions once a week when we could.

This meant we'd all be working a little harder, but after the change we'd seen in Makara, we owed it to all the kids try to give them much more attention.

~

I asked Sinet and Rithy what they knew about Makara's past. They told me Makara's father was mentally ill and his mum was extremely violent.

They had heard that the boys' mother had died, so the kids went to work illegally in Thailand. The Thai police caught Makara and Nimol and sent them back to Cambodia, where they were then sent to live at SKO. The two boys had an older sister and a younger brother, but they weren't sure where they were.

So the boys actually did have siblings? But why didn't we know where they were? And why were they separated?

As soon as I could, I sat down with Savenh and Jedtha to ask them about this.

'Almost all of the kids have some family,' Savenh told me, in an 'everyone knows that' tone. Everyone except me, it turned out.

'Almost all?' I was unable to hide my shock and bewilderment. 'Which ones? I thought these kids were orphans.' I suddenly thought back to the boy at New Dawn Orphanage. There seemed to be a trend here.

She went and fetched the kids' case files, which were written in Khmer. She went through them with me. I discovered that most of the kids had siblings they'd been separated from. Some of them even had parents, aunts and uncles.

'I don't understand,' I blurted in English, looking at Jedtha. 'Why did they go to SKO if they still have a mum and dad? And why were the siblings separated?'

Jedtha tried to explain: 'It's just how we do it in our country. If the family is too poor, it's better for some of the kids to go to an orphanage. They will get food there, and an education. It means the family will do better, without so many children to support. And when the kids grow up, the kids who are educated in the orphanage then help the rest of their family.'

'But . . .' How could I explain how wrong that sounded to me? 'But how do you choose which kids to take and which to leave behind? A coin flip? And the ones who are left behind, what happens to them? Are they just condemned to struggle through a life of poverty? And the kids who grow up in the orphanage, they won't be able to get ahead in life either. Even if they do get an education and then get a good job, they won't be able to escape poverty because they'll be forever financially supporting the rest of their family who were left behind. What does that achieve? And, I mean: "orphanage"—why on earth is it called an orphanage when they aren't really orphans?!' I put my face in my hands. Cambodia has got to be the most confusing place on Earth, I thought.

Jedtha and Savenh were just staring at me blankly.

'I'm sorry,' I said. 'I'm just really surprised.'

'Cambodia is very different to your country, I think,' Jedtha said again.

'It's just, *Loak Khrew*, isn't family really important in Cambodia? Don't most Cambodians end up looking after their poorer relatives?

A bit like you, no? You are supporting your brothers and sister on the small salary you get from CCT, aren't you?'

'Yes, it's very hard,' he agreed. 'I have a salary now but I'm still just as poor as I was before. It's a very sad situation, but they are my family and I can't stand to see them suffer, so I cannot say no.'

'Wouldn't it have been wonderful if your siblings all had the opportunity to get an education too so they could all find good jobs and support themselves?' I replied.

'That would be wonderful. Yes, I see what you mean, Tara.'

It wasn't an easy 'get' for Jedtha and Savenh—they'd grown up immersed in the system. But to their credit, they could see that bringing up the kids with their siblings made sense. Most of the kids, as far as we knew, grew up in a pretty desperate situation. It was highly probable that their siblings badly needed help, too. With a bit of effort, we could track down the siblings and reunite them with their brothers and sisters at CCT, which wouldn't be such a big extra cost.

As a start, we decided to look for Makara and Nimol's siblings. Full of youthful enthusiasm, I wrote up a report for our handful of private donors to help them understand the situation and what we were planning to do. We called it CCT's sibling reunion program.

In some ways, it was a step in the right direction . . .

13

Now that I had the sibling reunion program to raise funds for, and the whole 'family atmosphere' approach to keep us all on our toes, life at CCT got a little busier. But we never forgot the kids at SKO, and we were as determined as ever to put Rath in jail and see some justice for Sinet.

As soon as we had time, Jedtha and I went to the office of LICADHO, a Cambodian human rights NGO, to ask their advice. It was a typical Battambang office—a converted retail space with a desk up one end and a few seats up the other where customers could wait.

Jedtha met with one of the LICADHO managers. They talked quickly and earnestly in more formal Khmer, which I had a bit of trouble following.

Also, my attention was drawn to a trembling, distressed little girl who was sitting with a middle-aged woman in the waiting area. I'd never seen such a broken little person. The girl was tiny, with a soft, round face covered in scrapes and bruises. The pained expression on her face made her seem older than her years, which I guessed was around eight years old. She was trembling with fear and jumped at every sudden noise that drifted in from the street. When her aunt spoke softly to her, she froze and didn't seem to be able to answer. It broke my heart just to look at her.

I whispered to Jedtha: 'Sorry to interrupt, but is that little girl okay?'

Jedtha asked the LICADHO manager, who replied in a low, sad tone, 'She was raped by her cousin. He beat her badly, too.'

He and Jedtha went back to their conversation. Meanwhile, I was reeling from this information. I was certainly not expecting that response. I couldn't fathom how anyone could do that to a child.

I couldn't sit there and do nothing, so I left the meeting in Jedtha's capable hands and hurried off to the markets. I hunted down the biggest, cheeriest rag doll I could find and rushed back to LICADHO. If ever there was a kid who needed a friend, it was this one.

I put it gently in her lap. 'This is for you!' I said. The rag doll was almost as tall as she was.

'Say thank you,' the aunt said, smiling.

The merest shadow of a smile crept across the child's face. She pressed her little hands together and mouthed '*awkun*,' the Khmer word for 'thank you'.

'My name is Tara. What's your name?' I asked.

'Akara,' she whispered, so softly I could barely hear her.

Before we left, I asked Jedtha to find out what would happen to little Akara.

The human rights lawyer assured us she'd be kept safe under their care.

The next day, as I wrote my emails, as I took photos of smiling faces to send to our supporters, I thought of Akara. As I watched Sineit's serious face light up with laughter again after three days sick with fever, as I had another supportive little chat with Sinet, I wondered about that little girl. How was she doing? Was the cousin caught? What happened when a child was raped by a family member in Cambodia? Was she staying at the courthouse? Was she safe?

By lunch time, I couldn't take it anymore. I asked Jedtha to call, just to see how she was. My Khmer was improving, but talking on the phone was still difficult.

'Her aunt took her back home,' Jedtha reported back to me. 'The cousin was arrested. He will stay in jail until the hearing.'

'Can we go to visit her?' I asked. 'Just to check up on her?'

'Yes, sure we can,' said Jedtha. 'That would be a nice thing to do.'

Later that afternoon, he and I set off on the moto to visit the little girl's home.

The address we were given was about half an hour out of town, which can feel like a long way when you're on the back of a moto. Trees thickened around us until we pulled up at a cluster of decrepit pole huts nestled within a gloomy, jungly area near a bend on the Stung Sangker River.

A few children were hanging around and three or four adults sat under one of the huts, drinking and chatting. A plump guy in his fifties lounged in a hammock. He had no shirt on and rested a bottle on his impressive gut. They looked up as we approached.

Akara emerged from around the side of the house and ran up to greet us, her aunt following behind her. The girl didn't say anything, though, just looked up at me shyly, recognition in her eyes. You could still see the bruises all over her face and arms.

We said hello to Akara's aunt, who then invited us to sit down on a wooden plank near the shirtless drunk in the hammock. She sat down next to us and Akara squeezed herself timidly in between us, completely silent, clearly trying to make herself invisible. Her little hand crept into mine and she held it tightly. I gave it a reassuring squeeze and smiled at her.

'How are things going at the court?' Jedtha ask the aunt.

The older man in the hammock interrupted. 'Why do you come here asking this? She is my niece. Her parents are dead and now she's just a nuisance. She is causing our family a lot of trouble.'

'We met her at LICADHO and we just wanted to know how she was doing,' Jedtha explained.

'She's fine!' he barked, giving Akara's aunt a death stare. He was a scary guy and clearly very intoxicated. Akara's aunt got up, excused herself and left.

'Okay, we will leave you,' Jedtha said to Akara's uncle. 'Come on, we can talk more with her aunt,' he said to me quietly.

Akara kept hold of my hand as we went to find her aunt. We walked about fifty metres. Then Akara suddenly stopped in her tracks.

'What's wrong?' I asked. Her hand still squeezed mine tightly.

'I'm scared,' she said in a high-pitched little voice. Her cousin was in jail, but after meeting her uncle, it wasn't surprising. Even her aunt seemed on edge.

I crouched in front of the little girl and said softly, 'What are you scared of?'

Akara didn't answer. I looked up at Jedtha helplessly, hoping he could go into teacher/counsellor mode. He tried, but she just stared into the middle distance and wouldn't answer, her face closed, impassive.

'Akara,' I begged. 'You can tell me . . .'

'I don't want to stay here!' she blurted.

Her assertive tone was completely at odds with her cringing body language, the scrapes and bruises that I could see on her legs as well as her face and arms. This was a child who was so traumatised she was barely talking and this was what she had to say. I made up my mind in that moment. *I'm not leaving her here. I don't know what's going on, but she's obviously terrified . . .*

Jedtha asked her: 'Do you want come stay with us at our *onga* with other kids? We have—'

'Yes,' she interrupted.

I looked up at Jedtha, hoping that was going to be possible. She couldn't come to CCT without written permission from whoever had custody of her, and I knew that wasn't going to be easy to sort out.

Akara's aunt was sitting alone in a shed not far away. She'd overhead the conversation.

Jedtha pressed her for more information, and eventually she told us a little more about Akara. The girl's mother was an alcoholic. A few months ago she went to the river to wash some clothes with Akara and passed out, face down in the water. Akara couldn't rouse her and so she drowned, just like that, right in front of her daughter's eyes.

The aunt paused for a second to listen. Akara's uncle had company now and they were talking loudly, drunkenly.

Very quietly, she told us: 'Akara is very badly treated here. My brother and my nephew are very bad to her.' She went on to tell us about the rapes. Akara's cousin had taken her three times into the forest, raped and bashed her and then ran. Each time it was her aunt who found her, covered in blood and bruises, terrified and alone. She was so worried for Akara that she decided to take her to LICADHO to ask for help. Her brother was furious at her for reporting his son and for bringing shame on the family. The uncle was abusive too—he treated Akara like a dog.

She drew us in closer and said in a low whisper: 'Can you help Akara?'

Jedtha said softly, 'Yes, sister, we can. Don't worry. We just need permission from you and your brother.'

So the four of us—Jedtha, me, Akara and her aunt—went to talk to him.

He was immediately defensive. 'I haven't done anything wrong by this girl! No one here has done anything wrong!' I could practically see the steam shooting out his ears. 'I don't know why the police have put my boy in jail. He didn't do anything. This whole thing is stupid!'

He continued on like that, getting increasingly loud and aggressive.

I felt quite worried. This guy seemed so volatile, and the atmosphere was so tense that I didn't want to push him over the edge.

'If Akara comes to live with us, you will not have to pay to feed and clothe her anymore, and she will get an education,' Jedtha explained to the girl's uncle, in his usual calm and restrained tone.

'No, no, no, no, no!' the uncle snapped.

I felt Akara grip my hand tightly.

'But why not?' I asked. 'You can always come to visit her . . .'

'Just because!' he shouted. His bleary eyes slid across to Akara and he barked: 'Where do you want to live?' His tone was thick with threat.

Akara stiffened as if she was about to take a blow, but she answered with amazing force: 'I want to go live with the foreigner!'

My heart really started pumping then, because Akara had basically said: *Fuck you!*

Her uncle glowered at her. This was the moment on which everything turned. Losing face like this in front of Jedtha, in front of me—it wasn't good. Not for the uncle, and not for Akara.

So this was it. Akara had just put her life in our hands and we couldn't leave now.

I turned to Jedtha and asked in English: 'Can we get the officials from DoSVY here right now to help?'

Jedtha looked at the sky—the sun was going down. 'Tara,' he replied quietly, 'DoSVY don't work this late. And we are not safe in this village after dark. It is dangerous.'

'I know,' I said through clenched teeth. 'But, Jedtha, I'm not going to leave Akara here. I'll sit on this bench all night if I have to.'

'Yes—I know—we must help,' Jedtha said unhappily. I could see he was thinking: *Oh, fuuuuck . . .*

We spent another half-hour sitting there while Jedtha tried to negotiate with Akara's obnoxious, drunk uncle.

After a while, we all lapsed into a very long silence. It was hard by now to see much in the shadows of twilight. My arse was numb from sitting on the plank and my stomach was grumbling.

Jedtha suddenly leaned forward and said intensely: 'What if we give you some rice?'

I looked up at Jedtha in surprise. Was that a bribe?

To my complete astonishment, the uncle said: 'Okay.' (Probably because he was completely fed up with us by now.)

'Okay. I'll go get it now.' And Jedtha was off.

He roared away in the dark on the moto. I sat on the bench with Akara thinking: *Did we really just exchange a child—a child!—for a bag of rice?*

But the situation was desperate enough that I could see why he did it. In Australia you can rely on the child protection system to act in situations like Akara's. But here, there is no system in place yet.

The uncle poured rice wine down his gullet and rocked in his hammock, occasionally turning rheumy, hostile eyes on Akara and me. It wasn't the most comfortable evening of my life.

After about twenty minutes, we heard the hum of Jedtha's moto coming back. Like the superstar that he is, he reappeared under the house, staggering slightly under the weight of the fifty-kilo bag of rice. Akara slipped away with her aunt to pack her things. The uncle put his thumbprint on the temporary paperwork that we'd drawn up, muttering: 'Go, then.'

We said goodbye to Akara's aunt, put Akara between us on the moto and set off down the pitch-black roads back into Battambang. The girl clutched a little plastic bag against her chest, filled with all her worldly possessions. I chatted away to her, trying to say comforting things like: 'So we are going to CCT now—there are lots of kids who are very nice and you'll be very safe there. And shall we stop before and get some nice dinner? What do you like to eat? How about fried rice? Would you like ice-cream after dinner?'

She sat in silence, not responding to me at all. But as the lights of the town started to appear on the roads, I heard her utter a tiny squeak.

'What?' I asked, leaning down out of the wind so I could hear her.

'Never take me back there again,' she said in her fierce little mouse voice.

I gave her hand a squeeze. 'No, don't worry. You never have to go back there again.'

She nodded and held my arms even tighter and declared: 'And they can't come to visit me, either!'

We stopped off at the White Rose restaurant. Akara wolfed down a plate of fried rice with beef followed by ice-cream. She barely spoke a word. She was such a timid thing, but somehow still had this iron will. I hoped we could help her after everything she'd been through.

After she'd been cheered up a little by her dinner, we took her back to CCT. She was silent through all the introductions, but the other kids seemed to understand and gave us the space she needed. Savenh got her showered and into bed.

The next day, we took her to hospital to get all her injuries dealt with and provide further evidence to the police. Jedtha and Savenh also went to register her case officially with DoSVY.

That afternoon, after she'd settled down a little, I sat with her in the common room and explained how CCT works. 'So next week you can go to school. And we have extra tutoring after school, and on weekend we do art classes and PE and sometimes we go to the circus, or on a picnic or something nice. It's lots of fun!'

Little Makara bounced around us in his cheerful, slightly hyper-active way while I was explaining all this.

'And on Sundays we can watch TV!' he informed her in his gruff little voice. 'But if we fight we have to stop.' And then he added: 'I used to fight. But now I've stopped.'

~

Akara was still settling in when Jedtha pulled me aside and told me: 'Savenh just told me about a baby girl in her neighbourhood who is being badly neglected by her grandmother,' he said. 'They asked Savenh if CCT can help her. I think we should take a look.'

I wasn't confident we would have the resources to assist. We'd only just taken on Akara and our budget was already tight, but we couldn't just dismiss Savenh's concerns. She was CCT's social worker, after all. So Jedtha, Savenh and I went to check out the situation and see if there was anything we could do.

Savenh took us to a tiny wooden house in the street where she lived.

Sure enough, when we looked through the open front entrance we saw a very small baby inside, scooting around listlessly on her knees. She was less than a year old, dressed only in a ragged singlet.

I picked her up and she didn't protest. She was a mess, in desperate need of a bath. She looked malnourished, too. She had a pot belly, her ribs were sticking out and her hair was sparse and dry. She was also covered from head to toe in what looked like mosquito bites and the surrounding skin was red and extremely dry. It seemed to be pulled strangely tight all over her head, torso and tiny limbs—as if she were recovering from terrible sunburn.

Some neighbours appeared in the doorway, looking concerned. 'Do you know where her grandma is?' Savenh asked, adding for our benefit: 'They told me it's her grandma who normally looks after her.'

'Oh, she's probably off playing cards,' a woman said. 'I'll go find her.'

The other neighbours told us the baby was left alone most days, and this had been going on for months. They tried to help look after her but they were away at work most of the time.

The conversation was cut off when the neighbour returned, leading a very old, painfully thin lady with cropped silver hair.

'Hello!' the old lady cried, clearly surprised by all the fuss in her yard.

She and Jedtha had a long chat.

The old lady said that her daughter was a sex worker. She had taken off the day after the baby was born and never came back. The baby's name was Sovanni. The old lady had been trying her best to look after Sovanni for the last nine months, but she herself was sick with hepatitis C and looking after Sovanni had been hard.

When Jedtha asked her why she left the baby on her own so often, she just shrugged and said she needed to find money to feed them both, and she was too old and tired to take Sovanni along with her.

I was always amazed in those early days to see how open people were about the details of their lives, how matter-of-fact. Jedtha asked her if she had a gambling problem and again, without flinching, she agreed she did. She'd been gambling for years, so it was hard to stop now. She'd never planned to have such a small child to look after so late in life. As far as I could tell, she wasn't a bad woman, but the baby's situation was clearly desperate.

'Can you take Sovanni to live at your *onga?*' the old lady asked. 'She's a good baby. Doesn't cause any trouble. It would help me and be good for Sovanni, too.'

Savenh and Jedtha and I exchanged a look. We had the facilities and the infrastructure in place to help at-risk children—it was the reason CCT existed. How could we say no and leave the baby in this awful situation? So we contacted DoSVY to arrange the paperwork.

I just wish we knew then what we know now about how to deal properly with these sorts of situations. Perhaps we could have found Sovanni's mother and helped the whole family to stay together.

~

A few days later, we took Sovanni's grandma to the doctor to see if there was anything more we could do for her. But the old woman's health was much worse than we originally thought. She died a few months later.

We all took turns looking after Sovanni, but having a baby at CCT *was* a challenge. A lot of Sovanni's care fell to me—everyone else was so busy. So for the next six months she was with me almost all the time. As her grandma had said, she really was an easy baby to look after. She almost never cried and was fiercely independent. I often admired her stoicism, despite her rocky start. Perhaps, I thought, it was a case of what doesn't kill you makes you stronger. (I would find out later how wrong I was about that.) Still, looking after Sovanni was a *lot* of work. I developed a whole new respect for single parents!

Sineit was amazingly good with Sovanni and was a huge help to me. Sovanni absolutely adored her and beamed whenever she was in Sineit's arms.

Under our care, Sovanni grew plump and glossy and gorgeous. But she always remained fiercely independent. She was by far the smallest but had no problem shoving the other kids out of the way to get what she wanted.

I developed a special bond with Sovanni, but I worried a lot about what long-term effect having me—the young foreigner—as her main caregiver would have on the little girl.

I worried about the other kids, too. They were getting very dependent on me and the little ones were starting to call me 'Mum'. It's not uncommon in Cambodia for female caregivers to be given this name, but I was shocked the first time it happened. 'My name is Tara,' I told them. It wasn't a sentiment I wanted to encourage.

~

On the day we met Akara at LICADHO, the lawyer advised us to file an official report about Rath's attacks on Sinet with the Battambang police.

So Sinet, Jedtha and I went to the station and two policemen went through the motions of recording a detailed statement, which ended up being several pages long. Sinet had to spell out every last detail of each time Rath had raped her, which was awful—especially when everything she said was received with a sort of blank nonchalance by the policemen.

'Why didn't you report this when it happened?' one policeman asked, picking a bit of his lunch from his teeth.

'I was scared,' Sinet squeaked.

The policeman grunted. 'Well, that wasn't very smart, was it?'

I looked over at Jedtha in shock. *What a fucking arsehole!* I wanted to say. Jedtha just shook his head and gestured for me to stay quiet.

On the way home, Sinet's hands flew to her face. 'Oh! We just passed Rath's sister!' she cried, her voice shaking.

I patted her arm. 'Don't worry, we won't let anyone hurt you. The police have your report now and we'll get a good lawyer. Rath will be in jail soon.' I hoped with all my heart that this was true.

Our next step was for Jedtha, Sinet and me to drive out to meet with a well-respected lawyer, recommended to us by the assistant governor. His office was an ostentatious display of Khmer wealth, featuring beautifully carved and extremely uncomfortable wooden furniture.

Again, Sinet painstakingly went through the details of each incident. After asking lots of questions and taking copious notes, he told us that he thought we had a strong case. He seemed like a well-educated guy who knew what he was talking about. He was so confident that we could get a successful outcome, he declared, that he'd take on the case for a small upfront payment, and only charge for the rest if we won.

Very kindly, he told Sinet: 'Don't worry. We should be able to put him in jail for a long time for what he did to you.'

It was all extremely encouraging. We left feeling full of confidence that justice would soon be done and Rath would be locked away.

~

Not long after we met the lawyer, Jedtha and I attended the trial of Akara's cousin, who had raped the little girl in the forest so brutally.

The case was heard at Battambang's courthouse, an imposing building with a soaring ceiling and huge twin statues guarding the massive front door. If ever a building was designed to make you feel small, this was it.

An armed guard led Akara's cousin and one other man into the courtroom. They were chained together and dressed in blue prison jumpsuits. The guards made the prisoners sit on a wooden bench in the centre of the room, facing the judge.

Akara's cousin was tall and strong, and looked to me like he was about my age. It was clear that something wasn't right with him. He had his hand in his pants and was playing with himself while he waited for proceedings to start.

The other man was on trial for murder, and we had to sit through his case before we got to Akara's. The man had had an argument with a neighbour one night, which resulted in him sinking an axe into the back of the neighbour's skull.

I was horrified that Akara had to sit there and listen to the gory details. Characteristically, she coped by detaching, staring off into the middle distance.

After that case was finished, Akara's aunt was called to speak. Her voice was shaking as she gave her evidence to the judge. I was so moved and impressed by her bravery.

Then the judge called Akara up. I'll never forget how incredibly scared and tiny and vulnerable Akara looked up on the wooden stand. I hated that she had to do this right in front of her cousin and other members of her abusive family.

She was too intimidated to speak, so the judge asked me to get up and stand next to her. I held her hand and she managed to gasp out a couple of monosyllabic answers.

After another hour or so of proceedings, which I couldn't entirely follow, the court was dismissed and the men were led out of the court.

'So? What happened?' I asked Jedtha.

'He was found guilty,' said Jedtha. 'The judge said the reports from the doctor who examined Akara were very helpful.'

Jedtha explained the sentencing would happen later—he was expecting the cousin to be sentenced to fifteen years in jail. But when we got the report from the court, we found out he had only got eight! Apparently Akara's family had produced a birth certificate to show that the cousin was seventeen years and ten months old, so he was tried as a child.

Jedtha said: 'They probably paid for a fake one.'

I was outraged. Eight years for rape and attempted murder of sweet little Akara just felt like a joke to me.

'I can't believe that piece of shit got away with just eight years!' I lamented down the phone to Carolyn that afternoon. 'He should have his bloody dick chopped off for what he did to her!'

Carolyn agreed, but managed to calm me down by reminding me that eight years would be an awfully long time in a Cambodian prison . . . I couldn't deny that was true—I imagine that a prison in a developing country would be like hell on earth. But I'm not sure *anything* would have felt like justice for what Akara had been through.

~

Sinet's lawyer got in touch from time to time with updates on the case against Rath. The police had interviewed him, and of course Rath had denied everything. So now we were waiting for the case to be handed over to the court. It was certainly taking a long time . . .

Corruption is such a fact of life in South-East Asia that it becomes unremarkable. Even the travel guides for foreigners describe ways to bribe your way out of minor offences. Everyone talks openly about the problem of corruption in Cambodia—even high-level government officials. And sometimes it's understandable; it is no real secret that Cambodian police, teachers and government officials are paid so poorly that they are forced to supplement their salaries through corruption.

In all honesty, sometimes I did feel tempted to play the game just to get justice for people like Sinet and Akara. But Jedtha always says no, corruption is a slippery slope. And I know he's right. Supporting the rule of law in Cambodia has to be one of our key goals if we want lasting change to happen, so the process of how we go about our work needs to be just as important as the outcome.

~

Not long after the trial of Akara's cousin, Jedtha managed to track down Makara and Nimol's sister, a twelve-year-old girl named Sida.

I think Jedtha might've been Sherlock Holmes in a past life because he's a natural-born detective. Any time we need to find someone, he's on it like a bloodhound.

He found out that Sida had been labour-trafficked to another family in the boys' home town near the Thai border. He arranged for

DoSVY to come with us to pick her up. We took Makara and Nimol along to help identify their sister.

After driving for an hour, we pulled up at a compound of about twenty grass huts on the edge of a rice field. A small group of adults emerged from the huts with little children trailing behind them.

The boys ran ahead and threw their arms around a beautiful young girl who was with the group. Her clothes were ragged, her hair was ratty and her skin much darker than the boys', but I could see the family resemblance. I don't think I'd ever seen the boys so happy. Tears were rolling down the girl's face. She embraced the boys for several minutes before letting go. I blinked away a tear and went over to meet her.

The boys introduced me. 'This is Tara! We love her. She's really nice. We live with her at the *onga*.' We were in the middle of exchanging greetings when the boys interrupted again: 'Now you can come and live at the *onga* with us too!'

Meanwhile, Jedtha, Savenh and the men from DoSVY were talking to the extended family.

'Makara, Nimol and Sida's father is here,' Jedtha told me, pointing in the direction of the street.

I could see a man wandering around on the road in front of the compound, muttering away to himself and gesticulating madly.

'It's very hard in Cambodia,' Jedtha said. 'There's a lot of people with mental health problems but we have no way to help them.'

Certainly, it's not uncommon to see people with mental health problems on the streets in Cambodia. Unkempt people with no clothes on. People ranting to themselves. Like a lot of them, the boys' father didn't seem particularly distressed or unhappy.

Still. It was sad.

'And what about their mother?' I asked.

'We don't know where their mother is. She has been missing for a long time. Her mother owed a debt to a family who live about one hour from here. She couldn't afford to pay the debt, so she sold Sida to them for labour. Sida lived there for years, working for that family, but recently her grandmother bought her back. Now she has been living here for a few months but, even though it is her own family, she works very hard here, too. She has never been to school. We've explained to them now that trafficking and child labour is illegal and that every child has the right to go to school, so we're arranging for her to come to CCT.'

I looked back over at the boys and Sida playing together, still ecstatic to be in each other's company. It was hard to believe that she had spent most of her life being bought and sold like a slave.

None of the adults put up any objection to Sida leaving. When Jedtha told her she could come and live with her brothers she emitted a little squeak of happiness. '*Yes!*' She ran to pack her belongings.

That same day, we went to pick up Makara, Nimol and Sida's little brother, Sakana. He was only about four years old and had also been sold by his mother to a family near the Thai border.

It never fails to amaze me how keen Cambodian kids are to leave everything they've ever known to rush off and live in an orphanage. I suppose their attitude is driven by the adults. They all just see orphanages as a great opportunity.

~

In the weeks that followed, Sida took to life at CCT like a duck to water. She settled in and started school and worked hard to catch up. And she mothered her little brothers, of course. In no time at all she had learned to read and write and was topping her grade.

It was amazing considering everything she'd been through. She'd had to work incredibly hard when she was trafficked. Harvesting. Washing. Cooking. Cleaning. She suffered systematic abuse at the hands of the adults, too. Some of the things that happen to young girls in Cambodia would make your skin crawl. For Sida, it was about as bad as it gets—she needed surgery in order to make a full recovery from some of the injuries she'd received.

~

Around this time, my sister Noni and one of her best mates visited me in Battambang. It was great to see them.

Talking to them in English was oddly challenging at first. It was as if the gears in my brain kept seizing shut when I tried to swap from Khmer to English.

While Noni was visiting, we reunited two more kids with their siblings at CCT—Rithy's stepsisters, Jendar and Lai.

When we drove out to see how Rithy's family were doing, we found out that the children's parents were very sick with HIV. They'd been living in a tiny hut in such abject poverty that they'd sent eight-year-old Lai to live with her grandparents.

They were delighted to see Rithy looking so well, and pleaded with us to take Lai and Jendar to CCT.

The girls had a baby sibling, who was also very sick with HIV. We tried to get medical help for the baby but, tragically, she died from AIDS just a few months after we brought Jendar and Lai to CCT.

~

When Jedtha managed to track down the parents and younger brother of Amara, Maly and Chanlina, we took the kids on a short road trip to see how the rest of the family was doing.

We travelled to a village in the north, close to the Thai border. The village was called Prachea Thorm and, according to a story that ran in the *Cambodia Daily*, it was founded in response to a severe cholera outbreak in an overcrowded slum in the large, gritty town of Poipet. To manage the outbreak, thousands of people from the slum were resettled in the new village.

I'd heard that this large rural village still had a post-apocalyptic feel to it, all these years later, and that poverty and its attendant grim problems—drug abuse, domestic violence, crime and disease—were rife. And it was a dismal place indeed. Some people were completely homeless, without even the most basic of shelters. Others were bringing up whole families in tiny straw-and-scrap-metal structures that looked more like a kid's cubbyhouse than a home.

As we walked through the village with Amara, Maly and Chanlina, some of the local kids started to follow us. The three CCT kids seemed so out of place in Prachea Thorm—clean and well-fed, with shiny hair and glowing skin. The contrast between them and the ragged, malnourished village kids was stark.

The kids soon managed to track down the makeshift hut where their family lived. A couple in their fifties and a little boy came out when they heard Maly calling their names. They all looked absolutely overjoyed to see each other.

The parents doted on Amara, Chanlina and Maly the whole time and thanked me endlessly for looking after them. They struck me as very kind people who loved their kids. They were just poor, and not educated, so life was a horrible struggle. The whole family walked nearly twenty kilometres a day, every day, to work across the Thai border catching insects (a popular snack food) or scaling fish. Six-year-old Teng—who was just as bright and confident as his siblings—didn't attend school; he went to work with his parents.

Every day, hundreds of Cambodians spill across the Thai border to work illegally, because that's where the work is. (That's how Amara, Maly and Chanlina—and quite a few other kids—ended up at SKO: they were caught by the Thai police, who transferred them to the Transit Centre at the Poipet border, who then sent them to the orphanage.)

But even the work over the border doesn't pay well. The family made barely enough to put food in their mouths. Sometimes they subsisted on rice. They had no running water, no toilets and no healthcare. In those circumstances, everything becomes about survival. If you don't get up and find some money every day, you don't eat. If you get sick, you're screwed. It makes me crazy that human beings live like this in the twenty-first century. We have enough resources to go around. We can land a spacecraft on the moon. We should be able to work out how to overcome poverty.

While we were visiting, a man and woman dropped by to say hello. They were surrounded by a troupe of extremely familiar-looking children.

'Oh my god!' I gasped. 'They look so much like Tula and Mao!' Tula and Mao were Amara, Chanlina and Maly's cousins, and they also lived at CCT.

Sure enough, the couple were Tula and Mao's parents—and they had their other nine kids with them. My poor city-raised brain nearly exploded. How does someone have eleven children? How do you manage that? Seeing those familiar faces on all these thin, ragged little kids, reminded me of what Tula and Mao looked like when I'd first met them. It was heartbreaking.

Amara, Chanlina and Maly's parents asked us repeatedly if their six-year-old son, Teng, could come and live with us, too.

At the time, it seemed like giving Teng the chance to grow up with his siblings at CCT, where he could go to school and access healthcare, was the right thing to do. But it bothered me terribly, the thought of putting the kids in the van and leaving their parents behind. It was obvious that these parents loved their children deeply and would be perfectly capable of raising them if they could just get some help to climb out of poverty. But we had no systems in place to support a family, especially one that lived so far from Battambang city. We wouldn't have known where to start. And for the time being, getting Teng into school and giving him the same opportunities as his other siblings seemed like the next best option.

As word got around that Jedtha and I were in the vicinity, parents who lived in the little village kept approaching us, begging us to take their children to live at the *onga*. There were literally over thirty children lined up down the road, hoping we'd pick them to go with us. It was a strange and sad sight—a whole village wishing for their children to be taken away to a better life. And what was even more surprising was how keen the kids were to leave everything they've ever known to go with two strangers to the esteemed *onga*. I wondered if they even knew what an *onga* really was. Their implicit trust of foreigners was very worrying.

In the end we did take Teng with us. Jedtha also arranged for a sweet ten-year-old girl named Masa to come, too. He'd been told such appalling stories by the neighbours he felt she was at extreme risk of abuse. I wasn't sure I agreed, but the arrangements had been made by the time I knew what was happening.

~

On the way home to Battambang, the kids fell asleep and Jedtha and I talked softly about Prachea Thorm. We were both sobered by the things we'd seen that day.

I couldn't stop thinking about Teng's parents. It was wrong for the family to be broken apart just because of poverty. They clearly loved their kids—they were grateful because they saw CCT as a golden ticket. And Tula's mum and dad were the same. Human beings need to grow up in families, right? These kids should really be with their mum and dad, not at CCT.

Thinking about the injustice of leaving the parents behind, and the burden on Mao and Tula when they grew up and left CCT wasn't a nice thought. With nine siblings and a mum and dad living in poverty, Moa and Tula were growing up with a black cloud over their heads. When they started work as young adults, they'd have eleven people they cared about constantly needing their help. Even if they became doctors or lawyers, there'd be hardly anything left over . . .

Jedtha and I spent the rest of the journey discussing ways to help the families support themselves and then reunite them with all their kids. I loved the idea of the kids coming home every day to their real mum and dad.

14

So by April 2008 we had twenty kids at CCT. Having more kids meant more work—more fires to fight, emotional issues to manage and more individual wants and needs . . . And meanwhile we were trying to get justice for Sinet.

Life was getting stressful.

~

One of the hardest things for me at that time was coming to terms with the disparity between healthcare in Australia and Cambodia. In Australia, kids come home from school with the common cold. In Cambodia they come home with dengue fever. I always did what I could to ensure the kids got decent healthcare, but it always felt like the odds were stacked against us.

Sineit was still getting really sick all the time with low-grade fevers and spells of nausea, and had a generally poor appetite. She never got as sick again as she'd been at SKO, but every time she went to see her doctor at Battambang's public hospital, she'd return with a plastic bag full of unlabelled medication, which never seemed to help much. I wished there was something better available for her. After everything we'd been through, all we'd managed to achieve was better adherence to a treatment that she was already developing a resistance to . . .

One day when Kanya had period pain, she was given antibiotics (which you can buy over the counter in Cambodia) and told to take one whenever the pain was bad. It's no wonder antibiotic resistance is becoming such a serious public health concern.

To make matters even more stressful, the tiny trickle of funds from the regular donors wasn't quite enough to cover everything, especially now that we had more mouths to feed. And the other one-off donations we were relying on were getting harder and harder to come by.

By now, Sally had successfully set up our Australian charity, Green Kids Global, and was doing everything humanly possible to secure DGR status, so we could give tax-deductible receipts and set up an online donation system. She was also putting together proposals and plans to try to get corporate sponsorship for us. But it was hard—it seemed we just weren't big enough or established enough to attract major sponsors.

We were reaching a state of crisis. All we had to rely on was the small database of existing supporters who I would email and ask for money as I needed it. These supporters made great sacrifices to help us, but there was a limit to how much they could give. Soon we were living month to month, and Sally was still topping us up with her own money just to keep us going.

I had been living without a salary for almost a year. Sometimes, I was personally so desperate my friend Vicky Baron would put $50 in my bank account just to get me through—and she really didn't have much money spare herself.

My friends and family did all they could to spread the word. But the fundraising game was tough. Very tough. I remember nearly crying when I got yet another email from a kind-hearted soul in Australia wanting to send toys and clothing that her own kids had outgrown. This happens all the time—people wanting to send 'stuff' instead of money. I wanted to ring them and plead: 'We don't need your clothes or toys—the cost of postage to send them over here would feed us all for a week. We have a water bill and a power bill and a pathology bill to pay. Please, please, just send money!'

I did my best to make sure the kids had no idea of our financial woes. The last thing I wanted was for them to start worrying that their new home was not as secure as they'd thought.

~

All our hopes were resting on Green Kids Global finding a way to get DGR status. And after many months of effort, a promising opportunity came up. Rotary Australia World Community Service (RAWCS) said they could partner with Green Kids Global to provide us with DGR status. RAWCS were wonderful and incredibly positive about helping us. But, as with everything, there was red tape involved.

After a lot of negotiation, Sally called to tell me that before RAWCS could agree to the partnership, we needed a Cambodian Rotary club to sign a document approving CCT.

'Do whatever you have to do,' she said. 'Just GET THE DOCUMENT.'

So I jumped on a bus to Phnom Penh and presented our story to a group of Cambodian-based Rotarians. They all seemed very positive about approving us as a Rotary project, but the president of the club—a soft-spoken, academic-looking man from India—seemed to need more time. He said: 'We'll look over your proposal and consider it over the next few weeks.'

I couldn't help looking dismayed—we really couldn't afford to wait 'a few weeks'. So he suggested we have dinner that night and talk it over.

Later that night, at his family home, I told him more about CCT, and he told me he was very impressed. Then he went on to talk at length about his religious beliefs—the Baha'i faith. I listened, always curious to learn more about different belief systems. When he asked what I believed, I ummed for a moment and then politely tried to navigate around the question by saying that I had a great love and passion for science.

Before I left, he told me he'd be happy to sign the documents to have CCT approved. 'You can come by tomorrow and pick them up,' he said.

The next day I turned up at his place with a skip in my step. This was the ticket we needed!

'Hello, come in,' he said. 'Sit down and have a cold drink.'

He sat down opposite me with a pen and a little card in his hands.

'I'll get your papers for you in a minute. First, I'd just like to say how nice it was to share my faith with you yesterday. I know what you meant about having a love of science—and with Baha'i, all paths lead to God!' He pushed the little card in front of me and added: 'You can sign up to the Baha'i faith here and then I'll go and get those signed documents for you.'

Oh geez, I thought to myself. Feeling like I'd dug myself in too deep to backpedal now, I signed the card, collected the signed documents and went on my way.

On my way back to Battambang I kept thinking: *I can't believe I just converted to the Baha'i faith!*

~

Shortly after this, we had three awful scares.

1. The kids rode home from school one day crying and upset—someone had deliberately swerved at them in a car, clipping little Akara and knocking her off her bike.

    Akara! I nearly died when I heard this. The thought of the kids being hurt scared the hell out of all of us.

2. Jedtha was giving me a lift into town on the back of his moto. We were moving with the traffic along the riverbank when some rough-looking guys on a moto pulled in beside us.

    They sidled up very close alongside us, and I just had time to think, *This is weird, what are you doing?* before I saw them kick the back wheel of our moto out from under us. Jedtha and I went flying and landed on the road with a thump.

Two thumps, actually.

We were both badly shaken and covered in cuts and bruises, but, thankfully, the traffic flowed around us in the magical way that Cambodian traffic does.

I shot to my feet, spitting fire, and shrieked: 'Go after them!' in Khmer. Jedtha jumped straight back on the bike and charged off into the distance. So then suddenly I was left standing beside the road with no moto, and no Jedtha, covered in bloody scrapes and wondering why on earth I'd said that.

Rumours often fly around in Cambodia about people paying gangsters to despatch enemies by kicking them off motos. So the whole incident shook us up badly.

3. Not long after we were kicked off the moto, some people who were supporting SKO approached me, asking for the truth about Rath. They told me that Rath hated Jedtha and me with such a passion that he was always saying things like: 'I'll never forget what they have done,' and 'They will be sorry for what they did.'

Jedtha and I would joke about it sometimes—a case of you've 'gotta laugh or you'll cry.' I'd crack him up by pulling out my most badass Khmer: 'He thinks he can fuck with us? Bring it! Bitch!'

But the truth is, I've never feared and hated anyone like I feared and hated Rath.

~

The honeymoon was well and truly over. For a while there, it felt like Cambodia was conspiring against me.

I was so stressed I developed a strange rash, like a map of the world, on all my limbs.

When I google 'symptoms of culture shock', I now realise I was a textbook case. I spent many weeks feeling just like Wikipedia said I would: disoriented, worried, fatigued, lonely and anxious. All at once. All the time.

I didn't know what to do about all our problems except push on and push through—surely there'd be a light at the end of the tunnel sometime?

Jedtha worried constantly about me and wanted to hire security guards for my protection, but I felt at the time that we just couldn't justify the cost. Besides, as I kept pointing out, I had the dogs, and they were very loyal and protective of me.

We started talking about hiring Chan to be our driver—we'd be less visible and vulnerable in his car. Hopefully, we could put this plan in place when more money came through.

~

The thought of having Chan as a driver was a comforting one. He was my Cambodian brother, and I trusted him with my life. But one morning Chan's wife Mina came to CCT to drop off some washing I'd given her a few dollars to do. She was sporting a big black eye.

'Mina!' I cried, pushing her into the light so I could examine the ugly bruise. 'How did this happen?' It was distressing to see such a horrible thing on my friend's face.

'Oh.' She pulled away with a laugh. 'I walked into a stick. I'm clumsy.'

As soon as I could, I pulled Sinet aside and asked what she knew about Mina's black eye. She told me: 'Chan probably hit her.'

Hearing my fears confirmed out loud sent a shockwave through my system.

'Talk to the staff,' she said. 'They'll tell you.'

I rounded up Savenh, Heng, Davi and Jedtha and asked them to tell me what they knew about Chan. They were all—even Jedtha—tight-lipped at first. But I pushed, and eventually the truth came out.

'Everyone knows he is a very aggressive person,' Savenh said. 'He gets into fights a lot.'

The rest of the staff weighed in. They told me that before I learned to speak Khmer, Chan used to make nasty remarks about me, right in front of my face.

'Now he just does it behind your back,' Jedtha said. 'He's only nice to you to get your money.'

'Why are you only telling me this now?' I couldn't believe it.

There was a long pause. Nobody met my eye.

Jedtha was the first to speak, his voice soft and apologetic. 'He was your friend. We didn't want to upset you,' he said.

My god, I thought. *In all this time they never breathed a word about it. What else aren't they telling me?*

Discovering Chan's duplicity really rocked my foundations. Was everything I thought I knew about this country a lie? Could I trust anyone?

And as for Chan—knowing he was a bad guy who had deceived me all this time—it was like seeing a poisonous snake on the path ahead. I had to get myself and the kids away from him as quickly and quietly as possible.

~

Life kept getting harder. The stress was getting the better of me and I started feeling angry and bitter. I couldn't shake the resentment I felt towards the staff.

And our funding problems were becoming quite serious. I was so broke and often hungry, and I started to seethe when friends in Australia wrote cheery missives on Myspace about what a great night out they'd had. I couldn't help thinking: *If you gave us the money for that first cocktail, it would feed us for a whole day.*

In a casual conversation with some donors one day, I happened to mention that I was so broke I was mostly living off white rice and soy sauce.

Sally pulled me up on this. 'If you tell people things like that, people are going to think you are not good at managing CCT,' she scolded.

'But . . . it's true!' I protested.

'I've been sending you money!' Sally said. 'Are you sure this is not just your eating disorder being aggravated by the stress?' It's true that stress has always been a potential trigger for me, but at this point in time, my weight truly was the last thing on my mind.

'Sally, I'm very grateful for the money you've been sending. But after paying all the bills and giving the staff their salaries, there's nothing left. We don't have enough money, Sally. Do you understand? Not enough. NOT ENOUGH!'

I immediately felt bad for snapping at her. After all, she was practically CCT's biggest supporter at this stage.

Something had to give. Even if we started to make cuts, CCT's funding still wasn't enough to give twenty kids healthy, happy childhoods. I desperately needed an idea, a plan . . . something. I had to find a way to keep a reliable income stream coming in.

~

To add to the stress, Sinet's case seemed to be moving at a glacial pace. Sinet had been in to talk to the prosecutor at the court a couple of times. They also called Sineit and Kolab to give statements, as they were eyewitnesses to one particular night—a night when Rath raped Sinet while they were all sleeping in the same room.

Our lawyer warned us that these delays may be indicative of corruption. But still, he would try his best to keep pushing.

~

I started backpedalling my way out of my relationship with Chan. The plan was to ease away subtly, without provoking any drama, as in: 'I'm slowly moving away now . . . nothing to see here . . . okay, goodbye!'

It was devastating to have to end my relationship with Mina and the kids. Mina is a truly beautiful woman and the kids are remarkably bright and have so much potential. But in the end I decided there was nothing I could do for them. Mina would never leave Chan and I just couldn't have a person like Chan associated with CCT.

So one afternoon, I very gently told Chan I wouldn't be able to afford to bring him on as CCT's driver as we'd hoped. And I let Mina know that I would no longer need her help with cooking vegetarian food and doing my laundry.

It felt very unwise to go into my real reasons for letting them go, so I told them I didn't even have the few dollars that I was giving Mina (which was rapidly becoming true, anyway).

Chan was no fool. He sensed that something was wrong and called Sally and my dad, Peter. Had he done anything to make me angry?

The following Sunday afternoon, Sinet, Sineit and I were sitting around watching a movie when the phone rang. Sinet, in happy, confident mode, answered the phone for me.

I heard shouts blasting out of the phone—it was Chan's voice, sounding very angry. I put my ear close to the receiver and listened in. 'So you've turned Tara against me, too, have you, Sinet?' he thundered.

Sinet's demeanour immediately went from 'well-adjusted extrovert' to 'scared little victim'. Seeing her go into that state when she was scared always triggered the mother bear in me.

Outraged, I grabbed the phone. 'Chan!'

Chan went: 'OH!' And then, in the usual jolly, high-pitched tone he adopted with me: 'Hello, little sister!'

I said through clenched teeth: 'Chan, I heard every word you just said to Sinet.'

I could hear the shift down the phone . . . Then out came this voice that sounded like it was possessed by pure fucking evil, threatening me, our staff and all of our kids. 'You believe me! You think you can trick me, you little bitch . . . You made a big mistake!'

I slammed down the phone, my hands shaking. I knew Chan would come looking for me and I didn't want to have him anywhere near CCT or the kids. 'I have to get out of here!' I said to the girls and the staff.

In a panic, I hailed the first tuktuk to come down the road and bundled Ruby, Rosie and Franky inside. If Chan came by and saw that the dogs were gone, he'd know that I had gone too and the kids would be safe. There was a guard at CCT, but I called Jedtha from the tuktuk and asked him to get to CCT straight away. He could help the security guard protect everyone in case Chan did come looking for me there.

Then, desperate, I called one of my most-trusted friends in Battambang—Terry, the ex-donor representative of New Dawn. Poor Terry! I was in a terrible state.

'Terry! I've had a death threat from someone who says he's going to team up with Rath . . . I need somewhere to hide so he can't find me!'

'Come over,' he said without hesitation.

The tuktuk had barely come to a stop before I jumped out, threw a bunch of dollars in the tuktuk driver's direction and ran to Terry's front door with the dogs following behind me.

'I've got my dogs,' I said, as the four of us burst through the door. 'I hope that's okay!'

I tied the dogs up out the back and scuttled back inside, blurting out everything that had just happened.

'Fuck,' Terry said. 'This doesn't sound good!'

Terry's gatekeeper appeared at the door.

'Terry,' the gatekeeper said, 'I think Mr Chan and his son are circling the block with a motorbike and a tuktuk.'

'Oh my god—he knows I'm here!' I said, feeling like I was seconds away from full-blown panic.

Terry looked at me helplessly. 'This obviously isn't a good spot to hide out. You're probably better off at a hotel. We'll just have to get you to one without Chan knowing.'

So the dogs and I piled into the back of Terry's Camry. We waited until Chan and Ponlok started on their third lap of the block, then sped through the gates as fast as we could.

Terry dropped us at a nice hotel in town. I was so scared, I didn't give the reception staff the option to turn me away. I slammed a small pile of money on the counter and shrieked: 'I NEED A ROOM AND I HAVE DOGS WITH ME DON'T WORRY THEY DON'T BARK OR PISS INSIDE OR ANYTHING NOW QUICK GIVE ME THE KEYS! QUICK QUICK QUICK!'

For the next few hours it was me and the three dogs holed up in a tiny room, with a chill running down my spine every time I heard a tuktuk pass by.

I sent a message home, letting my parents and Sally know what had happened. My poor parents. I really didn't mean to worry them so much. But of course they were worried. Peter sent out a message far and wide calling for help to protect me. Paul Harapin, one of Green Kids Global's new board members, called the Australian embassy, who then called the chief of police in Battambang to have me placed under police protection.

I had to go to the station and tell the police the whole story. The police took down every last detail of the incident—including what my dogs looked like! One of them said: 'Ah, they've been circling the police station, too. We were wondering what those people were doing.'

They told me not to worry and dropped me back to the hotel. A policeman would meet me in the morning and take me and the dogs back to CCT.

I was utterly exhausted by the time I got back to the hotel room. My dogs were still there, waiting patiently. I felt considerably more relaxed now that I knew the police chief was looking out for me.

For the first time in as long as I could remember, I enjoyed a hot shower and cool air-conditioning, and curled up on a soft bed surrounded by three cuddly puppies.

What a strange day, I thought to myself as I drifted off to sleep. *I suppose I should start getting used to this—this crazy life down the rabbit hole, where things are never quite as they seem . . . Where kids in orphanages are not orphans, where your best friend turns out to be your mortal enemy and where, after a day spent in a living hell, you can wind up in a soft, clean, air-conditioned heaven on earth.*

And with that, I was sound asleep.

~

The next morning, as promised, the policeman arrived and took me and the dogs back to CCT. I'd been dealing with so much stress that it was a huge relief to suddenly have a tall, tough-looking policeman driving me around and hanging out in the yard at CCT.

The policeman's name was Meah. He had the bearing of a soldier, and Jedtha and I were impressed by his dedication and competence. He told us that he was impressed with us, too—he liked what CCT was doing.

Later that evening, the police at the station called. 'We've got him. Do you want to come in and press charges?'

When we arrived, Chan was sitting at a table at the back of the station with a policeman. He was crying uncontrollably.

'I'm sorry, *P'oun srey*!' he sobbed. 'I was drunk! I was at a wedding and I drank too much. Please don't send me to jail. I need to take care of my family . . .' He continued rambling but I couldn't make out what he was saying through all the blubbering and the snot.

I was tempted to feel sorry for him, but then I thought back to Mina's black eye and those chilling words I heard him hiss down the phone, and how long he had circled Terry's place and the police station after the wedding had ended. I had learned enough about Chan over the last few days not to necessarily believe his whimpering apology, but I didn't want a war. I decided not to press charges.

'Thank you. Thank you, *P'oun srey*!' he said as he got up to leave.

'That's okay, Chan. But please don't ever contact me or come near me or CCT again,' I said forcefully. 'Oh, and Chan? Be good to your family.'

He nodded glumly, and left.

'He's a weird guy,' the policeman warned me. 'Don't believe those tears. It was all a show.'

When we pulled into the gates at CCT, the staff hurried over to find out what had happened. I filled them in and concluded: 'So it's okay. It's over now. He won't have anything to do with me or CCT ever again.'

'I wouldn't be so sure,' said Savenh darkly. 'In Cambodia, people like him wait until they think you've forgotten . . . and that's when they get you.'

~

We decided to hire Meah as our second security guard. It would make us all feel a lot safer to have both a day and night guard at CCT.

Hiring Meah didn't mean I sailed through that big drama with Chan unscathed. I was terribly burned by it. I lost faith in my ability to work out who my friends were in Cambodia. And feeling like Jedtha and the staff had concealed the truth from me about Chan also really rattled me.

In my disillusioned state, I often wondered if maybe the little problems I had with the staff were about something darker than just a lack of experience or common sense.

For instance, sometimes it looked like Reaksmey just wasn't *trying* to do what we asked. We had to keep reducing his responsibilities. And I started to suspect that Heng, our cook, was skimming small sums of money off the food budget. The receipts she handed in sometimes looked quite dodgy, and they weren't adding up with the produce she was bringing back. I started to monitor her accounts more carefully, hoping I was wrong.

But by far the biggest issue with the staff was that the kids still didn't trust them, and, to be honest, at the time I couldn't blame them.

Shortly after the Big Chan Drama, some of the kids rang me when I was in Phnom Penh. They were scared and upset, because apparently Savenh, Davi and Reaksmey had sat them all down and said: 'When you have problems, don't tell Tara.'

Now what was going on? I wondered as I paced around the dingy little Phnom Penh hotel room. What were the staff trying to hide from me now?

I reassured the kids that they could *always* talk to me and tell me about anything that was troubling them. Then I rang Jedtha and gave him an earful: 'Why are the staff saying that? Is there some problem going on that I need to know about? No, it's not nothing. The kids are scared. They called me crying. Tell the staff we'll fire them if they ever say anything like that again.'

Okay, so I overreacted. The relentless stress had me at my wits' end.

I found out later that the staff had only been trying to say: 'Stop hassling Tara with every little issue you have, she has enough on her plate. Come to us and we'll help you.'

But the kids had been through a lot, too. It was no wonder that they had trouble trusting their carers.

~

By the middle of 2008, we finally fulfilled the quest to get DGR status for Green Kids Global (GKG) through RAWCS, which meant GKG could issue tax-deductible receipts. Now we could set up an online donation system and a proper admin structure. And, most importantly, we could accept donations without forcing our donors to jump through flaming hoops.

My friend Sally Reynolds got in touch to tell me she was going to organise a fundraiser in Australia. She wanted the funds to be split fifty-fifty between us and Charlie Teo's Cure for Life Foundation. Charlie Teo had been her sister Fiona's doctor. I had seen Charlie passing through the hospital corridors when Fee was sick and I knew that he was a respected neurosurgeon, but I didn't realise that he was also a

Mondulkiri elephant

CCT orphanage, 2009

Fun times

Battambang kids

Cambodian petrol station

Sinet graduating, 2012

Ruby, Rosie, me, Franky and Sinet, 2008

Max, Noni, me and Franky at home in Battambang, 2015

With Leangcheang (youth centre teacher), Kan (social worker), Sokunthea (preschool teacher) and kids at CCT's community youth centre no. 2

អាត្មាគតខ្ញុំ   ប្រុកបនប ⊔ច ⊔ច

ខ្ញុំមានគោឈ្មោលមួយក្បាល   កាច់ . ជាច់ . ប្ាច់ . សាច់

ឈ្មោះអាគ្មោត ។ គោខ្ញុំមានសម្បុរ   ប៉ាច់ . ទៅិច . ខុច . គិច . កុច

គ្មោត ។ វាមានមាឌធំខ្ពស់ ថៃ្មម   គេ្វាច . សេ៍ិច . ហ្ាច . កុ្ច .

គោម៉ិ⊔ុ⊔ចលត្ត ។ ដេ៍ម   ហ្ាច . ច្ច

                 ⊔រ⊔ស់អាគ្មោត ម៉ាៗ ។   ចៅម៉ាចចេះឈ្ាច⊔និ⊔សេ៍ិចនិច⊔ៗ

Literacy classes in action at CCT's community youth centre no. 1

Meal time at CCT's community youth centre no. 1

CCT nurses doing home visits to check up on a family

A family supported by CCT

CCT social workers visiting a foster care family

CCT's informational technology literacy classes in action

Peter, Sinet and me at the CCT Benefit Concert at the Enmore Theatre, Sydney, 2014

Carolyn and me at the launch of Carolyn's book, *Single White Female in Hanoi*, in 2011, while she was battling through chemotherapy

Battambang rooftops

CCT's restaurant, Battambang

Home with Franky, 2015

Storm clouds, Battambang

Psar Nat Market, Battambang

Sinet, BBC producer

bit of an Aussie celebrity. He'd been featured on several TV shows, including *60 Minutes, Enough Rope* and the ABC's *Australian Story*.

'I think doing a split event might work pretty well,' Sally continued. 'It could be a great opportunity for people who are already active in charity to hear your story. Of course, it would be best if you showed up in person and told the story yourself.'

Remember that plan I said I needed to solve the problem of CCT's unsustainable funding? Well, this looked like it might be it. I would go back to Australia for Sally's event and use it as an opportunity to do some serious hustling.

I said: 'Sally, you're a lifesaver! I'm so grateful you're doing this for us. And yes, I'll definitely be there.'

When Sinet heard I would be heading back to Australia to do some fundraising, she asked if she could come. 'I can help you,' she said. 'I know how to talk to donors. I used to talk to many donors at SKO. Once I even learned how to have conversations in Japanese so that a donor would help us.'

'Really?' I was impressed but also felt slightly disturbed. 'You should not have had to make money for SKO, Sinet. That was the job of the staff, like it is my job. I never want you to feel like you have to do anything like that for CCT.'

'Tara, I want to help. CCT is my home. I can't live without CCT. If I can help, please let me!'

You can imagine the effect those words had on me—it was like she lit a rocket under me. If I was motivated to secure CCT's funding before, nothing was going to stop me now.

'And I'm not a kid anymore anyway,' she reminded me. 'I'm over eighteen now!'

It was true. She was an adult and probably had more experience 'fundraising' than I did. And she had such a powerful story to tell.

But having a beneficiary, like Sinet was at the time, involved in fundraising activities is an extremely contentious issue for any charity that wants to uphold best practices. To this day we struggle with the conundrum of how to successfully raise funds without exploiting the kids or families to do it. The fact is, donors need personal stories to connect with. Personal stories help people to understand why they're being asked to give money, where their money is going and what's being achieved. Yet using personal stories from beneficiaries comes with a quagmire of ethical issues. For example, even if you get informed consent from an adult who is a beneficiary of the program, does the power imbalance at play mean that consent is truly ethical? And how do you make sure that the consent is genuinely 'informed,' especially when we're often talking across cultures—can a Cambodian with limited education properly grasp what it would mean to share their story on an Australian current affairs show, for example? We wrestle with questions like this constantly. It's one of the reasons we've changed most of the kids' names in the writing of this book.

I asked Jedtha what he thought of the idea of Sinet coming with me to help fundraise in Australia. To Jedtha, it was a no-brainer. We needed the money, she was an adult, let's treat her like an adult and let her help.

'I'll ask Savenh to organise a passport for her,' he said. 'She can arrange to get it done quickly.'

Getting things done in Cambodia's post-communist bureaucracy was an art form, but our staff always seemed to know how to navigate it.

'Maybe I'll talk to Chloe and see if she wants to fly over to help you while I'm away?' I suggested. 'She can also help look after my dogs.' Chloe was an old school friend who'd taught English at SKO. She and her mum were great fans of CCT and had done some fundraising for us. She was also a massive animal lover, so I could rest easy knowing that she was looking after Ruby, Rosie and Franky.

'That's a good idea,' Jedtha agreed.

And so it was decided. I started planning our trip. I knew our position was precarious enough that one fundraiser wasn't going to be enough to turn things around for us, so I got busy locking in meetings with other potential donors in Australia.

~

In the meantime, the issue of trust between me and the CCT staff, and the staff and kids, reared its head again. Sinet came to me one afternoon and told me that, even though they knew it was against the rules, some of the staff were smacking the kids when they were naughty. I never discouraged Sinet from coming to me and reporting problems. She was my eyes on the ground and she took that role seriously. Also, because we were only a couple of years apart in age, we were fast becoming good friends.

I couldn't stand the thought of the kids being disciplined like this under my watch. I understood that it was the way things were done in Cambodia, and in many other parts of the world. But I was never smacked as a child, and to me it seemed like an appalling way to communicate. The kids had been through enough, and I don't believe violence should *ever* be the answer. We'd spoken with the staff repeatedly about this, so it was disappointing to think they were ignoring the rules.

Jedtha suggested the two of us sit down with the kids and see what they had to say.

So we gathered them into a little circle on the floor and Jedtha said: 'Raise your hand if you've been hit by a staff member in the past few months.'

Every hand in the room went up, and little Nimol cried in an aggrieved tone: 'Yes! And Reaksmey pulled my ear!' He grabbed his ear to demonstrate.

The kids' grievances tumbled out one by one—they'd received smacks across the face, been dragged across the room by the ear . . . that kind of thing. It didn't seem to have been particularly traumatising for them, but to me it was unacceptable. I was just grateful that at least the kids felt safe and confident enough to share all this with Jedtha and me. It wasn't something they'd have done at SKO.

Knowing the kids were still being hit, despite my explicit instructions to the contrary, made my blood boil. To me, it was all just further evidence that I couldn't trust CCT's staff.

The next time the kids were out of earshot, Jedtha and I called a meeting with all the staff. It was raining, so we sat in a circle on the floor in the living room area.

As gently as I could, I told them I was disappointed to hear that some of them had been breaking the 'no hitting' rule.

Reaksmey looked at everything except me. Davi looked slightly mutinous.

Savenh said: 'We haven't been hitting the kids,' in a tone that meant: 'There, that's all sorted—let's move on.'

'The kids told us you have,' I persisted. 'I know you wouldn't hurt them but—'

'They're lying,' she said flatly.

The temperature in the room started to rise. 'They're *not* lying.'

'Then you misunderstood,' said Davi. 'You know your Khmer is not that good.'

I was getting frustrated. This wasn't the conversation I wanted to be having—I just wanted to resolve the issue. But Savenh and Davi were being unbelievably obstinate. And why the hell wasn't Jedtha saying anything?

'I *do* understand, Davi,' I informed her. 'The kids are telling us you're hitting them, and it upsets them.'

Reaksmey looked terrified, but Davi looked scornful. She snapped: 'Any child who says we're hitting them is stupid!'

I was trying to have an adult conversation here, but Davi kept subverting my efforts with this defensive nonsense. I could feel the mounting frustration levels building like a pressure cooker in my brain. I snapped. 'If I ever hear you say that again—and if I ever hear any of you are hitting any of the kids again, ever—you are fired! Got that? Fired!'

And then I burst into tears.

Everyone looked shocked. I had committed a serious faux pas. Losing your cool in such an explosive and uncontrolled way is considered to be a disgraceful loss of face in most Asian cultures.

It definitely wasn't my finest moment, but it was the culmination of over a year of stress. That outburst was to cost me dearly in the months to come.

~

Life went along fairly normally for a few weeks.

We went back to the lawyer to see what was happening with Sinet's trial. He assured us the police commissioner had been true to his word and a date would soon be set for the hearing, but it was unlikely it would happen before our upcoming trip to Australia. We just had to be patient.

I was kept busy tightening up processes where I could. I didn't want the staff—and Chloe—to be inundated with work when I was gone.

Then Sinet informed me that Reaksmey had once again smacked one of the kids.

We had tried really hard to help Reaksmey cope with his role. We'd reduced his responsibilities more and more over time, so he could manage while continuing to study at university. But he kept coming up short. We'd given him warning after warning, and now he'd broken the rules again, after I'd made it crystal clear that we wouldn't tolerate any hitting.

Jedtha talked to him about it and Reaksmey admitted it was true. He told Jedtha the job was just too much for him and caused him too much stress. It wasn't that Reaksmey wasn't a good person. He was a very nice boy. But he was young and the role just wasn't right for him. So, regretfully, Jedtha and I decided we'd have to let him go. But Jedtha couldn't face firing his nephew himself. 'You'll have to do it,' he said. 'I can't. He is my family.'

I sighed. 'Okay, I'll do it then . . .'

It was awful. Reaksmey hung his head forlornly and just nodded quietly as I spoke. He said he'd seen it coming for a while. I wished we'd had the funds to help cover the costs of his studies, but it was way beyond our means at that time.

While we were licking our wounds over the loss of Reaksmey, we also had to face up to the fact that my suspicions about our cook, Heng, were right. She *was* stealing money from the food budget. Not an awful lot of money, but the change she was getting at the markets definitely wasn't making it back to CCT.

Whenever I asked her about it, she'd always come back with some vague excuse—a different one every time. We tried to give her clear warnings and change the process to make her more accountable, but it kept happening.

We had—and still have—a zero tolerance policy on corruption at CCT, so eventually we had to let her go, too.

~

A week or so later, it was time for Sinet and me to set off for Phnom Penh on the first leg of our journey to Australia.

I tried to prepare the kids well in advance for our departure and kept our goodbyes very light and cheery. Even so, saying goodbye was tough. All the kids cried.

As we travelled to Phnom Penh, they kept calling to tell me they missed me already. Jedtha told me they'd cried themselves to sleep for the next few nights. The kids' sense of safety in the world seemed to depend so much on me. It was a concern.

Sinet was sorry for the kids, but her eyes were alight with excitement—her first plane trip, her first trip outside Cambodia.

I was too nervous about the fundraiser to feel excited. I've never been what you'd call an enthusiastic public speaker. But Sinet seemed unfazed. I asked her multiple times whether she was *sure* about wanting to share her story—it was a lot to share, a lot to open up about. She'd always reply: 'Yes, I'm sure. I want to help. CCT is my home and it is my future and I am not losing it.' Of course, she was a little nervous too. She wrote out her life story on palm cards and worked hard to get the English pronunciation down pat.

We picked up Chloe from Phnom Penh's busy little airport and took her out for dinner. Chloe was going to stay in Battambang for six months, so she'd be there when we got back from Australia, but it was great to see her and have a short catch-up before I left.

We went to a cafe to scoff tofu and vegies and I briefed her on everything that had been happening at CCT. The sibling reunion project, the kids' health, everything that had happened with Chan and Rath . . . 'But we've got round-the-clock security at CCT now so you don't need to worry,' I assured her. 'And I'll be just a phone call away, and Sally Power will be visiting in a few weeks.'

'It'll be fine,' Chloe said. 'I can't wait to see the kids—and the dogs!'

After dinner we went back to the cheap hotel room we were all sharing. Sinet fell asleep as soon as her head hit the pillow, but Chloe and I got into one of those deep and meaningful late-night conversations.

Once I started talking, I couldn't stop—it was such a relief to have a sympathetic ear. I told her all my worries and anxieties over funding. It looked like my future was going to be one long, unending hustle for money . . . (Turned out I was right about that.)

I nearly broke down in tears as I told her all this. The reality of helping children in Cambodia meant witnessing and working among desperate poverty, abuse, corruption and crime. The first eighteen months of CCT's existence had been a real baptism of fire. In hindsight, I can see that I was quite traumatised by it all. I'd been running on pure adrenaline for months.

'Let's hope you can get a good rest in Australia,' Chloe said. 'You seem to really need it.'

15

Sinet's first glimpse of Sydney was on a beautiful clear morning in October 2008, as our plane banked over the sparkling blue of Botany Bay. Compared to the bustle of Cambodia, Sydney was shiny, clean and modern, with massive buildings, amazing beaches, stunning harbour vistas and unimaginable wealth.

It was great to be around familiar faces, to sleep in my old room at Peter and Sue's place. It was fun to introduce Sinet to all of my old stomping grounds, my friends and our family's dogs. Everything in Sydney was exactly the same as it had ever been, and that familiarity was comforting.

But I was still so wound up inside that anyone who was foolish enough to ask: 'How are things going over there?' got a teary twenty-minute diatribe about everything we'd been through.

And I worried constantly about the fundraiser. Everything was riding on it being a success. But who was really going to care about our story? And even if it did go well, it seemed highly unlikely that we'd get enough new supporters to keep CCT afloat for the months and years ahead.

I was starting to seriously dread the speech I was going to have to give—I was already emotionally fragile and I knew that would only be amplified when I was up on a stage, standing at the podium. I was going to burst into tears and ruin the whole thing. I wished someone else, not me, could do the talking.

My head was full of all of these fears and worries when I got a cheery email from Chloe, letting me know that everything was going well, and the kids and the dogs were fine. Also, she'd been offered a dog and cat by some locals and could she take them on? They badly needed a home.

I wrote back rather frantically: 'Chloe—I'm sorry, but I'm afraid not. We have too many mouths to feed already. Right now we just can't afford it.'

I was sure she'd understand.

~

Sally Reynolds told me she was expecting about fifty or so people to come to the fundraiser. Fifty people! I'd never spoken in front of a crowd that big before. My anxiety grew and grew. By the time the night of the fundraiser rolled around, I was almost mute with terror.

When Sue, Sinet, Noni and I arrived at the small art gallery in Surry Hills, the place was packed. It seemed Sally's strategy of sharing the fundraiser with Charlie Teo's Cure for Life Foundation had worked well. More than a hundred people had turned up. The smart, glamorous Sydneysiders left Sinet and me feeling terribly unsophisticated in our polyester specials sourced from Battambang's markets, with Cambodia's dust still on our shoes.

During the welcoming drinks, whenever people asked me about CCT and the kids I started misting up with tears as I tried to answer. I quickly realised I just *couldn't* speak to a crowd in the state I was in . . . I had a bowling ball in my stomach that wasn't going anywhere.

I croaked at Sue: 'I'm not doing it—I can't.'

Sue looked at my face and immediately got it. She said: 'Okay. Don't worry, sweetie. I'll say a few words for you.'

So when my name was called, Sue heroically stepped up to the microphone and ad-libbed on my behalf. 'Tara's feeling too emotional to speak, so I'm going to tell you about the work that my daughter is doing in Cambodia . . .' she began. She told the story of how we'd rescued the kids, and how proud she was of me. She concluded: 'When people ask me why we should help people in Cambodia when you can help people at home, I tell them that when Tara was in Battambang she saw that something needed to be done about the poverty she witnessed. Wherever you are, if you see a need that should be addressed, you should do something. We should all do something.'

She started crying, and everyone applauded, which made me feel better about how tearful I was. The sympathy in the room spurred me on to be brave, so I stepped up to the microphone. It was excruciating, but I managed to elaborate on Sue's depiction of events over the previous eighteen months and share some stories of the trials and tribulations—and also of some of the bittersweet times. I even managed to get a few laughs from the crowd, which was enormously encouraging. I ended by explaining how much we desperately needed their support to give the kids the futures they deserved.

Then I introduced Sinet—one of the bravest girls I'd ever met in my life.

It was a small, intimate room, so emotions were contagious. By the time I stepped away from the microphone some people were already dabbing at their eyes.

But Sinet was amazing. Beyond amazing. It turned out she was a natural at public speaking. With tears rolling down her cheeks, she slowly delivered her heart-rending story. As soon as she finished, she was greeted with deafening applause. Everyone—I really do mean everyone—was crying. Some were even pulling out their hankies and blowing their noses.

For Sinet, receiving such a heartfelt ovation from the people in that room helped her to see what a brave, inspiring and extraordinary young woman she is, and to turn a series of traumatic events that had been a source of terrible shame for her into something she was proud of surviving. She realised that she could be a role model for the many other young girls in Cambodia who have lived through similar horrors. It was a life-changing moment for Sinet.

Sally Reynolds then stepped up to the mic to invite neurosurgeon Charlie Teo to speak. Everyone turned to look up at the mezzanine level of the small gallery, where a tall, fit-looking guy in his forties stood. Charlie called down: 'I'm sorry—I can't follow that. What an amazing story. These girls deserve all of your support tonight.'

People started coming up to me and saying incredibly kind, generous things. I felt very moved and humbled by the reaction. I wished Jedtha had been there, because a large portion of all that praise belonged to him, too.

Charlie introduced himself and we had a quick chat. He was a very down-to-earth guy, and he listened intently to everything I had to say about CCT.

'I'm gonna help you,' he said, handing me his card.

Thanks to Sally's incredible efforts, the night was an outstanding success. People dug deep to buy the donated artworks and raffle tickets.

Some incredible musicians donated their time, too. The Aussie-Israeli pop star Lior settled at the microphone and announced that he was dedicating the song he was about to perform to Sinet.

Sinet and I had no idea who he was, but soon the whole room was spellbound, singing along to his hit song, 'This Old Love'. I looked at Sue and thought: *Far out, even my mum knows the words! I really have been away a long time.*

He came over to speak with us for several minutes and instantly became Sinet's biggest celebrity crush. He is still a dedicated supporter of CCT and we're very grateful for everything he's done for us over the years.

~

I was blown away by the response we got at the fundraiser and hoped it was an indication of what was to come—because we still had a *lot* of fundraising to do to make CCT viable.

For the next few weeks, our lives were all about rushing from one meeting to the next. Sinet and I met with people who had attended the fundraiser, almost all of our existing donors (whom we only knew via email at that stage) and with many of our donors' friends and colleagues. We told our stories over and over again to small groups of people at cafes and restaurants, in people's homes and offices.

The meetings proved successful. We got twenty new regular supporters on board. One very kind-hearted businessman wrote us a cheque for $20,000 on the spot. I came out of every single meeting thinking: *YES! We can do this!* I felt profoundly grateful for every dollar we received. None of these people had to part with their hard-earned cash. The privilege of seeing such extraordinary acts of human kindness is still one of the best parts of my job.

I wanted to give something back to our supporters. We didn't have the money to get anything professionally printed, so Sinet and I got a bunch of my old, unused black art books and spent our evenings cutting and pasting photos to create little CCT scrapbooks as 'thank you' gifts.

I couldn't believe it. Everything was going to be okay.

~

Charlie Teo took Sinet and me out to lunch. Charlie is a freak of nature. He's one of the world's top neurosurgeons, performing amazing feats of surgery on patients when other surgeons have given up hope. He has a passion for kickboxing and motorbikes, and he is the founder of the biggest brain cancer research foundation in Australia.

He was very easy to talk to and listened intently to our stories. He said he'd plan a visit to CCT as soon as he could. He also said: 'I'm going to contact ABC TV for you. The guys at *Australian Story* will do a great job of representing you.'

It was a big promise—the documentary show *Australian Story* had done huge things for Charlie's foundation, as far as I understood. It seemed like a great opportunity, but one I never quite believed would materialise. That was, until I got an email from one of their journalists asking to meet with Sinet and me while we were in town.

We met the journalist at a cafe in Bondi Beach. She was a tall, elegant woman with a kind face. 'I've heard some amazing things about you from Charlie,' she said. 'I'd love to hear more!'

I launched into the spiel I'd been giving everyone over the last few weeks. She seemed to hang on every word and said lovely flattering things like: 'It's such an amazing story! You're such an inspiring/brave/incredible girl!'

I was so encouraged by the journalist's interest I couldn't shut up. When she asked me what made me go to Cambodia I told her my deepest darkest secrets. My teenage struggle with anorexia, my disappointment with the film industry, the dark feelings that had overwhelmed me after my grandmother's death . . .

She said: 'You're amazing—honestly, I'm just so blown away. This will make a terrific story!'

I left the meeting thinking: *Great, that's in the bag.* Of course I realised the journalist had to put it to her bosses first, but I'd given it my best shot and I had the sense that her enthusiasm was genuine.

I knew this was a brilliant opportunity for CCT, but I didn't stop for a moment to consider the impact it was going to have on me personally. And in hindsight I can't believe I overshared so much. I'd behaved like I was talking to my long-lost best friend, not a journalist.

Peter, Sue and Sally Power were instantly supportive of the idea of appearing on *Australian Story*. 'This is exactly the kind of show we should be doing, Tara,' Sally said. 'It could be life-changing for CCT and the kids!'

It sounded wonderful, but we didn't even know if the documentary would go ahead, let alone if it would actually help raise any money.

So Sinet and I returned to our hectic schedule of meetings and talks with potential donors, focusing on the funding. We needed to raise as much as we could if CCT was going to survive.

~

Chloe emailed to let me know that things at CCT were going along well, but Sida had caused a small furore with the staff. Apparently Meah had come down on her quite hard for being late. She promptly informed him that if he ever spoke to her like that again: 'I'll tell Tara and she'll fire you!'

Okay, so I'd have to have a chat with Sida. It wasn't great that she was rude to Meah, but I thought it was quite good to hear that our once shy, beaten-down girl felt safe enough to stand up for herself. I saw it as a small victory. We must be doing the right thing if the kids felt safe enough to speak their minds and weren't intimidated like they were at SKO.

I felt nothing but buoyant and confident about the future as the departure date for our trip back to Battambang approached. Sinet and I couldn't wait to head home in triumph.

~

Throughout these busy weeks in Sydney, I spent whatever spare time I could with Carolyn Shine.

We quickly developed a lovely relationship that bounced along in text messages and late-night dinners at her place. She had so many passions: music, linguistics, tropical plants, art, animation, cats, vegetarian cooking, physics, scepticism, travel . . . There was no denying, I'd developed quite the crush on her by now.

Every spring, Carolyn's large circle of musician friends hold a get-together they call Floranaelia at a friend's house about an hour north of Sydney. They set up tents, light campfires, eat incredible food and play mind-blowing music together for three epic days. This year, it was to be held just a few days before I was due to fly back to Cambodia with Sinet. When Carolyn invited me along, I performed some quite advanced feats of mathematics to make the room in my schedule to go.

I'm so glad I did. It was a magical weekend.

Carolyn was in her element, her quick dry wit and infectious laugh at the ready. She had a sense of curiosity and humour that lit up a room. I was amazed by her ability to maintain close friendships with so many people. And her friends were an amazing community—musicians, writers, scientists, intellectual hooligans . . . they suited me down to the ground. I felt completely at home with them.

Over the course of the weekend I was pretty chuffed to find out that she was into me, too. It was just a casual fling, but I was on cloud nine. I managed to extract a promise from her to come and visit me in Battambang soon.

~

The day after the party, I was back at Peter and Sue's place, sleeping off the mother of all hangovers, when Peter knocked on my bedroom door. 'Tara, I need to talk to you. It's important.' His tone was heavy and serious.

I staggered out of bed and followed him to the living room, going 'What? What's going on?'

He sat down opposite me on the couch, and took my hand. That was not a reassuring gesture. It made me think: *WHAT the FUCK is going on?!*

'I have something to tell you.'

That was even worse.

Then he said: 'Tara, I know you're looking forward to going back to Cambodia, but it looks like you might not be able to. There's been some trouble at CCT. You're being accused of breaking a number of Cambodian laws . . .'

'*What?*' Was this some bizarre joke? Peter wasn't that closely involved with CCT at this point—what on earth could he know that I didn't?

'The allegations are coming from Jedtha and Davi,' he continued. '...And Chloe.'

The blood drained from my face and I felt like I was going to faint. Or vomit.

Peter started running through the list of alleged crimes.

First, they accused me of possessing pornography, which is illegal in Cambodia.

I couldn't believe my ears. 'What? What pornography?!'

It turned out that Chloe had gone through all my stuff and had given the staff a box set of the Showtime TV series *The L Word* that was among my small collection of DVDs. She'd also given them a pop art image of a mouth that I'd been playing around with in Photoshop. *The L Word* is a primetime commercial TV show and the picture was my clumsy effort to teach myself how to apply coloured filters in Photoshop.

The other 'crime' I'd apparently committed was taking Sineit, Makara and various kids to Phnom Penh and Siem Reap for medical treatment. According to the emails Peter had received, Jedtha had said: 'It is highly illegal in Cambodia for a foreigner to take Cambodian children anywhere on their own.'

According to the staff, they could have me arrested and jailed at Phnom Penh airport for either of these crimes.

The accusations were so ridiculous it was laughable—except this was no laughing matter. The staff were seriously pissed off, it seemed. It was hard to understand what was happening, but Davi was quoted as saying: 'If I ever get fired, I will definitely tell the authorities about Tara.' They'd completely convinced Chloe that they could have me sent to jail if they chose.

Apparently, while Sally Power was visiting, Chloe and Jedtha had gone to her with a litany of complaints about me. Sally, wondering if Chloe might have some kind of personal beef against me, asked Chloe to type it all up and email it to her so we could all try to sort it out.

Peter gave me a printout of the list of complaints that Chloe had sent to Sally. To give you a taste of what I was up against, here is the list (verbatim) of the things that Chloe said about me, followed by my responses to them. I have to preface this by saying that while none of these accusations would hold water in a court of law, they are admittedly examples of bad practice caused by a lack of staff, funds and professional expertise.

1. Tara is running CCT. She has taken all the staff's jobs and their files for herself. Apparently her taking all the documents and keeping them is illegal. For example, the medical files should be with the nurse et cetera.

2. For a foreigner to take kids to Phnom Penh is illegal. It isn't her job, but the job of the employees.

3. She administers medicine, which the nurse should do. I'm so-so on this one as the nurse is bloody hopeless and I think Tara would do a better job.

4. She flat-out spoils the children. She is ruining them beyond belief. She gives the children anything they want. It doesn't matter what it is. Money, food, movies on Sundays, video games which Rithy is highly addicted to. All the kids have too many clothes—they don't need them. All the dorms have fans in them, which they don't need. They're extremely resentful of me because I don't buy these for them. If I do it is much rarer than they're used to. The kids don't want to study or play outside at all now, just watch TV and play videos and games. Giving children phones, money, presents etc. is just not necessary. CCT could be running on a quarter of its costs and supporting four times as many kids if we cut this out.

5. The kids have been led to believe that the staff are now lower beings and if the children don't like them, they're fired. This has led to the children threatening staff, not listening to staff, being rude, all of this I have witnessed. The children are definitely running the show. I am so afraid they will not be able to reintegrate into society. The spoiling etc. is not exactly illegal but if DoSVY or any other NGOs found out they would give Tara and CCT a really hard time and most likely take the children away.

6. The dogs full stop are a disgusting waste of money. I know she loves them but no money should be taken from CCT to pay for them as I could support probably two children for every one dog that she has. They are better-fed and taken care of than the children.

7. The obsession with medicine and doctors is also a waste of money. I think they should most definitely be looked after in this department but the staff are telling me she is forever taking blood, going to Phnom Penh buying medical supplies etc. Also taking Sovanni to Phnom Penh for her vaccinations is costing around $600. And Jedtha said Battambang has way cheaper alternatives to this.

I'm not going to launch into a huge diatribe defending myself. The most important thing to take away from this disaster is that Chloe did actually make some salient points . . .

I wanted to give the kids the same upbringing that I had been lucky enough to have, but Chloe's remark about reintegration was spot on. These days I understand that I was setting up an unrealistic standard of living that would create problems when it was time for them to move on to independent living.

And the issue raised about foreigners taking children to

Phnom Penh is, more than anything, an indication of my failings as a leader. My team should have felt able to communicate their concerns with me—this would have been in the best interests of both CCT and me. Because, although it's not illegal for foreigners to take unaccompanied minors on excursions, it's certainly not best practice. Even as the managing director of CCT, I would not do this today—our current child protection policy states that children must be accompanied by the child's guardian as well as a CCT social worker or nurse.

The one thing I *will* defend is the points raised about my dogs. Those dogs were and still are a very crucial element to my overall safety in Cambodia. On a trip to Phnom Penh in late 2014, without the dogs with me, three men grabbed me on the street one evening, strangled me and attempted to rape me. Luckily I got away and managed to actually help catch and arrest one of the three men. Safety is an issue to take seriously in Cambodia. Cambodians keep dogs as a means of protection because it's effective. Almost every expat I know who's lived in Cambodia long term has experienced house burglaries and robberies. In the nine years I've been living in Cambodia I haven't been broken into once because of the protection my three beautiful dogs provide.

The other issue—and it's just as important—is that in those early days in Cambodia I was very isolated and those dogs brought, and still bring, immeasurable happiness to my life. They contribute significantly to my overall wellbeing in Cambodia. Before I was receiving a salary, I relied on a bare minimum of funds from CCT to feed myself and my dogs, and I used to feel bad for how little they had to eat. As soon as I began receiving a modest salary, I of course began to cover my dogs' costs myself, and this has been the case ever since.

~

With the benefit of time (and perhaps a little more wisdom), I can see what important lessons these accusations held for me.

But back in 2008, having them fired at me from afar felt like a knife in my back. CCT was not operating in line with best practices on a number of issues, but I felt that those shortcomings weren't a result of only my wrongdoing. We were a team, and the mistakes we made, we made as a team. And threatening me with jail was outrageously cruel. I was deeply hurt and felt very betrayed.

Chloe went on to explain that she'd withheld the 'evidence' that she'd found in my room in an effort to protect me. But the staff told her it didn't matter. If they told the authorities I owned 'pornography', the authorities would believe them.

Despite the absurdity of these charges, there was enough darkness in that threat to scare me half to death. The thought of not being able to go back to Cambodia, of not seeing the kids again and of leaving things on this horrific and humiliating note made me sick to my stomach.

There were a lot of other bullet points about Sinet, too, which were too outrageous and cruel to repeat here. As Chloe put it: 'The staff have really got it in for Sinet, so I'm not sure what is and isn't true.'

My friendship with Sinet was, apparently, a great source of angst for the staff. Their biggest beef seemed to be around a welcome sign I'd asked Sinet to make when my grandfather, Michael, had visited Cambodia several months earlier. According to the staff, she'd disrupted the afternoon's activities to get it done, without first asking them for permission. I was mortified that asking her to do something that seemed so small to me had created so much conflict.

But it seemed that, in the staff's eyes, Sinet couldn't do anything right. When she got good marks in school, it was because she was 'bribing the teachers'. When I asked her to go grab my bag for me, she was 'seen stealing from Tara's wallet'. When we set up a bank account for her so she could get a visa for Australia, they immediately accused her of corruption.

The way they'd turned on her left me bristling with anger. How could they do this to a young girl like Sinet, who'd been through so much already?

Young unmarried girls certainly are quite put upon in Cambodia—
they're expected to be meek and submissive and virginal, to work
hard and look after their families and to disregard their own needs
and ambitions. (The Cambodian youth of today are slowly changing
this, though.)

Although Sinet was a typical good, meek little Khmer schoolgirl
in many ways, she had a confidence about her that had helped her to
survive everything she'd been through, and to be 'mother' to all the
kids through the tough days at SKO. She was a natural leader with
a great talent for just getting on and doing what needed to be done.
Although perhaps not an ideal situation, she was the heart of CCT and
the kids trusted her above everyone else. Sometimes she was the only
one they listened to and the only one they talked to. So, by default, she'd
become the voice of the kids. She'd come and talk to me when there
was a problem because she trusted me. She had been hurt by too many
Cambodian adults in positions of power and had learned not to trust
them. And, at that time, the staff still hadn't managed to earn her trust.

Perhaps I didn't help much in that regard because the staff hadn't
done a great job of winning my trust either. I had never been in a
position before where I had to be a leader. It was all brand new to me,
I was still very young and had a lot to learn.

Feelings of disbelief, confusion, hurt, anger, sadness and despair
flooded over me in waves as I tried to process it all.

'I can't believe Chloe and Jedtha are involved in all of this,' I said
to Peter through bitter tears. 'They know what Sinet's been through—
and what she's still going through with the court case. And look at
everything she's done on this trip. She's done so much for CCT.'

Sinet was always talking about how much CCT had changed her
life—how it was the best *onga* in the world. And now our team were
being unthinkably horrible to her.

'I'm not sure Jedtha *is* on board with these accusations,' Peter said.
'He doesn't seem to agree with everything the staff have said. There
are a lot of different angles to this whole mess. I think he can't cope

with conflict and he doesn't know how to react. And as for Chloe—her head seems to have been completely turned by the staff. Does she have a history of this kind of behaviour?'

'This is not the Chloe I know,' I said bleakly.

I moved from the couch to the kitchen table, feeling like I was going to vomit. 'So do you really think they can arrest me at the airport?'

Peter looked worried. 'Let's find the best legal advice we can get before we make any decisions,' he said.

I dropped my head into my hands, shattered. I agreed that we couldn't make any decisions just yet, but I knew I wouldn't be able to relax until we did.

I heard Sue's key turn in the front door—she was arriving home from my grandmother's place.

Whenever anything bad happens in my life, Peter and Sue take on quite stereotypical roles—Peter gets angry and protective and kind of: 'Oh no! You've messed with the wrong family!' And Sue turns very warm and gentle and motherly.

'Aw, sweetheart,' Sue said, stroking my hair away from my face. 'I'm so sorry this has happened. It's just not fair.'

She evoked such a deep feeling of childhood comfort in me that I just dissolved into tears again. I'd never been on the receiving end of anything like this before. I'd never been so betrayed by people I liked and who I thought liked me. And the fear that I might not see the kids again . . .

If ever the universe could somehow conspire to bring about the Worst. Hangover. Ever. This had to be it. I staggered to the bathroom, locked the door, vomited, and then lay on the bathroom floor for a long time.

I didn't want to go back out to the living room or my bedroom, because I knew Sinet was having a lovely time in the front room watching YouTube videos, oblivious to everything that was happening. I wanted to keep it that way. I wanted to protect her from as much of this as I could.

My phone buzzed. It was a text message from Carolyn. *How are you feeling? Up for dinner tonight at mine?*

Not so good, I texted back. I followed with a short novella outlining what had just happened.

The phone immediately buzzed with her reply: *I'm on my way.*

Fifteen minutes later, she texted to say she was parked outside our house with a bottle of red wine. I went straight outside and sat in the passenger seat for several hours, drinking straight from the bottle until I was numb. I hate red wine, but I adored Carolyn. In that moment, she felt like the only good thing left in my life.

~

Over the next few days, Sally got in touch. She'd been burned by the whole thing, too. She felt that the problem with the staff was fundamentally a clash of cultures. I didn't disagree with that assessment, but it didn't make it feel any less personal, less hurtful.

It was good to have the support of the people around me. As always, when I really needed help, my family were 100 per cent behind me. And because they cared about the kids as much as I did by now, the kids were our main concern.

We got in touch with a Khmer friend who worked for an NGO in Phnom Penh to ask if he could recommend a good lawyer. He put us in touch with a Khmer lawyer whom he said was one of Phnom Penh's best and most respected.

We emailed the whole story to the lawyer and waited anxiously for his response. He wrote back assuring us that no, I wouldn't be arrested at the airport, so we arranged to meet in Phnom Penh.

Peter decided, like the hero he is, to book a ticket and come back to Cambodia with Sinet and me. I can't overstate my relief at hearing this.

'We'll get through this together, sweetie-pops. They should've thought twice before deciding to fuck with the Winklers,' he said with a cheeky grin.

We were hoping we could also talk to Chloe when we arrived back in Cambodia, but we got an email from Jedtha saying that she'd packed up her stuff and left.

Chloe and I didn't speak to each other for many years after she left Battambang, but recently we got in touch and talked about what had happened. She gave me an honest and generous apology and said she'll always feel guilty about the part she played in it all. If it's her punishment to have the whole episode put in this book, she'd cop it on the chin. (I appreciate the offer, but I've changed her name here anyway. I don't want to punish Chloe, or anyone actually. I've only included this whole thing because the lessons learned by me are too important to leave out.)

Chloe explained that she'd been robbed shortly after she arrived in South-East Asia and she was diagnosed with post-traumatic stress after she returned to Australia. She said it's no excuse, but she'd have been thinking more clearly if she hadn't been suffering from that background stress. And then the staff came to her with all their concerns and they were incredibly convincing.

Matters like this are never black and white. Chloe and I are now on good terms again.

16

I was filled with dread as we set off for Sydney airport. The triumphant return I'd been imagining a few days earlier was such a long way from my current reality. Despite having all these new donations, new supporters and an *Australian Story* documentary on the horizon, going back to CCT now felt like the last thing in the world I wanted to do.

We had an extra forty kilos worth of donated items that friends and donors had begged me to take back for the kids. Carolyn and I had sat up into the night parcelling them up. It should have been fun, but with all the fear and uncertainty and hurt and anger I was feeling, it had just felt like a chore.

We begged the guy at the check-in counter in Sydney to let us take the excess luggage—and as soon as he heard about CCT, he said: 'That's fine, guys, no worries. It must be pretty crazy over there.' We all looked at each other and said: 'That's truer than you know.'

I turned away from the counter to see that Sally Reynolds had come to see me off. I had a few minutes to sit down and tell her about everything that was happening.

When the time came to go through immigration, we were both in tears. She pulled out a little pouch of worry dolls that Fiona had given her. 'I think you need them more than I do now,' she said.

That made me cry even more. Leaving Sally and my mum and the safety and security of Sydney—and people who actually *liked* me . . . that was very hard.

The flight to Phnom Penh seemed to take even longer than usual, thanks to the heavy waves of dread that kept crashing over me.

~

Nobody jumped out of the crowd to arrest me at Phnom Penh, so we went straight to a hotel and settled in. Peter and I then had yet another passionate bitch session about Chloe and the staff. My temper got the better of me and let's just say I got a little carried away . . .

It takes quite a lot for me to lose my temper, but when it happens, I do so rather spectacularly. I think I inherited this tendency from Peter. He can be as fiery as me. But in Phnom Penh that day, when I started to really lose it, he sat me down with his serious face on and gave me a little talking-to.

He said: 'Tara, I'm very happy to be here in Cambodia with you and I'm very happy to help you through this. But there are some things I need from you. I need you to turn down the intensity, and I need you to stay calm. No more histrionics. If we're going to get through this, we have to hose it down—not fan the flames.'

I thought back guiltily to all of my venomous outbursts of the last few days. Peter was right: it was time to leave all that behind now. I promised him—and myself—that I'd keep a cool head. After all, the last thing I wanted to do was make things any worse. And my dad would kill me if I didn't!

This was the point in my life where I realised that the less drama you have in your life, the better. And while I haven't exactly rewired my fundamental nature, I always do aim to stay calm and professional under stress.

~

The next morning we left Sinet at the hotel with her nose in a book, and Peter and I went out into busy Phnom Penh to meet with Jedtha at a cafe. I knew I'd have difficulty reining in my anger, so I asked Peter to help mediate. The plan was to work with Jedtha to help identify the issues and accusations that truly worried him. Later that day we'd work through the list together in our meeting with the lawyer.

Walking in and seeing Jedtha sitting at a table was hard. Knowing him so well—his kind, gentle face, his habit of fidgeting when he was stressed—it meant that part of me wanted to greet him like the friend he had once been. But a bigger part of me felt decidedly unfriendly and unsympathetic. *How could he have done this to me?*

Peter kept things polite and businesslike, and between the three of us we made a list of all Jedtha's concerns.

It seemed that Jedtha's main issue was that I'd been doing so many things that were 'highly illegal' because the law—according to him—was different for foreigners and locals. These things included taking the children to Phnom Penh for medical treatment, and owning a pornographic DVD and picture.

'Jedtha, you do realise that this is *not* pornography,' I hissed.

Peter shot me a quelling look and said: 'I'm sure the lawyer will help clear that up. But, Jedtha, can you please explain to us why you never told Tara that taking the kids out of Battambang was illegal in the entire eighteen months that she was working at CCT? If that's true, you put her in a dangerous position.'

'Well, yes, I don't know,' Jedtha said, clearly flustered.

We tried asking the question a few different ways, but he just couldn't give us a straight answer.

Peter asked about a lot of the comments in Chloe's letter, but Jedtha said he didn't know anything about them. He said that while the kids did have some behavioural issues, as far as he was concerned, that was a normal part of working with children in orphanages. He said he didn't believe that I'd ever wasted money and never thought my dogs, who were mostly living on leftovers and rice, were an issue.

But, oh dear—he had a lot to say about Sinet. Davi and Savenh had told him a bunch of stories that didn't even have the tiniest seed of truth in them—crazy stuff like: 'Sinet hit Sakana, drawing blood. When Makara and Sakana told Tara, Tara said: "Oh well, Sakana deserved it because he's spoiled."'

I felt like crying and laughing at the same time.

~

Peter and I headed back to the hotel to wait for our appointment with the lawyer.

I gave myself a metaphorical pat on the back for staying calm through that meeting with Jedtha. It hadn't been easy, but I could see that things did go better when I didn't fly off the handle.

I could also see that Jedtha was approaching the whole thing in a reasonable way. He abhors conflict and doesn't know how to deal with it. But he was doing his best to work through it with us. The problem was, I didn't know where it was all heading. The thought of going back to CCT was frankly nauseating—but I couldn't abandon the kids, and I was pretty sure none of our new donors would keep supporting CCT if I walked away.

Sinet was sitting on her bed in the hotel room writing in her journal when we got back to the hotel. She looked up with interest and a little concern—she knew something was up, but she didn't know what it was.

With the future so uncertain (and the fact that we were good friends), I felt it was unfair to leave her in the dark. So I sat on the bed opposite her and told her the broad brushstrokes of what had happened. I didn't burden her with too many gory details—but I wanted her to understand why I might not be returning to live in Battambang.

She took the news so stoically I was worried—surely the thought of going back to an orphanage where the staff had accused you of all kinds of nonsense should be extremely upsetting? I asked her point blank: 'Are you okay to go back to CCT?'

She returned to her writing and said mildly: 'Yes . . . because I know you will always be there for me.'

Her simple faith and trust in me broke my heart. I couldn't, *couldn't* abandon her and the other kids.

~

There was a part of me that couldn't help but feel pleased to see Jedtha squirm in his seat when he met our new lawyer.

Jedtha is a big shot around Battambang—tall, well-spoken, educated and respected. But our new lawyer, Sok Hy, was something else again. Sok Hy is a highly educated, global-citizen type. He got his bachelor's and master's degree in law in Cambodia and also completed a training course at the Australian National University in Canberra. He worked in the Cambodian senate for almost five years and was a consulting expert in the process of drafting Cambodia's improved legal system. He has worked as a criminal and corporate lawyer on high-profile cases throughout Asia and now works as a commercial and banking lawyer.

After introducing himself and outlining his considerable credentials, he worked though the list of accusations against me that we'd created with Jedtha that morning.

His brow furrowed into lines of complete bewilderment as he read the documents.

'There's no legal grounding whatsoever for any of these accusations,' he said. At one point, a little smile tugged at the corner of his mouth. 'This is quite funny!'

He read on, and turned to Jedtha. 'Okay, so can I see the evidence you say you have?'

Jedtha dropped the DVD case and the coloured picture onto the table. Sok Hy picked up the picture and his eyebrows shot up. 'This is a person's mouth, with some colours on top.' He dropped it dismissively and picked up the DVD. 'So is this pornography?' he asked.

'No,' I said, rather assertively. 'It's a popular, primetime TV series—I'll pull up the synopsis for you on my laptop.'

He examined the DVD cover and read the online synopsis. 'This is a TV show,' he sighed. Then he added, 'Anyone who thinks this is evidence of anything is stupid.'

By now, Jedtha was so out of his depth he could barely string a sentence together. I felt a tiny bit sorry to see him in such a state. But a bigger part of me was jubilant. I felt so vindicated.

Now that the business was over, Sok Hy pushed the paperwork aside and we all settled down for a chat. He asked us a lot of questions about CCT and told us a bit more about his life. He said he was very appreciative of our work in Cambodia and felt a strong affinity with us.

He said: 'I think you should go back to all the people who are carrying on with these threats and say: "I'm not a child. I have a lawyer. And if I hear one breath of this ever again I'll be seeing you in court. And if you don't believe me you can give my lawyer a call."'

Sok Hy has remained a great supporter and pro bono lawyer of CCT. We're very grateful to have him on our team.

~

Now that the fear of being thrown into jail had dissolved, the full realisation of what lay ahead of me began to sink in. The CCT team was broken. I was broken, too. I just could not face the thought of going back to Battambang, where people like Rath and Chan made death threats against me, and people like Davi had threatened to put me in jail. All the fight had gone out of me.

The best plan I could come up with was to stay in Phnom Penh, where I would manage donor relations, and occasionally make trips to Battambang to check that the donors' funds were used as intended. I'd have to find a job—I couldn't justify taking money from donors if I wasn't working full time at CCT. I'd have to see if it was possible to make a life for myself away from CCT, while still upholding my responsibilities to the donors and, most importantly, to the kids.

I told Peter all of this and he said: 'Come on, don't give up on me now.' He gave me a friendly nudge. 'We can get through this. I'll come with you to Battambang and help you deal with Davi and Savenh. Once that's behind us, we can focus on moving forward.'

His calm assuredness gave me a little injection of energy. It did sound like a good plan.

~

Passing the imposing black statue that towers over the turn-off into Battambang raised strange, conflicted feelings in me. I was home. I desperately wanted to see the kids. But I was dreading the looming confrontation.

When we arrived in Battambang, we checked into a hotel and Jedtha came to meet us to discuss the next course of action.

We wanted to fire Davi and Savenh. Jedtha was clearly nervous about this idea. 'Maybe possible to give them one more chance?' he asked. 'I think we won't have this problem again.'

'But don't you agree that they deserve to be fired?' Peter asked. 'If you want Tara to help you run CCT, how can you expect her to work with them?'

Jedtha suggested that perhaps we could just fire Davi. 'Savenh is a good social worker—she's good with the kids,' he said. 'She's known them for a very long time now. Also, Savenh has worked with us from SKO days. We can trust her.' Jedtha continued: 'Or maybe we can just move CCT to Phnom Penh? That could solve the problem.'

That suggestion didn't come totally out of the blue. Jedtha and I did sometimes fantasise about moving CCT to Phnom Penh. We felt so paranoid about Rath and Chan—and Rath's network of 'relatives'— that making a fresh start didn't seem like such a bad idea.

But Peter thought we were both mentally defective. 'Is that going to be your solution every time you have a problem with staff? Instead of dealing with the situation, you'll just move cities?'

Jedtha was getting agitated. 'Please, we can't fire Savenh. I promise we will not have any problem from her. I agree we should fire Davi, but not Savenh. Not Savenh.'

We had to give Jedtha something—it was only fair. So we agreed that we'd just fire Davi and then see how things went.

'But it will be difficult,' Jedtha warned us. 'She will not want to accept.'

'Well . . .' said Peter. 'We'll try to do it very sensitively, so she won't lose face. We won't put any blame on anyone, just tell her that we don't have the funding to keep a nurse on anymore. Keep it as stress-free as possible.'

Jedtha nodded. 'Okay. You try that. It may be okay. I will arrange for us to meet her this afternoon.'

~

When we arrived at CCT the kids squealed and ran at us, jumping up and down and flinging their arms around me and Sinet. I started to cry. How could I leave them?

I gave them all a big hug. Little Akara wiped away the tears that rolled down my cheeks.

'Oh, I missed you all so much,' I said in Khmer, trying my best to smile. 'I brought some presents from Australia for you all, but I need to have a meeting with the staff first, okay?'

'Okay!' They skipped away, beaming.

We asked Davi to join us in the main downstairs common room. Peter and Jedtha and I sat in a circle on the floor with her. Having to sit opposite Davi set my limbic system into overdrive. I wanted to yell: *You fucking bitch! Look what you've done! You've wrecked everything— you'll be without a job and CCT will be left broken!*

So it was probably best that I didn't do any of the talking.

I let Jedtha do the translating for Peter. I figured she might accept this news more readily from an older, white male than she would from me.

Davi sat very still, her face blank, but with a defiant gleam in her eye.

Peter broke the rising tension in the room by clearing his throat. He said: 'Davi, I'm very sorry, but I'm afraid we don't have enough funds for a nurse anymore. So I'm afraid we have to let you go.'

Jedtha translated to Davi. She shook her head and said: 'No. I don't agree.'

Jedtha translated this for Peter, who was shocked into silence for a beat, his eyebrows shooting sky-high. He sputtered: 'What do you mean she doesn't agree? We don't have the money. It's as simple as that.'

Jedtha translated this back to Davi, who shook her head vehemently.

'She still won't accept it,' reported Jedtha.

It was a real face-palm moment. I looked at Peter with eyes that said: 'Oh, fuck it. She's impossible and I'm too tired for this.'

Peter gave me a reassuring tap on the knee, leaned forward and said: 'Look, tell her she can come back to work tomorrow if she wants, but she's Not. Gonna. Get. Paid.'

When that seemed to fall on deaf ears, Jedtha said: 'We need to give her some money. In Cambodia we do like this.'

I rolled my eyes.

'Oh,' Peter said, sounding a bit surprised. 'If this is a cultural thing, why didn't you mention it before? How much does she want, exactly?'

'I think maybe five hundred US dollars is good amount,' Jedtha replied meekly.

I was loath to give this bitch any of the money we'd worked so hard to raise, but it was a way to get her to leave without adding to my ever-growing list of enemies in Battambang. So we agreed. At least now she would go without causing any more problems.

Davi picked up her handbag and left without another word. I was glad to see the back of her, but also deeply sad that it had come to this.

I clambered to my feet, and went out to call the kids into the common room. Peter and I handed out the donated gifts I had brought back in my oversized luggage and watched the kids play with their new presents for a few minutes. Then it was time to break the news to them.

'Okay, everyone. Please stop playing for a minute I have something to tell you . . .' I started crying before I could even get the words out. The happy expressions on their faces faded away and were replaced with looks of deep concern. 'I have to go and live and work in Phnom Penh now, so I won't be at CCT every day anymore.' My voice quivered as I spoke. One by one, the kids all started to cry. 'But you know I love you all very much and I will never leave forever and will come and visit on the weekends as much as I can.'

In hindsight it was really a terrible thing to do to them. I would one day come to learn just how traumatising it was for the kids.

Even at the time, I hated that I was crying. I knew I was only contributing to the levels of distress this news would bring, but I couldn't help it. I could see Sinet trying to be stoic up the back of the room, but with the intense emotional charge in the room, tears were running down her cheeks too.

Even today, if I ever cry at CCT, everyone else will cry with me— the kids and all the staff, too. And then we all laugh and cry at the same time, because it's so funny and sweet.

But this wasn't funny or sweet. It was awful. I felt like such a failure.

~

If my life were a movie, this would be the place to insert a 'sad and lonely in Phnom Penh' montage. It would start with Peter helping me move my bags into a tiny, $5 a night hotel room that I called 'the dog box'. (Picture those horrible concrete cages people put greyhounds in and you get the idea.)

Then zoom in on Peter's face as he looks around the hotel room with a kind of 'Oh dear, you poor kid' expression . . . Then jump-cut to me, dissolving into self-pitying tears. There was a part of me that wished Peter would say: 'Why don't you come home and get back into your film career, Tara?' Not that I would have. But I wished someone would just say it, offer me an out so I could feel I had a choice, that I had chosen to be here . . . alone in my dog box.

Cross-fade to me saying goodbye to Peter at the airport, me looking completely and utterly destroyed as he walks through the gates. In that moment I felt so very small in a very big, scary world.

Then dissolve to me sitting in a bar on the riverfront trying to drown my sorrows by drinking vodka so cheap and nasty it was more like turpentine. I couldn't even get past the second glass. My head slumps into my hands. *I can't even manage to successfully drink my sorrows away—am I destined to fail at every fucking thing I try to do?*

Cut in a few scenes where I sit (alone) in cafes applying for jobs and trying to keep up with donor communications for CCT. Add a truly awful dinner with an aid worker who I thought was a potential friend, but who was only trying to get into my pants and tried to do so quite forcefully.

Cut to me walking home alone through the streets of Phnom Penh as the rain falls in sheets, drenching me to the bone.

Zoom in on an SMS from Carolyn, which says: *I'm so flattered that you feel this way about me, Tara. I adore you and would do anything for you. But I'm afraid I don't feel quite the same way.*

Yep. Lovin' life.

~

It was the loneliest time of my life. I was in limbo—completely cut off from *both* my old lives. I missed the kids. I missed Franky and Rosie and Ruby, who were now under Sinet's care at CCT. I missed Carolyn. I missed Peter, Sue and Noni. I missed my friends. The grief and isolation consumed me.

But it did give me time to lick my wounds and think.

I spent a lot of time reflecting on the role I'd played in the whole mess. Where had I gone wrong to make my team turn on me in such a vicious way?

There had been a lot of fear of being fired coming across in all the accusations, so perhaps the way I'd gone about firing Heng and Reaksmey had been culturally inappropriate. Or perhaps losing my temper in that meeting had a much bigger knock-on effect than I'd first thought . . .

If you lose your temper like that in Australia, it's not good, but you might eventually be forgiven. But you absolutely can't show anger like that in Cambodia. It's just a no-no—anger must be suppressed unless you want to end up on the receiving end of some serious passive-aggression.

Here's what the Lonely Planet guide says about Cambodia: 'No matter how high your blood pressure rises, do not raise your voice or show signs of aggression. This will lead to a "loss of face" and cause embarrassment to the locals, ensuring the situation gets worse rather than better.'

Yeah, that's pretty much what happened. I've seen some awful cases where foreigners trip over this unwritten rule—like a woman I know who yelled at her landlord and ended up getting locked out of her house forever.

In the staff's eyes, I'd completely humiliated myself. And in threatening to fire them—and then firing Reaksmey and Heng—I'd humiliated them, too. But also, I had destroyed any sense of safety they had within CCT. If a leader makes their team feel unsafe and untrusted, things will inevitably start to unravel.

As the author and leadership expert Simon Sinek once said: 'We evolved into social animals, where we lived together and worked together in what I call a circle of safety, inside the tribe, where we felt like we belonged. And when we felt safe amongst our own, the natural reaction was trust and cooperation. There are inherent benefits to this. It means I can fall asleep at night and trust that someone from within my tribe will watch for danger. If we don't trust each other, if I don't trust you, that means you won't watch for danger. Bad system of survival.'

I mused on all sorts of theories during this time, but hiding away in Phnom Penh meant there was no way I could follow up on any of them, so they rolled around and around in my head, keeping me up at night.

Other expats listened sympathetically to my story and said things like: 'Yeah, one of the hardest things about working in Cambodia is working with Cambodian people!' One Australian running another children's organisation in Phnom Penh told me he thought Cambodian people were actually incapable of loving their children . . .

Hearing these sorts of negative sentiments about Cambodian people and Khmer culture wasn't particularly helpful. It only served to justify my feelings of anger, resentment and mistrust. And sometimes these sorts of sweeping generalisations come at you under the banner of sophistication, of 'cultural edification'.

After everything I'd been through, I wasn't quite sure what to believe.

~

The beginning of November 2008 brought with it a three-day public holiday for Bon Om Touk, the Cambodian Water Festival. The festival—which dates back to the twelfth century—celebrates a real wonder of nature: the reversal of the flow of Cambodia's most important body of water, the Tonlé Sap lake and river system.

For most of the year, the Tonlé Sap River flows towards the Mekong River (which runs through China and much of South-East Asia). But when the monsoon season arrives in June, the Tonlé Sap River actually reverses direction. This is because the Mekong rises, causing tonnes of water to flow back into the Tonlé Sap. The Tonlé Sap River swells by up to ten times its size in this period. All kinds of good things happen from there—fish stocks increase, the fields are watered, and silt deposits fertilise the soil. Phnom Penh is the focus of the festivities, so the city goes absolutely mental for the entire three-day holiday.

I decided to escape the craziness and head back to Battambang to spend Bon Om Touk with the kids.

Being back in Battambang felt like arriving home—I had really grown very fond of the sleepy little town. And after the shitty time I'd been having in Phnom Penh, it was wonderful to see the kids again. We spent the three days playing games, listening to Cambodian music and just hanging out.

When it was time to go back to Phnom Penh, I realised I simply couldn't. How could I go back to that dark, lonely city? But how could I stay in Battambang?

I decided to take Peter's advice and move forward. I needed to find a way to let it all go, to forgive, to own up to the role I had played in the problems, to learn my lessons and then continue on with the mission I had taken on the day we rescued the kids.

Fulfilling my responsibilities is important to me. I'm not a martyr, and I believe that everyone's entitled to the best life they can make for themselves and to seek out the things that bring pleasure and happiness. But responsibilities are responsibilities—kids, family, pets . . . They come first, no matter what. The responsibility I took on the day we rescued the kids was not something I took lightly—I knew it was a lifelong commitment. So I suddenly felt extremely guilty for having left them over a bruised ego.

Jedtha seemed over the moon to hear that I was sticking around. I realised how hard things had been for him in my absence, trying to manage on his own. I didn't think it was wise to rush back into working at CCT again, so my plan was to find a job and support myself while I continued to manage CCT's donor relations. It would still be a part-time volunteer role—but much easier to do from Battambang.

With the help of my Aussie friend Terry, I managed to find a job teaching English at the University of Battambang. (Yes, I did find it rather amusing that I'd managed to bypass being a university student and move straight onto being a university teacher. Such is life down the rabbit hole.)

My next task was to find a cheap, safe place for myself and the dogs to live. My salary at the university was only a couple of hundred dollars a month, so I didn't have much of a budget to play with.

I cycled around the streets of Battambang in search of 'for rent' signs in curly Khmer script. Eventually, I found a little attic in this old Khmer guy's home. He seemed a lovely man—his family had all relocated to America, so he was happy to have some company. The attic was a bit decrepit, with gaps in the walls and floor, but it was cheap, and even had a little bathroom and balcony.

What I hadn't quite considered was how hot it would be living in an attic in Cambodia. I only had one floor-standing fan that seemed to prefer to look at the floor. I bought a room thermometer from the local bookshop and put it on the wall above my desk. While punching away at my keyboard, I would watch as the mercury rose—often climbing several degrees above the 40°C mark. I had to take regular fan breaks, squatting on the floor in front of my downward-facing fan just to cool down.

But putting aside the heat, I didn't mind living in the attic. I decorated it with quirky odds and ends I found around Battambang, and cheap, multicoloured fabric that I turned into curtains.

Ruby and Rosie and Franky weren't thrilled. My landlord had a couple of scruffy little dogs of his own who wouldn't allow my dogs to enter their territory. So Ruby, Rosie and Franky were mostly confined to the house or my balcony.

But at least they could sun themselves during the day and curl up on my bed at night. It was so good for me to have them around again.

~

I soon found myself thoroughly enjoying being back in Battambang. It's such a pretty, friendly, easy little town to live in. Life flows along at a much more relaxed pace than in Phnom Penh, and after everything I'd been through the quiet life felt good.

My job at the uni kind of sucked, though. It reminded me of the stuffy, sterile environment I'd hated so much at school. Also, truth be known, I wasn't all that good at it. Hardly surprising, really. The education system in Cambodia still relies heavily on rote learning. So while the students couldn't string a sentence together in English, they were experts on the twelve different grammatical tenses. I appreciate good grammar and spelling, but when the students quizzed me on the difference between past perfect tense and past perfect progressive tense it felt like a big neon sign was flashing above my head saying FRAUD! FRAUD! FRAUD!

That's probably why, over time, I gradually let myself get pulled back into taking on more work at CCT. This was what I was good at.

At first, I spent the bare minimum amount of time at CCT, just keeping our new donors informed about where their money was going. I took photos, made short videos, wrote up reports and letters of thanks. This meant spending more time with the kids, which was a balm to my sore and bruised soul.

And although Jedtha, Meah and Savenh and I were still coldly professional with each other, I could see that they genuinely did want to mend fences. Especially Jedtha. He clearly felt awful about everything that had happened and wanted to have me back full time. And it wasn't just the security of funding he was after; he missed having someone to bounce ideas off and share in the decision-making. Until he (in my eyes) threw me to the wolves, Jedtha and I had been good friends and a good team. We worked well together.

One of the most daunting tasks required at CCT was updating (and in some cases creating from scratch) the huge volume of policies, procedures and forms CCT needed in order to comply with government requirements and ensure we were operating in line with best practices. I wasn't quite ready to come back full time, but I agreed to step up my involvement and help with this task. So we put aside our differences and soon I was working more hours at CCT than I was at the university.

We had to rework and draft dozens of new policy documents, including guidelines for general operations as well as a child protection policy and a code of conduct, redrafted by-laws, HR policies and finance policies, and updated case files for all the kids. Then we had to actually implement these policies to ensure the whole team understood them—and that there would be zero tolerance for any form of abuse or corruption at CCT. We also had to draft position descriptions for the new roles we needed. Then draft job ads. Then interview and draw up work contracts and ensure new staff were up to speed with all CCT policies, and on and on it went . . .

It was a daunting task, and really, we only made a start. But on the upside, CCT was soon back in full swing. Additions to the team included: a new house mother, an eternally bright and chirpy soul named Rouet; a new house father, Samnang; a new cook, Noit; and a Khmer arts and literature teacher, Journ. Having new people in the mix, untainted by past events, injected a new spirit into CCT. There were no more jokes or chummy little chats between me and the team, but I started enjoying the atmosphere there much more after that.

~

Around this time, Kanya's older sister Kolab, who had left SKO before the rescue and who we were helping to support, graduated from beauty school in Phnom Penh and moved back to Battambang.

By now I'd met the girls' mother. She was a sweet and devoutly Buddhist little lady who was badly crippled after being beaten by the girls' father. She would almost bowl me over every time I met her, showering me in hugs and lots of Khmer kisses—the ones where they try to inhale you with deep sniffs.

When the kids' father died, their mother and her three small grandchildren, whom she was supporting, fell into desperate poverty. For a long time, unknown to us, Kanya gave every cent of her pocket money to her mother.

CCT had just made an investment in Kolab's education so she could become independent, but now she had a mother who was too frail and sick to work and three little nieces and nephews who were really doing it tough. This meant that as soon as Kolab started to earn an income she'd be giving almost all of it to her mum. However, the salary Kolab would earn as an entry-level beautician would not be enough to support herself and four others. So she would have to find a second job, and maybe even a third, as do so many Cambodians who live below the poverty line.

If Kolab was solely responsible for supporting the whole family during this pivotal time at the beginning of her career, she would almost certainly struggle to get ahead in life. One day in the future, when her little sister Kanya has finished school and is earning a decent wage, the burden on Kolab might be a bit less. But even then, things would be hard going for both girls—especially when their own children came along.

In Australia, by paying tax we all financially contribute to support-ing disadvantaged communities and people who can't work. We do this not only out of humanity and to protect the most vulnerable in our society, but because we know that there are dire consequences for entire communities when people with no alternatives are left without any means of survival. An elderly woman with no income and a dis-ability, who was the primary carer for her three grandchildren, would definitely fall into this category. But for now, because social services in Cambodia are so inadequate, it's predominantly NGOs who fill this gap. I wanted the girls to be free to build a better life for themselves and the families they would have in the future without being held back by having to help their mother raise their nieces and nephews. So we provided a modest living allowance for the girls' mum that would enable her to support her grandchildren. The girls could then see that their family was okay and focus on building their own futures.

This was the beginning of CCT's family preservation work—where we finally developed the sibling reunification program into what was *actually* required in order to keep families together. Today, we have much more structured systems in place, which include a framework to manage the support payments that CCT provides.

~

In mid-November, the prosecutor at the Battambang court called and asked Sinet to attend a meeting with Rath at the courthouse.

It was quite a scary time for both of us.

We hired an extra daytime security guard so that the CCT staff and kids would be protected at all times. The guard helped to escort Sinet and the other kids to and from school throughout this period. I didn't feel particularly safe in my attic at night, but at least I had the dogs.

Jedtha found out that Rath had recruited another dozen or so children into SKO to make up the numbers he'd lost. I could hardly sleep at night thinking about those poor kids used as commodities to raise funds. It was incredibly frustrating that over the past eighteen months we hadn't been able to get his operation shut down. All of our hopes hung on getting a successful prosecution, but we still had a long way to go. We hoped this meeting with the prosecutor would be the final step towards getting a fair trial.

On the day of the meeting, Sinet remained very calm and resolute, even though the imposing courthouse and uniformed officials were incredibly intimidating for her. But Rath didn't even turn up. Jedtha told me he heard that Rath had gone to the border, ready to escape to Thailand if the court issued a warrant for his arrest.

The prosecutor quizzed Sinet on the details surrounding the evidence she had provided about each of the times Rath had raped her. She answered everything clearly and accurately, as she had every time before. Her story didn't waver and she never hesitated or flinched as the prosecutor pried into the painful details. I watched her with a sense of mounting horror at what they were putting her through, but I was also in awe of her courage and strength.

But we never did get a trial.

Maybe this was due to corruption. Or maybe the evidence really was just insufficient.

We continued to live under a dark cloud, constantly worrying about what Rath or his people might do to us.

We were all terribly disappointed.

~

I very much wish we'd been able to see justice served for Sinet. It definitely would have been better for her if we had. She struggled with it for a long time. It was hard for her to feel safe in Battambang, knowing that Rath was still out there, and still running SKO.

~

In time I came to learn that the corruption at SKO was not an isolated or even uncommon occurrence.

But in the days before I understood this, before government and independent reports revealed some shocking truths about orphanages in Cambodia, we just continued on, doing our best to connect the kids with siblings and family where we could, but ultimately believing we were still doing a good thing by running a 'good orphanage'.

We had a lot to learn.

~

Not long after Sinet's case was closed, one of CCT's most dedicated supporters asked me to bring a few of the kids to a fundraiser for CCT that she was putting on in Singapore. It would be our biggest fundraiser to date and she would be taking care of all the logistics and organisation of the event, so all we had to do was turn up! It was an enormously generous offer that would bring a huge injection of funding, our biggest to date. We agreed without hesitation.

However, 'just turning up' would still be quite a big undertaking. We'd have to get passports issued and book flights and inform Social Affairs and pull the kids out of school for a few days ... But if the event was successful, we figured it would be worth it, and it would be *such* an exciting experience for the kids.

I was pretty insistent that Rouet, our house mother, would have to come, too. If taking kids to Phnom Penh by myself had been an issue, I would certainly not be taking them out of the country on my own. We decided to choose five kids who had been putting in the most effort at school, and who we thought would be best equipped to handle the trip. That turned out to be Makara, Tula, Mao, Rithy and Sinet.

Rouet and the kids had a ball in Singapore—Rouet's mind was blown by all the big buildings and her enjoyment of the adventure was contagious. The fundraiser, too, was a huge success. Having those adorable, polite, charismatic little children up on stage performing 'You Are My Sunshine' definitely won over many hearts that night.

But taking the kids to help me raise funds isn't something I would do today. Even at that time, I remember looking at the kids onstage and feeling slightly uncomfortable about it. Even though they had agreed to do the fundraiser and were excited about it, they were clearly nervous and a little bewildered by all the attention. I wondered if they actually did want to be there, up on the stage with all eyes on them. Had they agreed just to please me? How could they have known in advance what that was going to be like?

Eventually, I came to understand that there are some important ethical questions to be posed around using children in this way to incite people to give money. Kids in some orphanages perform like dancing bears night after night for tourists and supporters. For these visitors, the experience doesn't feel harmful because the kids look like they're enjoying themselves—indeed, some of them genuinely do enjoy it; a lot of kids actually volunteer to perform.

Similarly, when NGOs get kids to speak to the public about their histories of poverty and abuse, it can be a powerful experience for the audience, and many children volunteer to take part. But using kids to raise money for an organisation that they are supposed to be a beneficiary of is a big burden to place on their small shoulders.

Especially when the subtext is clearly: 'Look at how poverty hasn't crushed their sweet little spirits thanks to the wonderful NGO supporting them!'

The problem is that it is almost impossible to use beneficiaries to raise money without perpetuating 'poor third-world people saved by a Western NGO' stereotypes. And stereotyping can do terrible harm to people's confidence and sense of themselves. Becoming poster children for the issue of poverty can also harm their reputation in the community they live in and impact on their future employment prospects.

This dilemma gets thorny because, in order for people to care enough to give money, they need to understand the problem. How do you help people understand poverty without showing them what poverty looks like?

I do understand that this issue is not black and white and there are exceptions. Even today I'm constantly caught in the tug-of-war between needing to raise funds and wanting to protect CCT's beneficiaries from exploitation. I know if I did paint depressing stories of the kids' lives, or make them sing and dance for donations, we'd raise a lot more money. But the beneficiaries of any NGO have a right to dignity and privacy. And Cambodia deserves better than the 'poor third world' tropes that present a distorted image of what is, in reality, a beautiful and diverse country.

Today, our policy is that only our staff can help us with fund-raising events—this includes Sinet, who is now a part-time casual member of the CCT team. When we do tell stories, we change the names and identifying details to protect privacy. We try very hard not to use stereotypes and to show only dignified, empowered images of our beneficiaries. It's never straightforward. Even with adult beneficiaries, there's a big question mark around whether they're truly able to provide ethical, informed consent when asked to appear in a photograph or video or have their story told in print. But today we have policies and guidelines on identity protection and informed consent. They help guide us and our beneficiaries through the process of informed consent to ensure best practices are maintained.

Even so, it's a difficult line to walk and every time it comes up, we really wrestle with the ethics of it.

~

I was still trying to process my mixed feelings about taking the kids to Singapore when I got back to CCT. So it was a particular shock to me to discover that there were suddenly three more kids at CCT.

They were lovely kids, incredibly sweet and well mannered. But where had they come from?

'A village chief called DoSVY about a family who were struggling to support their six kids, so DoSVY asked us to investigate,' Jedtha explained. 'The parents are good people but very poor. Savenh and I agreed to bring three of the kids to CCT.'

I was quite stunned to hear this—I thought Jedtha and the rest of the staff fully understood what we were trying to do with our new family reunion projects.

'But—oh dear. But *Loak Khrew*, we want CCT to keep families together, not split them up, remember?' I spluttered. 'Poverty is not a good reason for children to be taken away from their parents and put in an orphanage. And what about their siblings who were left behind? What will become of them? Are they now just sentenced to a life of poverty?'

It was a horrible situation to be in. After everything we'd just been through, the last thing I wanted was to have to veto one of Jedtha's decisions. It just goes to show how deeply hard-wired the reflex to put children in orphanages is in Cambodia.

Jedtha had just done the right thing as far as most Cambodians saw it. A 2011 UNICEF report found that over 90 per cent of Cambodians believe that children should be sent to live in orphanages if their family is too poor to support them. The thinking is: *They'll get fed, they'll get healthcare, they'll get an education . . .*

This is a sad and quite recent change in attitude. In Cambodian culture, family is extremely important. Cambodian people are likely to remain living in multi-generational households their entire lives and traditionally Cambodians have cared for vulnerable and orphaned children through informal kinship care (which just means being cared for by a member of one's extended family—aunts, uncles, grandparents, adult siblings or family friends).

But this culture of family-based care has been eroded by a belief that orphanages are the best way to ensure a good future for disadvantaged children.

The flaws inherent in this way of responding to poverty are bigger and deeper than I suspected at the time. I was only just starting to catch on to the fact that parents in Cambodia were reflexively putting their kids into orphanages in response to the problems posed by poverty, not the lack of family. The issues with separating kids from their families were not an easy 'get' for anyone—especially for Jedtha and the staff, who lived in a world where, for decades, residential care had been widely seen as the only option.

But Jedtha listened with an open mind and took it all on board. We decided we should go back out to the village where the kids' family lived to meet the parents and assess the situation properly.

~

The following day, Jedtha, Savenh and I jumped on the motos and travelled down a dusty dirt road to a village about an hour out of Battambang city. We pulled up out the front of a traditional wooden home on stilts.

The parents of the three new kids were outside preparing food; their father was stoking the fire while their mother chopped vegetables. We sat down on a wooden log and chatted with them.

They were very sweet-natured people who loved their kids. They explained that they had farming skills and even some land of their own behind the house. They hoped to farm it, but hadn't been able to raise the capital to buy the water pump and other equipment they needed to get started. With six children to support, they were really struggling. Sending three of the kids away to a place where they'd be fed and educated seemed like their only option.

But all they needed to start generating more income and keep the family together was some extra farming equipment. That was it! We agreed to buy them the equipment, as well as some bicycles so the kids could get to school—this would cost us far less than keeping the kids at CCT and it would mean the family could stay together.

Both parents were overjoyed with this idea and excited to have their children back. The kids were delighted, too.

When a family is too poor to support their own children, the answer should never be to remove the children from their family. The solution is to empower the family to be better able to care for their own children. And it is significantly more cost effective to support children in their family than to support them in residential care.

Once Jedtha saw with his own eyes that this approach was much better than just bringing kids who still had homes and families to CCT, he was able to explain it to the rest of the staff and put it into practice himself.

~

Around this same time, the Commune Leader of a village about twenty minutes out of Battambang asked us to take in a fourteen-year-old girl to live at CCT who'd recently been raped. The girl lived with her mother in a small village, but the perpetrator lived nearby and the mother was desperate to protect her daughter.

When the mother met us, her face lit up with hope. 'Please please will you take her with you to the *onga*?' Her attitude seemed to be: 'Thank you, good white person! Please save my daughter and put her on the path of opportunity!'

It made me want to cry. It was such a typical example of the help-less, defeated attitude I was starting to see everywhere. I understood her plight but taking this young girl away from a loving, protective mother was not the right thing to do. The perpetrator needed to be removed, not the victim!

There was a time when we'd have snatched the young girl up and 'saved' her by taking her away from her family and community. But we knew better, now. So we worked with this family to help them report the case to the police and get the girl's attacker arrested. And it worked. Getting a perpetrator convicted for rape is difficult, but it's not impossible.

Even if we hadn't been able to get a successful conviction, we could have assisted with temporary, alternative accommodation for the mother and her daughter, engaged the support of their community and commune leaders, and provided counselling and rehabilitation to the perpetrator. There are always other steps that can be taken to avoid the unnecessary institutionalisation of children with loving families.

I'm always saying to my team: if you want to see the problems that might result from a particular approach or practice, scale it up. When you scale it up as a thought experiment in your head, the potential problems start to jump out at you.

When you see a child in a high-risk environment, like this young girl who'd been raped, removing her from the situation to keep her safe feels like the right thing to do. But what happens if you remove all the children in Cambodia who are living in high-risk environments and put them in an orphanage? You'll find yourself institutionalising a very large percentage of the population, separating them from their families and communities. If a large percentage of the population grows up in an institution, the community pays a huge price for this in the future. Growing up without a good role model of what a family looks like affects people's ability to parent the next generation. So the problems are passed on and the intergenerational cycle of poverty continues.

We learned this lesson once before in Australia—we call it 'The Stolen Generations'.

17

In late November 2008, I drove down to Phnom Penh to pick up Charlie Teo from the airport.

I couldn't believe a busy guy like Charlie would really make time to visit us, but here we were, on a Thursday afternoon, me and the famous brain surgeon, driving to Battambang in CCT's van with Bob Dylan blasting from the car stereo.

Charlie loved every minute of the drive. The lovely rice paddies, the truck-boys riding on top of sky-high semitrailer loads of plastic bottles, the tractors towing metal cages full of commuters. We saw a three-metre blue teddy bear attached to the back of a bicycle, a guy carrying a sow upside down across the back of his motorbike, a cloud of brightly coloured helium balloons floating above the back of a moto... Charlie was mesmerised.

We stopped for petrol at a stand beside the road. I paid the guy who ran the stand and he promptly handed me a used Coke bottle full of petrol.

Charlie was amused. 'Is this how everyone here sells petrol?'

I just smiled. I knew it seemed strange, but it was just part of everyday life to me.

'Where do you want to stay?' I asked on approach to Battambang. 'The hotels here range anywhere from five to a hundred dollars a night.'

'I'll just crash with you,' Charlie said.

'Oh, you'd be very welcome, of course, but I'm not exactly set up for visitors. I don't even have a spare couch to offer you,' I suddenly felt very self-conscious about my living arrangements.

'Do you have a spare pillow? I'll just sleep on the floor. I often get home late after a long surgery and just pass out the floor. I'm not fussy.'

'Okay . . . if you're sure,' I replied. 'I've also got no air-con and no mosquito nets . . . Don't say I didn't warn you!'

After doing a quick turn around Battambang's scary roundabout-god, we went to CCT and introduced Charlie to the staff and the kids. He soon had the kids giggling and stepping on each other's heads to get his attention.

A visit from Charlie turned out to be like a visit from Santa—if Santa was a super-fit, motorbike-riding neurosurgeon with a broad Aussie accent and a drawer full of speeding tickets.

When the sun started to go down, Charlie said, 'What time do the kids have dinner? Let's take them out!'

So we ferried the kids to an all-you-can-eat Korean barbecue place in town. It was terrific fun.

We dropped the kids at CCT after dinner and headed back to my dark, hot little attic.

On the way Charlie was raving. 'The kids seem so happy! You're doing an amazing—' He stopped mid-sentence. 'Why are you driving like an old lady?'

'The headlights have blown,' I told him.

'You've got to be kidding me!' Charlie grinned. 'You're crazy!'

Charlie's a fellow dog tragic, and I had spent a good part of the drive to Battambang raving about them. The dogs cried and sang with joy as they heard me getting out of the car.

'Oh, they've missed you!' Charlie observed, as he followed me up the rickety steps. Rosie cried, span in circles, jumped in the air, rolled over—all in one fluid movement. Franky howled and wagged his tail so hard his whole body was wiggling.

Charlie fussed over the dogs as I unlocked the door, hoping I'd left the place in a decent state. The dogs bolted in after me and Charlie followed.

'Well, welcome to my humble abode,' I said, snatching up some dirty clothes I'd left in a pile on the floor.

'Yep, it's certainly pretty humble,' he said with a rueful smile.

'You sure you're happy on the floor? It's not too late to take you to a hotel.'

'Nah! Just chuck me a pillow and I'll be out like a light in minutes,' Charlie said.

As I drifted off to sleep, surrounded by my three sooky dogs, I thought to myself: *Man, my life is weird. There's a world famous neuro-surgeon sleeping on my floor.*

~

The next day, Charlie insisted we take the van to a mechanic to have the lights fixed. Then he bought a bunch of tools from the markets in town. He set to work repairing the fittings on my door so that it closed properly. Then he made a bunch of minor repairs to the CCT house, too.

While he was playing Mr Fix It, he got me to tell him more about CCT and my plans for the future. He seemed completely bowled over by everything he heard. He was so vocal and genuine it was incredibly uplifting. It's often hard to see past the flaws in your own project. Incessant problem-solving ends up being the default focus. This was the first time I really saw CCT through someone else's eyes.

That night I took Charlie to the Riverside Balcony Bar. We ate burgers and mingled with the expat crowd a little.

I struck up a conversation in Khmer with one of the local bar staff who immediately did a double take.

'Are you Khmer?' she asked sounding a bit confused. 'Is your mother Khmer or something?'

'No, sister, I'm Australian.'

'Wow! Unbelievable! You speak Khmer so well! How long have you been here?' she asked.

'About a year and a half.'

'A YEAR AND A HALF?!' she shrieked, slamming her hand down on the wooden bar. 'That's unbelievable!' Then she turned and said to Charlie in English, 'Your friend, she's amazing! She speaks Khmer so beautifully—she sounds just like Cambodian people!'

'Why does that not surprise me?' Charlie said, giving me a nudge with his elbow.

I won't deny I was pleased that happened while Charlie was there.

We talked intently about CCT for some time that night. Then he said: 'You know, I really like your approach. You're obviously a natural leader, and your focus on long-term gains rather than short-term satisfaction is really quite astounding—especially for someone so young. I think it will stand you in good stead in the years to come. I know things are a bit tough right now, but I have a feeling there are great things to come for you and CCT...'

'Oh, wow,' I mumbled, feeling quite stunned by such generous feedback.

'I'm going to help you,' Charlie declared.

~

The next day I put Charlie in a taxi back to Phnom Penh. His visit—and his enthusiasm, encouragement and praise—was just the boost I'd needed.

'I'll be back again soon,' he promised me. 'I'll bring the whole family next time.'

Then he pulled a card out of his pocket and handed it to me. It was a gold credit card.

'Pull out a thousand dollars every day and don't stop until it's empty,' he said. 'You need to stop teaching at the university and focus on CCT. When I get home I'm going to donate enough funds for a salary for you so you can move into a decent house. Your dogs need a yard and you deserve some basic comforts, too. It's important for the longevity of you *and* CCT.'

At first, I was almost too gobsmacked to speak. 'Oh. My. God . . .' was all I managed to say as I held the card limply in my hand.

Charlie just laughed.

'Charlie! My goodness!' Now the words tumbled out of me. 'I don't know what to say . . . This is just unbelievable. And amazing. Holy shit!'

Charlie laughed again. 'You deserve it. Trust me.'

I was still gushing my appreciation as his taxi pulled away.

Having someone give me such a vote of confidence, just when I had been struggling so badly . . . It was completely transformational. A big wave of adrenaline rushed through me. With that sudden surge of energy, I turned and bolted up the stairs, and proceeded to leap around my little attic like an idiot, much to the delight of Ruby, Rosie and Franky.

~

As soon as Charlie got back to Australia, he fulfilled his promises. He made an incredibly generous donation to CCT and an ongoing donation that allowed for me to live modestly but comfortably for several months to come and (yippee!) give up my job at the university.

It was like being sprung from prison. My brain started racing with all the things that we needed to do—and that we could do now.

Thanks to Charlie's sponsorship, and at his suggestion, I moved into a new house with a lot more space and natural light, and with a yard for the dogs. I didn't have a stick of furniture, so I rattled around the big echoing rooms. But it was definitely more comfortable than the attic.

Carolyn, who had gone quiet since the SMS exchange in Phnom Penh, started sending me regular emails again. Those emails had me bouncing out of bed in the morning so I could send off a reply before heading to CCT. The happiness I got from that crush fuelled me all day long. Every time anything remotely interesting happened, I'd make a mental note to include it in my next email, or use it as an excuse to text her.

Soon we were sending emails and texts back and forth all day and night. Even though I knew there was a risk that she'd shut it down again, I couldn't help but get swept up in the romance of it all. I was so love-sick I lost my appetite, couldn't sleep, and in every spare moment was lost in a daydream—I was addicted to that dopamine rush of seeing a message from her pop up on my phone.

~

About a month after Charlie's visit, I got an email from an Australian expat named Gerard ('call me Baz') Basili. Baz, a pharmacist, was working as a volunteer with the Sihanouk Hospital of Hope in Phnom Penh, educating staff and improving operations at the hospital's pharmacy. He'd heard about my problems getting decent medical care for the kids from some other expats in Phnom Penh (who I'd met through Charlie). He said that if CCT needed any medical-related assistance, he'd be more than happy to help.

Baz is an upbeat, larger-than-life boy from Perth. His first self-appointed task was to review all our medical processes and medical files and review all the treatment plans for the kids with chronic illnesses. He made a special trip up to Battambang to conduct the assessment.

By going through the files, he discovered that the results from Nimol's viral load test for hepatitis B were a cause for great concern and the medication we'd been provided seemed to be having no real effect. Makara's viral load wasn't great, either. But before I had a chance to start wringing my hands over this revelation, Baz had delivered calm, matter-of-fact reassurance that all would be well. Both boys just needed to be put on an antiretroviral regime and monitored regularly. Fortunately, the other kids with hepatitis B were doing well, but he also put them on to the schedule for regular, ongoing monitoring.

It was such a huge relief to finally have someone on board who was so very experienced and capable, not just in the field of medicine, but also on the ground in Cambodia. Baz has endless empathy for Cambodian people and is always willing to help, without ever wanting anything in return.

He helped us put new policies and protocols in place and establish a triage system. He then set up a simple yet comprehensive home pharmacy at CCT with good-quality, registered drugs. He provided training for the staff and me, and made a second copy of all the medical files. That meant that no matter where he was, he could always look things up and offer recommendations and advice, and ensure the treatment being provided by local doctors was following best practice. For me it was as if not just a breath, but a tornado of fresh air had blown through CCT.

The best part of Baz's visit was when he sat down with Sinet's sister, our gentle, sweet Sineit.

Sineit understood all too well what it meant to have HIV. She had seen both her parents die in terrible pain from AIDS. She was often sick and knew that, like her parents, her days were numbered. She had come to accept that she'd never have a husband or child, but she couldn't stop dreaming of being a wife and mother herself one day. She devoured romance novels and spent all her spare time helping to 'mother' the youngest kids at CCT and had developed a particularly close bond with Sovanni.

Sineit, Baz and I sat around the pink stone table in the CCT court-yard. I translated as Baz said: 'Sineit, I have some very good news for you. There are new HIV treatment regimes available at the Hope Clinic in Phnom Penh. I've organised for you to be treated there.'

I translated this, and Sineit smiled politely and said, 'Thank you,' in her soft, sweet voice.

'If you follow the doctor's instructions and do your best to take good care of your health, then you can expect to live a long life. A normal life, with good health and almost no effects of HIV.' Baz grinned.

The tears began welling up in my eyes—and hers—as I translated. 'And one day, when you have a partner, we can help you have a baby. And we can make sure that both your partner and the baby remain HIV negative.'

Sineit burst into real tears now—tears of surprise and joy. That set me off too; even Baz was weeping by now.

All the tough times I'd been through since moving to Cambodia suddenly melted away. It had all been worth it.

Sometimes, doctors ask me if I have a medical background, because in those early days of CCT I became something of a walking encyclopaedia of tropical medicine. But I was just trying to ensure the kids were getting adequate healthcare, and that required a very steep learning curve. It had been stressful and utterly terrifying at times. Having Baz on board changed everything. After two years of feeling like I was battling through it alone, I finally had a dedicated medical professional on my side.

These days CCT has a local team of Cambodian medical professionals running our medical outreach program. Baz is still on our medical advisory board, helping the team to access quality healthcare. It is a still a very challenging task.

~

I was still on a high from Baz and Charlie's visits when an ABC producer named Ben Cheshire got in touch. He said they'd made up their mind—they *would* like to feature me on the *Australian Story* program.

A wave of anxiety crashed over me. I knew I couldn't say 'no' to an opportunity like this to reach new supporters, but just the thought of being on TV made my heart start racing. For the first time in a while, a familiar feeling seemed to come over and tap me on the shoulder ... *'Hey, maybe you should skip dinner tonight.'*

~

Having new funds in place—and knowing more were coming—meant we could take the risk of investing in some much-needed support. Our most pressing need was to have a consultant in child psychology come and do a full assessment of our practices, and advise us on how we could best support the kids going forward.

Essentially, all the kids were doing quite well in their day-to-day lives. They were happy and playful and came home from school each day with stories of success. They were also starting to get pretty good grades. Most of the kids amazed me with their resilience, and seemed really well-adjusted. But others did show worrying signs of inner turmoil.

Many of the kids wolfed down their meals in a desperate hurry, as if terrified the food would be taken from them. Some of the younger kids would playfully bite and smack me and the other staff in an attempt to get attention. There were some instances where kids wouldn't think to mention that they were sick or in pain.

Rithy was still hoarding things. Under his mattress, there always seemed to be a stockpile of seemingly useless junk. He was also painfully shy, often finding it very hard even to make eye contact.

Makara had improved a lot since our trip to Phnom Penh. He was still telling the kids not to fight, and would declare piously that children shouldn't play with toy guns, because guns were bad and hurt people. He was going out of his way to be the 'good boy' he knew we wanted him to be. But from time to time that temper would still surface and give everyone an awful shock.

Some of the kids—like Akara, the little girl we'd met at the lawyer's office—were still extremely aloof and withdrawn. Akara could barely speak above a whisper and would never join in with group activities.

Whenever we left the CCT grounds for an excursion, she would get panicky and have to run to the toilet over and over again. I could set my watch by her little voice crying, 'Tara! *Chu ju ait!*'

She also fidgeted an awful lot, and was unable to sit still for very long. She'd constantly stand up, adjust her pants and sit back down, only to repeat the action a couple of minutes later.

One day, the school called Savenh to inform us that Akara had collapsed in the playground and was completely unresponsive. Another kid had been pushing her on a swing and didn't stop when she asked her to. Akara had just fallen off the swing into unconsciousness.

Savenh and I rushed her to hospital and called Baz en route. I was terrified that she had concussion. But the doctor confirmed that there was no head injury. He said it was just a panic attack.

Just a panic attack! I thought to myself. *What sort of panic attack makes a child fall unconscious?!* I worried about her constantly.

My dream of finding a child psychologist in Cambodia had long died, so I looked for options elsewhere. I'd been very impressed with the therapist I'd seen about my eating disorder when I was in Australia a few years earlier. Her name was Anna, and she was now doing further studies at Lancaster University, specialising in work with traumatised young refugees and asylum seekers. She had a keen interest in eastern and cross-cultural psychology.

She agreed to fly over and undertake the assessment as part of her studies.

I was excited about Anna's upcoming visit. I was also amazed and humbled that someone who knew the gory details of my eating disorder—something I still felt so deeply ashamed about—would think me worthy enough to know and help, outside the walls of a therapist's office.

~

It was lovely to see such a familiar and comforting face when Anna arrived in Battambang. The night she arrived, we went to dinner at the White Rose to discuss her plans for the workshops with the staff.

'I'd like to base some of the initial sessions on attachment theory,' Anna told me in her soft Mancunian lilt. 'We'll draw on the staff's expertise to ensure these workshops are culturally relevant, of course, but I do think this is our best starting point.'

She reached into her backpack, pulled out a couple of books and pressed them into my hands. They were titled *Nurturing Attachments: Supporting children who are fostered or adopted* by Kim S. Golding and *Why Love Matters: How affection shapes a baby's brain* by Sue Gerhardt.

I scanned the backs of the books while she explained. 'Attachment theory is one of the major ideas underpinning modern-day developmental psychology. It explains how the relationships we form in childhood with our primary carers have a direct impact on the way our brain develops. We're all born with a need to form long-lasting, affectionate attachments. If a child has at least one secure, ongoing relationship with a stable adult—someone who loves them and makes them feel safe—they're likely to grow up into well-adjusted adults. The adult doesn't need to be at the child's beck and call—that can cause problems too—but they do need to be there for them and attentive *most* of the time.'

Anna then went on to explain that kids can fail to form secure attachments as a result of neglect, abuse, abrupt separation from parents or a high turnover of caregivers.

I thought guiltily about how we'd been doing things at CCT—firing staff, hiring new staff, the shift work of the current house parents, all the coming and going I had done . . . It had been obvious that there was something unhealthy about how the kids attached to the adults in their lives and now I was beginning to understand why.

I started bombarding Anna with more questions, but she gestured for me to keep eating my dinner. 'Don't worry,' she said. 'We'll go through all of this in the workshops. If you like, you and I can do separate sessions, just the two of us. We'll be able to move through all the material a lot quicker that way, and then you'll be able to help explain it to the staff.'

I went home that evening and read for hours, devouring the words on those pages as if I was reading a thriller, bouncing from one epiphany to the next. I was desperate to know more, to understand more.

Human beings and their problems are, of course, far too complicated to cover in a few textbooks. We should never swallow any one theory or study whole—it's good to question, to be sceptical—that's how science works. But the books did give me a completely new way of thinking about where some of the kids' issues might have been coming from.

And attachment theory—at least for now—is a widely respected way of understanding and treating the problems that manifest in childhood development. At the time, the case studies in Kim S. Golding's book about how attachment disorders manifested in children who had been separated from their parents rang eerily true to me. Several of them did sound like the kind of experiences some of our kids were having.

> Marcus finds it very difficult to stay still or concentrate on anything for very long. He can become excited or angry very easily and then becomes very difficult to manage . . . Sometimes Marcus feels very sad. He cannot cope with feeling sad; when he was little, feeling sad did not lead to comfort. Marcus has learnt that he can stop the feelings of sadness by being angry.

This case study was about a little boy who had developed a 'disorganised-controlling attachment relationship', which happens when primary caregivers are frightened, or frightening to the child. This seemed to correspond with what Makara went through as a child.

Then there was the case study of a little girl with an 'avoidant' attachment pattern.

> Catherine behaves [towards her foster parents] as if she does
> not expect them to be available and responsive. She makes few
> demands on them, plays on her own, and if upset makes little
> fuss . . . A few months after she came to live with them [her
> foster father] took Catherine to the dentist. He was amazed to
> be told she had a nasty abscess at the back of her mouth; she
> had given no sign of discomfort.

This did sound rather like Sovanni, the baby we'd picked up from her grandmother. She never cried—she'd just go off and soothe herself if she was upset. This kind of fierce independence is unusual in Cambodia, which is a very baby-oriented culture as a rule, but this little girl had suffered terrible neglect before she came to us.

The next case study was of a child with an ambivalent-resistant attachment pattern. In this case, the caregiver is *sometimes* responsive, but is *usually* insensitive, unresponsive and unavailable.

> Zoe learned to demand attention, expecting inconsistency and
> unpredictability . . . [She] works so hard at getting attention
> that she knows she is a nuisance. When her parents or teachers
> get frustrated with her this just confirms that she is naughty
> and that she won't get attention when she needs it . . . It is as if
> they think 'I don't know if you will be there when I need you so
> I am going to make sure that you are there for me all the time.'

One of our little girls, Jendar, fitted that description. I used to call her 'cheeky monkey'. She'd smack your bum if you paid attention to someone else and not to her. She'd shower you in hugs and kisses and sing little songs that went: 'I love you, I love you!' It just seemed like cute, cheeky behaviour, so it was upsetting to think that there might have been something dysfunctional behind it all.

The next case study was about a little boy with a 'non-attachment' style. This happens to kids who are subject to severe neglect.

> Luke expects little of parents but looks for attention indiscriminately from the range of people he meets during the day . . . At six, Luke is still not properly toilet trained. He will wet or soil his bed but appears not to notice . . . Luke eats voraciously, whatever is put in front of him. He also tries to secrete food in his bedroom, hiding it in unlikely places . . . Luke's impulsivity can lead to situations that are very alarming . . . [Luke's foster parent] fears that Luke would go with anyone that held out a hand at the right time.

Oh dear—I'd met so many children in orphanages that could have fit that description since I'd arrived in Cambodia . . .

Of course, it's unwise to go around diagnosing and pathologising children when you don't have formal training, but it was helpful to understand the kinds of issues that the kids might be facing, now and in later life, if they weren't brought up with secure attachments.

I couldn't wait to see if Anna could help us put all this knowledge into practice.

~

The workshops went painfully slowly at first, because some of the concepts were so hard to translate into Khmer. We hired a translator to facilitate the meetings, and Jedtha and I helped out where we could.

Anna began with the key ideas behind attachment theory and the different ways attachment disorders manifested. Then we talked through some specific cases of the kids at CCT who the staff were most worried about.

I was still keeping the staff at arm's length, so it was a bit of a revelation to me to see how enthusiastic they all were about helping the kids. They seemed to really love having the chance to talk through some of the challenges they were facing, and to get Anna's expert opinion on ways they could work through those problems. After finding it all such a revelation myself, it was wonderful to see the lights go on in everyone's eyes.

Given how cold I'd been feeling towards Savenh, our social worker, it was good for me to see that she was genuinely inspired. She was one of the first to go: 'Ah! I just thought Jendar was naughty! But actually, she's trying to get attention because she's worried she'll be abandoned again!'

Jedtha was right about Savenh, it seemed. She truly was very enthusiastic about understanding the kids.

I remember seeing the moment our new house father Samnang's brain exploded. He was sitting on the floor, holding his chin while Anna talked, his face intense. He suddenly put a hand up and yelled: 'Wait, hold on, oh my god, I've just got to stop for a minute. This is so *deep*.'

We all laughed, because it was so true.

Anna explained to us that a lot of the behaviours we were seeing in the kids were unconscious 'safety behaviours' which were likely to have originated from earlier traumatic experiences, like being abruptly separated from family, or like the neglect and sexual abuse that happened at SKO. The only way to really help them grow out of these behaviours was to ensure that these kids could establish a secure attachment to a parental figure.

'Kids who have secure attachments feel safe and know they can trust and rely on their caregivers,' Anna explained. 'Having a loving and stable primary carer lets children form a secure attachment and grow up to be happy and well-adjusted, and able to form healthy relationships of their own. They'll be more independent and have a lower chance of developing anxiety and depression and other mental illnesses. But the problem is, forming secure attachments is hard for children to do when they're living in an institution. More than sixty years of research has shown that growing up in institutions creates attachment disorders, which can lead to mental health issues and all sorts of other problems later in life.'

'An institution?' I queried nervously. This was the first time I'd heard that word used to describe CCT. 'CCT's an institution?'

'Well . . .' Anna paused. 'It's very clear that you and your team are trying your best to provide a happy environment for the kids, but, yes—there's no getting around the fact that CCT is providing a form of institutional care. Having twenty-plus kids in one home, sleeping in dorms, house parents on rotating shifts . . .' Her voice trailed off, probably in response to the devastated look on my face.

I knew that orphanages weren't good. But I think that on some level I was still hoping that the kids who were genuine orphans could grow up to be healthy, happy people if we made CCT the best orphanage it could be.

But Anna was saying that attachment disorders were created by the mere fact of living in an institution—not just by abuse.

The staff were paid to be there. They had to go home everyday to attend to their own families, their own lives. It wasn't humanly possible for them to have the dedication of a real family. The mere fact there was a different adult coming on to the shift every eight hours meant that the kids couldn't attach properly. And staff come and go—employee turnover is a reality of the workplace. But even if I lived full time at CCT and never had to come and go myself, it just wasn't possible to properly parent that many kids. One person just cannot adequately hold the role of the sole stable adult in the lives of dozens of children.

Anna kept talking but my mind was elsewhere now. How would I fix this? How could we give each of the kids the family they deserved? *They should never have been taken away from their families in the first place.*

And that was the big tragedy in all of this. We were always talking about 'the CCT family', but most of these kids already had families. Even the kids who had lost both their parents might have had aunts, uncles, grandparents, cousins or older brothers and sisters who could have looked after them if they'd had a little help.

Naturally, I'm only human and I did of course feel tempted to get defensive, but there was no time to indulge it. I knew by now that being defensive never serves any good purpose. I just had to get busy finding a way to solve these problems . . .

STEP 3

Do something better

18

'Orphanage' is a label that can be extremely deceptive. Given that children are being placed into orphanages because of poverty and not because they're orphaned, the label 'orphanage' is not really accurate for many of the institutions that use it. Today, 'orphanage' is just a euphemistic term given to a widely used model of residential care—that is, care that children receive in an institutional setting by paid staff, rather than by their own immediate or extended family members, or other family-based carers such as foster carers.

There are various terms used to refer to residential care for children, including orphanages, children's homes, boarding schools, children's villages, safe houses, rehabilitation centres and shelters, to name just a few.

Residential care is problematic when the parent–child bond is severed unnecessarily and when it is seen as a permanent solution.

Of course, sometimes, residential care might truly be necessary. If a child isn't safe at home, and if all possible opportunities for kinship care have been exhausted, the child may need to be placed in residential care. But this should be the absolute *last resort*, not the first. And in these situations, trained professionals should be working with the family to empower them to work through their problems until they can take back the responsibility of providing non-violent, safe and loving care to their children. And in the few cases where there definitely aren't any other alternatives, placing a child in residential care should still only be a *temporary* measure until a permanent family-based care solution can be found—through family reunification, local adoption or long-term foster care.

In short, no matter what the circumstances, research has shown that family-based care, including parental care, kinship care, foster care or local adoption, is *always* better than caring for children in an institutional setting.

Some institutions will use deceptive labels in an attempt to avoid negative connotations and simply call themselves a 'family'. But just because you call an institution a family, doesn't make it one.

~

In our one-on-one sessions, Anna naturally slipped into the role of counsellor. She could see that I was still really hurting over the accusations and threats the staff had made while I was in Australia. We had a lot of long talks about it during the week she spent with us.

Together, we pondered the differences between Australian and Cambodian culture. I told her my theory that the cultural faux pas I'd committed, combined with amateurish leadership, may have been a catalyst to the fallout.

She suggested that also, in Cambodia, life is all about attending to the social hierarchy, being respectful of your elders and focusing on 'the greater good'—meaning family and community. The sociological reasons for this are obviously complex. People have a lot of theories about why there are such differences between 'eastern' and 'western' thinking. Maybe it comes down to religion, or climate, or economic development or agricultural practices. Maybe it's just life in a fairly rural community. Whatever the reasons, these differences meant that, in the staff's eyes, 'good' children should be sweet, meek

302

and obedient. Because my point of view was naturally quite 'western', I valued individuality. I wanted the kids to be confident and brave enough to go against the grain. I wanted to see them come out of their shells and stand up for themselves and what they believed in. It was no wonder we'd clashed.

'Honestly Tara, you do need to reconnect with the staff,' Anna told me. 'If you want to achieve any of the things we've discussed, it's going to take teamwork. You've got to stop working through Jedtha and get everyone united. I can see you have the capacity to be a good leader. Don't let pride get in the way of that.'

It took a little while to accept this, but I knew she was right. We had so much work ahead of us, I had to find a way to forgive the staff and trust them again, and give them reasons to trust me in return. I wasn't sure if the staff would accept me back in a leadership role, but I had to give it a shot.

~

A week or so after Anna had returned to England, she sent me her official report, with all her observations and recommendations.

While there was nothing in the report we hadn't discussed in person, seeing our erroneous ways printed in black and white wasn't the best feeling in the world.

First, our child protection practices needed strengthening—we were allowing un-vetted visitors and volunteers to interact with the kids, we weren't following adequate safety procedures when it came to the kids travelling in vehicles (we were just following cultural norms, but I could see her point), we let them play in the yard with the gate open and with safety hazards like open water urns and coconut trees around, the list went on . . .

The next issue was that our social work practices were not up to standard—our case file management was poor, we didn't have a safe reporting system in place for the kids to confidentially report complaints or concerns, we didn't have professional supervision for our social workers, and we were working too independently of DoSVY.

Anna urged us to strengthen the communication between staff to allow for better teamwork, and to try to foster a family atmosphere at CCT as much as possible.

She *did* write many really lovely, glowing things about CCT. She praised our commitment to providing a well-rounded education, the gentleness and enthusiasm of the staff, the encouraging move towards sibling reunion and family support, the commitment to healthcare, the weekly excursions and the balance of time spent studying versus playing.

She also wrote: *Tara's ability to reflect on her own role within CCT and to be open to feedback is one of her great strengths and supports her in being flexible and open to change and improvement.*

I hoped I could live up to that description.

~

In the weeks that followed, Jedtha and I pushed forward, trying to work out how to put Anna's recommendations into practice. Her report and the principles she taught us became our new blueprint for running CCT.

But even though we were working to make CCT the best it could be, finding out that even the 'best' institutional care can create attachment disorders haunted me. I tracked down some of the research that Anna mentioned to try to better understand the problem.

Everything I learned just confirmed my worst fears. Growing up in an institution, deprived of loving parental care, has been shown to impair the development of a child's brain and can lead to growth and speech delays, higher incidences of hyperactivity, difficulties forming relationships in adulthood, clinical personality disorders and an impaired ability to re-enter society later in life.

When you compounded all of this with the fact that orphanages tore apart families and didn't help at all to break the cycle of poverty . . . then what were we doing here? What was the point in trying to make CCT the best orphanage it could be? It would still, fundamentally, be an institution.

~

The fact was, the kids needed to grow up in loving and supportive families—not inside the walls of an institution. We needed to reunite them with their own families, or otherwise find ways to support them in family-based care.

Realising that this was the only way forward was an incredibly daunting idea. It meant giving up every picture we'd had in our heads of what CCT should look like: the eco-village idea was out, even creating a 'family atmosphere' at CCT wasn't going to cut it.

The biggest, most daunting obstacle was that Cambodian families who gave up their kids did so because of poverty. It would be an enormous undertaking to find ways to help them keep their kids or take their kids back. It was going to take time, money and a big serving of humble pie for me.

Basically, we had to change the whole model of CCT and, in doing that, admit that the way we had been doing it all this time was a mistake. How was I going to explain that to our donors?

They had signed up to support an orphanage. We had been telling them that CCT was a really *great* orphanage. Now I had to tell them that even good orphanages aren't good for kids. Would they still want to support CCT? Or would they withdraw their funding? Would changing the model mean the end of CCT?

But despite the risks inherent in changing direction, the best interests of the kids had to come first. We'd just have to make the changes slowly and carefully and make sure all of our supporters came along on the journey with us. We'd have to take baby steps and communicate the new direction well. We certainly weren't going to be able to transform CCT overnight.

The good news was that a lot of what we were doing was already on track—bringing siblings together, the small amount of family support we were already providing, and not taking in more children who already had family. These were all very positive steps.

But oh my god. There was still an incomprehensible amount of work to do.

~

We drafted up our first attempt at a strategic plan and moved forward with a project that we called our Family Reunification Program.

We needed to do proper family tracing for all the kids and then conduct risk assessments on their families to see if it would be safe for the kids to go back to living with them. Then we'd need to work out how the kids could continue to access decent healthcare and education . . .

We decided that Amara, Chanlina, Maly and Teng should be the first to begin the reintegration process. Having met their parents the day we visited them at Prachea Thorm, we knew they were good candidates—they were kind-hearted people who adored their children. So we raised some funds to rent a modest house for the family in Battambang and to set the parents up with a small food stall business. The kids could then move back in with their parents and CCT could continue to support their healthcare and education. And if the business went well enough, the parents could begin covering these costs themselves.

It sounded simple enough—but the challenge of life in Cambodia is that just when you think you have a handle on something, it'll turn around in a totally unexpected way and you'll be left back at square one.

While I was busy thanking donors for the wonderful support they were offering to bring this family back together, the kids came to me to tell me they didn't want to move back in with their parents after all.

'Tara, CCT is our home now. We haven't lived with our parents for a long time. We hardly even know them anymore. Please don't make us go!'

Oh man, I thought to myself, looking at the appeal in their eyes. There was no way in the world I was going to send them away from the place they felt was their home and have them experience even more abandonment.

This family-based care thing was going to be even more complicated than I'd expected.

~

When we're young and idealistic, we're prone to seeing the world in black and white:

'These people must be terrible because they trafficked their kids/ their kids are picking through garbage/working as beggars/not going to school etc.'

Actually no, many of these families are simply living in desperate poverty and have no other options.

'Orphanages, even the good ones, are bad for kids. Let's reintegrate them back to their biological families!'

Actually, sometimes, after living apart from family for so long, the kids are hesitant to go back. Or sometimes there's no high school back in their home village so the parents want their kids to stay and get a good education.

Nothing is black and white. When a family is broken apart, it's not easy to put it back together again. The parts don't fit anymore. That's why it's so important that, wherever possible, we keep kids with their families in the first place.

I knew that reintegrating the kids against their will wasn't going to result in good outcomes for anyone involved. And I needed the kids to feel safe, so I informed the donors of the hiccup and let it drop until I could work out what to do next.

~

Today, the CCT team know how to conduct reintegration professionally, safely and effectively. We follow MoSVY's Policy on the

Alternative Care for Children and we have a long, careful process for reintegration.

First we conduct family tracing—a process of locating the children's biological family through discussions with commune leaders, neighbours, other known relatives and the children themselves.

The next step is to conduct a number of risk assessments and family assessments to work out if the family can provide a safe and stable environment for the kids. Then, in consultation with the children and the family, we create a case plan that outlines the most practical steps for reintegration.

Then it's time for the kids to slowly get to know their family again, typically through short, supervised weekend visits, accompanied by their social worker. Over time, those visits tend to naturally extend to full days and then to overnight stays.

After the kids feel comfortable spending the weekends with their family and can see that nothing else in their lives has changed, they usually decide that they'd like to move back permanently. Our social work team are responsible for conducting this process, alongside DoSVY, the local commune leaders and village leaders. We always let the process be guided by the kids and their families. And, thankfully, it does work.

In more recent years, Amara, Chanlina, Maly and Teng were successfully reintegrated back with their family in Battambang. Sadly, their father passed away due to a long battle with diabetes, but their mother is doing well, working as an assistant at CCT's preschool. Maly is studying nursing at university, and Teng, Amara and Chanlina are still in high school, acing all their exams.

Interestingly, one of the barriers that initially stopped those kids from wanting to move back with their family was because—as you may have guessed already—the standard of living at CCT really was 'too high'.

Yep, those video games, cable TV and personal devices, and that endless supply of donated clothes and toys, came back to haunt me. These things can be enough to prevent a successful reintegration.

The unrealistic living standards in 'good orphanages' set children up for a big shock when it comes time for them to transition into independence. Most of the time, they cannot possibly sustain the same quality of life they were used to without the ongoing support of the organisation. This creates a culture of dependency and, as a result, the children resist reintegrating back into society or back into their families.

By striving to give the kids the same privileged childhood that I'd been so fortunate to have, I created even more problems for them. I just hadn't taken the time to fully understand the negative impacts these actions might have had in a completely different economic and cultural setting.

19

Not long after Anna's visit to CCT, we had to start thinking about how to occupy the kids during the Khmer New Year holiday in April.

These days we run an educational holiday program at CCT, but back in early 2009 we thought it sounded like a great idea when one of our donors offered to fund a holiday trip for the kids. We picked out a few options and had a big meeting with all the staff and kids to vote on a location. The majority decided that they'd like to see the famous Bou Sra waterfalls in Mondulkiri, a province in far north-east Cambodia.

I had heard about the beautiful, untouched forested landscapes, the windswept valleys and the cooler climate of Mondulkiri and was keen to check it out myself. I figured that we could make the trip an educational experience and teach the kids about the importance of wildlife conservation and protecting the environment. So I wrote to the Elephant Valley Project in Mondulkiri and asked if we could visit while we were there.

The Elephant Valley Project was set up by a British guy named Jack Highwood to help rehabilitate captive, working Asian elephants in Cambodia. Elephants are still used for transportation, logging, hunting and tourism, especially in the more sparsely populated north-eastern provinces. The trouble is, a lot of elephant husbandry knowledge was lost with the Khmer Rouge and the rapid changes happening in Cambodian society.

The project's 650-hectare sanctuary is now a place where these elephants can go for medical treatment, rest and recuperation, and retirement. Retired elephants are slowly rehabilitated back to the natural jungle habitat that's being conserved within the sanctuary.

The project provides jobs for the indigenous people who live in the area, and provides training and employment for new and existing mahouts (elephant keepers) using humane, sustainable animal husbandry practices. I thought it would be a magical learning opportunity for the kids.

Jack wrote back to say we were very welcome, so we planned our itinerary, booked the bus and got packing.

It was going to be a long trip. The road to Mondulkiri wasn't sealed at that time, so it would be about seven or so hours on the bus to Phnom Penh and then a further twelve hours from there on to Mondulkiri—with a bus full of carsick kids. Yaaaaay. I was looking forward to Mondulkiri, but dreading the journey.

Nevertheless, we set off (with everyone dosed up on travel sickness medicine), and by the time the bus got to Phnom Penh, the kids were in the zone. They sat quietly, reading books, eating snacks and taking little naps all the way up the long dirt road to Mondulkiri Province. I did pretty much the same.

Many hours later, I came out of my bus coma to see that it was raining and the greenery that bordered the road had thickened into dense jungle. We were getting close but still had to cross some of the most mountainous terrain in Cambodia.

The dirt roads quickly turned to mud. The bus started to labour, until the driver pulled it to a full halt. He and the two 'bus boys' (the extra staff who support the driver) jumped off the bus and put chains around the tyres. These worked like snow chains, providing extra traction in the slippery mud. Soon the bus was moving again and we all let out a sigh of relief.

We made our first long ascent up the mountains, but when we reached a small plateau, the bus shuddered to a halt again. The next climb was a lot steeper.

'No problem,' said the bus driver. 'Everybody get out and walk and I will drive behind you.'

We all spilled out of the bus and proceeded to slip and slide our way up the next ascent. We weren't the only ones who had to walk. All the other vehicles on the road were in the same situation, so there were quite a few other people making their way up the mountain on foot, while the buses and trucks struggled noisily around us.

We trudged up one ascent, and then another. And then another. Our spirits started to flag as we found ourselves wading through knee-deep, sticky, slippery mud. Anna's words of caution regarding child protection and safety rolled around in my head . . . I dreaded to think what she'd be saying if she could see us now.

Journ, our Khmer literature teacher, was the only one who was completely unfazed. He kept stopping to take in the spectacular views of the mountains around us, crying out like YouTube's 'double rainbow guy': 'Wow! This is amazing! SO amazing! In my whole life I have never seen anything so BEAUTIFUL! WOW! Oh my god, WOW!'

He had us all in fits of laugher. Everyone stopped to lift their gaze from the river of mud to take in the awe-inspiring view. It was as if the jungle knew it had an audience—the storm clouds that had brought the rain put on a spectacular lightning show, crashing over the jungle-clad mountains.

As we soldiered on, I kept counting the kids and calling out for everyone to stay together. I was relieved when we were finally able to get back on the bus. Unfortunately, that relief was short-lived. Only a few hundred metres down the track, the bus got stuck and we had to get back off again and walk. This happened three times.

By the third time, I started to get a bit concerned. It was starting to get dark and it was cold. Mondulkiri has a microclimate with considerably cooler temperatures than the rest of Cambodia. We trudged ahead of the bus, our muscles groaning with the effort of wading up a mountain through a river of mud. At the next plateau, we were told to wait for the bus. So we waited. The sun disappeared below the thick canopy. Still we waited. And waited. But there was no sign of the bus.

I was idly wondering whether there were still any tigers left in the jungle when Jedtha came striding up to me through the mud, looking stressed. 'The bus is stuck,' he said. 'Everybody needs to go back and wait on the bus while I try to get to Mondulkiri and find another vehicle.'

I felt my pulse quicken. I was starting to feel genuinely concerned for our safety now, but I was relieved that Jedtha was stepping up and making decisions, because I was really out of my depth in this jungle landscape.

'Okay, everybody—let's go!' I shouted. I did a headcount as everyone started making tracks back down the hill to the bus, and realised that some of our group had charged on ahead.

Jedtha hailed a pickup truck that seemed to be making slow but steady progress through the mud river and convinced them to give him and Meah a ride into town. He was just stepping into the tray of the pickup when I called, rather frantically: 'Jedtha! Rouet and the five little kids are up ahead!'

'Okay,' he called back. 'Come with us to find them. Then you can take them back to the bus.'

I quickly told Samnang what was happening and asked him to make sure everyone else got on the bus and stayed on it. Then I clambered into the tray of the truck with Meah and Jedtha and about six other people who were also hitching a ride.

We were all covered in mud from head to toe. It was almost funny seeing Jedtha, who was always so neat and dignified, in such a state of disarray. But before I could make a joke about it, the truck wheels screamed as they spun through the mud and the truck leaped violently forward. I was flung to the back of the tray where I hung on for dear life as it skidded down the slope.

Then the sky opened and the rain came thundering down.

I parted the curtain of wet hair plastered across my face and squinted ahead through the rain as the truck was washed down the mountain by the river of flowing mud. Thankfully I didn't have much further to go—I could see Rouet and the kids in the distance, surrounded by other people.

Just as we were nearing the bottom of the descent, the truck lost traction and started veering sideways towards a sheer drop on the right-hand side of the muddy road. Everyone in the tray immediately scrambled over to the left side of the truck and hung off the rim of the tray, like a bunch of terrified Indiana Joneses. The pickup truck swerved the rest of the way down the descent and finally came to a sticky halt in the mud at the bottom.

I stayed there, welded to the truck for a moment while I processed the amazing fact that I was still alive. The gloomy, sludgy road through the jungle was by now lit up only by the small chain of trucks still attempting to clamber up the mountain.

Rouet and the five kids seemed relieved to see us. 'Oh Tara! This is crazy, right?' Rouet smiled broadly.

I nodded in emphatic agreement and opened my arms to Jendar, who had flung herself at me—probably for warmth as much as comfort. She wrapped herself around my torso like a koala bear and wouldn't let go.

A few minutes later, Jedtha waded through the mud towards us. 'I don't think you can go back to the bus now—it's too difficult,' he said. 'You should all come with us in this truck to Mondulkiri. Then we'll find a vehicle that's equipped to handle these roads to come back for the others.'

We looked at each other over the heads of the kids and in that moment everything changed—all the weirdness of the months and weeks since my trip to Australia melted away, and I realised that I had complete faith in Jedtha's ability to navigate us through this. I was impressed by how calm, decisive and confident he was. Whether he felt it or not, he seemed to be in control of the situation, which meant I was free to focus my attention on making sure the kids were okay.

I took the hands of Makara and Teng and began walking towards the truck that Jedtha had lined up for us to travel in.

The new truck was bigger, but it still struggled to get through the mud. It heaved, skidded and lurched up the next slope through the rain. Then it got bogged, its wheels spinning with a fountain of mud being thrown up in its wake. Jedtha would usher us off and we'd walk a way up the mountain until he found another truck for us to hitch a ride on, and we'd repeat the process. It started raining again. We were on and off the back of about five different pickup trucks before we finally reached the top of the mountain and could hitch a ride all the way into town. All up, it took us five hours to get off that mountain.

We were in quite a state when we finally arrived at a guesthouse in Mondulkiri town—shivering, exhausted and more mud than human.

Jedtha and Meah rushed off to mount a rescue mission for the rest of the kids and staff still on the bus. We were all worried sick about them. There was no phone signal in the jungle, so there was no way to communicate with them. Even if they were perfectly safe on the bus, they'd still be cold, hungry and miserable.

Rouet took the shivering kids off to have a warm shower. But what would they change into? I went down to reception, looking like the loser in a mud-wrestling match, and tried rather tearfully to explain our situation. The woman at reception took pity on me and supplied everyone with clean dry pairs of pyjamas. Then they had a big, hot meal sent to our rooms.

I sat and waited and tried not to let my imagination run away with me.

About an hour later, Jedtha and Meah arrived back at the guest-house, upset and defeated. It was just too wet and dark now to get a vehicle to drive back for the rest of the team on the bus. We barely slept a wink for the rest of the night, worrying about everyone still stuck on the bus in the jungle.

Yeah, it was an epic fail as far as child protection goes.

~

Early the next morning, we got hold of Jack, the founder of the Elephant Valley Project. He picked us up in a rough old truck equipped with big, thick tyres that scorned the mud.

I want me one of these! I thought, as Jedtha, Jack and I set off to retrieve the rest of the kids and staff.

The poor bus looked very tiny and vulnerable, stuck in the mud at the bottom of a steep hill in the middle of the mountain range. You can imagine how overjoyed everyone was when we pulled up beside them. They'd had an uncomfortable night on the cold, smelly, muddy bus, with disconcerting sounds coming from the jungle outside. None of the adults had slept at all.

Jack did several trips, shuttling everyone into town for comforting hot showers and not one, not two, but *three* servings of breakfast.

The capacity of Cambodian people to bounce back from life's little dramas never fails to amaze me. Once they were stuffed to the gills with food, everyone was cheery and keen to put the night behind them. So we set out for the elephant sanctuary in high spirits, ready for another adventure.

Mondulkiri is one of the most beautiful places in the world to experience pure, unsullied nature. With the thick, unspoilt jungle, stunning mountain views and a range of very different indigenous minority groups, it was like arriving in a whole new country.

For the next three days, the kids, staff and I learned how to care for the elephants while following them through Mondulkiri's gorgeous jungle with its huge variety of plants, birds, insects and animals.

Elephants love to swim and it was magical to watch them swim in the sanctuary's many waterholes, and to see them interact with the environment and each other, just as they would if they were truly wild.

Away from the stress of case files, of policies and reports, and of the demands of fundraising, my eyes were opened to how wonderful my team really was. We all spent more time chatting and laughing together than we ever had before. The kids kept exclaiming: 'I'm so happy I could die!'

Samnang has this incredibly loud, wonderful belly laugh. Even now, every time he laughs, I laugh at his laughter. Savenh and I sat side-by-side on a rock and watched while Samnang and the kids had a water fight in the Bou Sra waterfalls. Samnang's laughter as the kids splashed him set Savenh and me off into fits of giggles. All the awkwardness and resentment between us just disappeared.

Today, the kids remember the trip as just a fantastic adventure. Despite the hellish journey getting to Mondulkiri, even the staff say they feel lucky to have visited the region while it was still so isolated.

~

That trip to Mondulkiri ended up being much more than just an activity to pass the time during the kids' school holidays. The rift between me, Jedtha, Savenh and the rest of the staff was now a thing of the past. Jedtha had regained my trust and I was impressed to see what a good leader he could be, and what good people Savenh and the rest of the team truly were. It was such a relief to find we were all friends again.

Jedtha and Savenh have both since told me they feel awful about the falling out we had during Chloe's visit. I have completely and wholeheartedly forgiven them both and also apologised for the part I played in bringing on the conflict.

In the months that followed, the culture at CCT completely trans-formed—the motivation levels, work ethic and camaraderie of the team was palpable. I'd wake up in the morning and bounce out of bed, looking forward to seeing everyone at work.

CCT is still like that, and we work hard to make sure our workplace culture stays that way. Life's too short not to enjoy your work and the people who you do it with. Of course, there were challenges, but I had learned that you are only ever as good as your team. I learned that people will go above and beyond for you if they are made to feel safe, if they are trusted and given the opportunity to try and fail, to learn and grow.

The task we had ahead of us, to change our model from an orphanage to family-based care, still seemed incredibly daunting. But I made sure that I let the team know that I believed in their potential, and their ability to rise to the enormous challenges ahead.

I had more hope than ever before that if we worked at it, we could find the solution together.

~

Several weeks after we returned from Mondulkiri, Carolyn came to visit me in Battambang. It had been a long time since I'd had a proper break from CCT, and even though my spirits were high, I was tired and needed some time out. So I took the opportunity to have a few days off.

Like me, Carolyn was bowled over by Cambodia's raw, awe-inspiring beauty—and the gobsmacking sights you see as a matter of course every single day.

I took her to the Angkor Wat temples in Siem Reap. We sat in Ta Prohm temple, just the two of us, watching the sun go down and the sky turn into pastel swirls of pinks and purples. Sitting next to Carolyn in the enchanted temple, surrounded by twinkling fireflies under a fairy-floss sky . . . I felt like I was lost in some magical fantasy world.

Back in Battambang, Carolyn gave the kids music lessons with a little weighted keyboard she had brought with her from Australia.

It was a surprise to everyone to see how our shy, quiet Rithy blossomed under Carolyn's tutelage. He learned to play incredibly quickly, and was soon her star pupil. Carolyn was so impressed, she gave him the keyboard when she left.

It was transformational for Rithy to find a way he could express himself, and discovering that had a natural talent for music was a huge boost to his self-confidence. Over the next few months he changed from a boy who was happy to go unnoticed to a little creative genius, excelling at music, painting, drawing and dance.

I fell in love with Carolyn on that trip. It was so effortless to be together, talking, laughing, putting the world to rights. Seeing how she loved Cambodia, the kids and even my dogs had a powerful effect on me. I was crazy about her. And, finally, she seemed to be returning my affection in full.

When Carolyn returned to Australia, she stepped up her involvement with CCT. She started helping with the writing and proofreading for our website and she tapped into her enormous network of friends to raise more funds.

She was in touch every day, sometimes several times a day and sent me long, romantic, enthralling missives. She wrote songs about her time in Cambodia with me . . .

I'd never felt so loved, and so in love.

~

I was collapsed in an exhausted heap on my bed when I got the text from Carolyn.

I'd been up since three that morning, at the local pagoda with the kids for the P'chum Ben festival. My phone had run out of battery life and by the time I got home and charged it, I was tired, hungry and not in the best mood. And then a text from Carolyn buzzed through. Excellent! That would cheer me up.

The text read: *So I slept with Chris last night. I think we're going to try and give a real relationship a go this time.*

I had a sudden, uncontrollable urge to put my fist through a wall. I didn't give in to the impulse, but I did feel such a flash of anger that I smashed my tiny, piece-of-shit Nokia phone onto my tiled bedroom floor.

Those bloody phones are almost indestructible, so to my intense annoyance, it just bounced and landed on the other side of the room, still fully intact. The screen, with that fucking message still on it, lay on the floor mocking me.

I'd met Chris before. He was a quiet person, a brilliant musician. I knew Carolyn was in awe of him, but I had definitely not seen this coming.

It was the way she told me, blunt and out of the blue, that really cut me. I couldn't even bring myself to reply.

~

I started asking myself why I was investing so much time and effort into a long-distance relationship that mostly only existed in cyber-space. What was the point?

My life was here, in Cambodia. Maybe I should focus my attention on the people around me, build relationships with people I could actually connect with in real life, instead of staring at a screen all the time?

I never did reply to that text. I never let myself cry, either. I convinced myself that the relationship wasn't good for me, and that it was time to move on.

But of course, underneath the pride and the bravado, I was hurting badly.

~

Around this time, the *Australian Story* producer, Ben Cheshire, started to email me ideas for the documentary. He said something like:

> We'd like you to talk about why you're in Cambodia. We need to really delve into your deeper motivations, so the audience can

> understand what's driving you. Otherwise the story won't have
> any depth. From what you said at the first meeting, it sounds
> like you were struggling with anorexia and depression, and
> going to Cambodia and helping the kids is what saved you?

Oh boy. Having my eating disorder addressed so directly like that really threw me.

At that point in my life, it was something that I still kept very private. My family and some of my friends knew it was something I struggled with, but it certainly was not up for discussion, let alone something to be aired on national television.

What once had seemed incredibly challenging—opening up about myself publicly—now started to feel completely fucking impossible.

I was also concerned by the idea that I'd be sending out the message that a young person with depression or an eating disorder or any other mental illness should run off to a place like Cambodia to be 'saved' by trying to 'save' others. I'm sure most mental health professionals would agree that if you're struggling with a mental illness, the last thing you should do is isolate yourself in a foreign country and cut yourself off from established support networks—especially in a country like Cambodia, where there are very limited services in place to respond to mental health crises.

Even back in 2009, before I truly understood the harm that unskilled volunteering can cause in developing countries, I was concerned that I'd be encouraging lost young souls to race off to seek out redemption in Cambodia.

And the elephant in the room, of course, was that I couldn't very well go on TV and talk about being 'saved' from my eating disorder when I was still, to some degree, in the grip of it. The pressure of being in the spotlight, of having my story exposed in the media, and the total lack of control I had over the whole process ... meant my eating disorder was soon back in the driver's seat again.

An endless torrent of controlling thoughts flooded my internal world. I skipped meals and fuelled myself on black coffee. I didn't even bother trying to fight it. I knew how powerful those thoughts could be and I had so much to deal with, it felt like the only thing I could do was just go along with it, just to keep the constant white noise at bay.

But I couldn't back out of doing *Australian Story*. We really, really, really needed the money and this, we hoped, was our Big Chance— at the time, it was the only way we knew of that would connect us with new supporters. The thought of blowing this chance, of letting everyone down because I was 'scared of the spotlight' was unthinkable. I had to do it.

So on I went, coping as best I could.

~

Sally, naturally, wanted to create some buzz around the *Australian Story* episode. She started emailing through requests for me to do more media appearances. I flipped into panic mode and lost my temper with her.

I felt terrible about it, but my life felt like it was slowly spiralling further and further out of my control. This sense of losing control exacerbated my eating disorder, which in turn made me feel even *more* out of control. And on the vicious cycle raged.

Thankfully, Ben emailed through a request for us to embargo all other media until my story went to air. That brought me some relief, for a while, anyway.

'What's going on with you?' Peter asked on Skype one day. 'You're being a bit crazy about this whole *Australian Story* thing.'

'I really don't want to do it anymore, Pete,' I confessed. 'I'm really freaking out that I won't know how to answer all their scary personal questions!'

'Now calm down,' Peter said. 'I'm sure it won't be all about you— they'll mostly focus on CCT and your work. And you talk about all of that very well.'

'No, it's an *Australian Story*, about an Australian. That's me! They've told me it will be focused on me. They've told me they want me to open up about my deeper motivations and the fact I had an eating disorder!'

(The fact that I *had* an eating disorder. I couldn't even refer to my eating disorder in the present tense to my own dad.)

'Oh, I see,' he said, sympathetic now. After a long pause he said: 'I agree it would be better if they didn't focus on the eating disorder stuff. It's a shame they already know about that.'

'I know. I'm such an idiot! I can't believe I opened my big mouth. But it's done now.'

'It's okay. We can fix this. We just need to think more about the reasons that you were so drawn to Cambodia so they don't try to connect the dots on their own. Do you have any theories?'

'I don't know, Peter,' I groaned. 'I just was. One thing led to another and, voilà!—here I am.'

'The problem is, that answer won't make for an interesting story,' Peter said. 'I understand it's not a simple question to answer, but have a think about it. Susie and I will think on it, too. And don't worry about how you'll come across on camera. You'll be great! Everyone will love you, my sweetie-poppins. How could they not?'

I rolled my eyes at this, but I was feeling much calmer, and very grateful to have such a wonderful, supportive dad.

Even all these years later, my theory about the 'why' of how I ended up in Cambodia is still pretty hazy. It's a combination of so many factors, so many variables, so many sliding door moments. It's kind of impossible to hang it on any one event or personal trait. But musings on the complexity of life and any one given human personality don't come across particularly well in a half-hour TV story.

Later that night, Peter rang back and said: 'Tara, do you think it's any coincidence that the country you've ended up dedicating your life to is recovering from a holocaust? You and the kids at CCT are both the grandchildren of holocaust survivors. Do you think that might be significant?'

I thought: *Well, yeah, of course.*

Whenever I hear a Cambodian talk about the war, my thoughts always turn to Nagy. The first time I went to the Tuol Sleng torture prison and the Killing Fields, the horror of it all felt uncomfortably close to home. For this reason, I *still* find it difficult to hear or read stories about the Khmer Rouge genocide.

It was not the whole answer, but it was definitely part of it. I emailed Ben and he said they'd certainly be interested in exploring that during the interviews.

I relaxed slightly. I hoped it would be enough of a 'deeper motivation' to keep them from prying into the more personal parts of my story.

~

My anxiety levels were still sky high in August 2009, when the *Australian Story* guys—producer Ben Cheshire and cameraman Quentin Davis—arrived in Battambang. I had discovered that they'd been doing some very thorough background research, talking to people like Geraldine Cox, officials from DoSVY and MoSVY and other expats in Cambodia to ask their opinion of me and CCT. I started feeling intensely paranoid. What sort of story were they planning? I had no control at all over how the final story would look. The first time I would see it would be with the rest of the world, when it went to air.

As well as being plagued by insecurities around my eating disorder, I also had serious performance anxiety—which is what you get when you're a diehard perfectionist. I only had a few short sound bites to get across everything I wanted to say about CCT. What if I forgot a crucial piece of information? What if I accidentally said the wrong things? Given I was so nervous about it all, I knew I wouldn't be as articulate as I wanted to be.

Fortunately, Ben and Quentin were laidback people, incredibly easy to get along with. But it was a busy time—they worked to a strict schedule with mandatory set breaks included. While they had their 'occupational health and safety breaks', I'd be running from pillar to post, trying to organise everything they needed for the next shot.

Filming the re-enactment scenes was a *very* weird experience. Predictably, I felt intensely self-conscious every time the camera was pointed my way. Acting isn't one of my natural talents, so when they asked me to gaze sadly through the orphanage gates, or when I had to stand on one of Battambang's bridges and 'look pensive', I just felt like a total loser.

'Look left . . . look right . . . look left again,' they called out, while I stood awkwardly on the bridge. The camera they were using was an absolute monster—at least a metre long with a lens that was bigger than my head. Onlookers gawked, wondering aloud if there was some Hollywood event going on.

The kids, by contrast, took to it all like ducks to water.

I was worried that the re-enactment scenes might be traumatic for them, so the staff and I spent a lot of time in the lead-up explaining what the film crew wanted us to do and why. We did our best to make sure they understood that participation was completely optional, so I was relieved to see that a few kids felt comfortable enough to say no, they were too shy to go on TV.

When we picked up the kids who'd volunteered to shoot the rescue re-enactment scene, we were surprised to find they had dressed themselves for the part! They had put on their old SKO clothes, teased their hair and literally rolled around in the dirt to try to emulate what life was like at SKO. They were beside themselves with excitement.

We had found a shed that looked a bit like the main building at SKO. The plan was for the kids to wait inside while Jedtha and I drove around the block in a bus. That way the cameras would be rolling to capture the start of the scene—pulling up at the orphanage with the officials from DoSVY.

The whole way around the block I felt even more nervous than usual. The kids all seemed happy and relaxed, but how would they feel when the cameras were rolling and the pressure was on?

'Okay, action!' called Ben, giving the kids their cue.

The kids ran out of the building towards me, and I could see tears—real tears—streaming down their faces. I almost yelled: 'Stop the cameras! This was a terrible idea! The kids are upset!' But in an instant, they had bowled past me and onto the bus. I hurried after them, only to find them all sitting on the bus seats, laughing—literally rolling around in absolute hysterics!

'Why were you crying?' I asked, feeling very confused. 'Was that too hard?'

'No, it wasn't hard!' Nimol boasted proudly. 'While you were driving around the block we were telling stories about what life was like at SKO so that we could cry for the camera.'

'Who told you to do that?' I demanded.

'No one,' Sinet said. 'We just wanted to do good acting!'

I laughed in amazement.

The bus circled the block and pulled up again where Ben and Quentin were waiting.

'Can you do it again?' Ben asked. 'We need to get a different angle.'

'Argh! We've got no more tears left!' the kids cried, bursting into laughter again.

'I'd prefer no tears anyway,' I said. 'Those tears nearly gave me a heart attack!'

~

Just before the film crew arrived in town, the local NGO that provided psychological health services to adults got in touch. They wanted us to take three kids to live at CCT. The kids had been orphaned and left in the care of their older sister, Mohm. They told us that Mohm had been really struggling, and for various reasons was no longer able to care for her younger siblings.

Jedtha, Savenh and I went out to meet the little family and discovered that their situation was undeniably grim—Mohm was barely out of her teens and was having trouble coping. She had an aunt living next door who was also poor and doing it tough.

We agreed it would be best if the three children came to CCT. But we weren't about to separate the family and leave Mohm behind. We couldn't send her to school, but we could offer the chance to learn to read and write in CCT's supplementary education classes and, when she was ready, we could put her into the vocational training course of her choice.

Mohm and her siblings seemed delighted by the idea, so we suggested they take a few days to prepare before we came out to their village again to pick them up.

On the very day we'd be picking them up, the film crew was scheduled to be following us around, filming our work. We weren't quite sure how to handle this situation, other than trying to make sure Mohm was fully aware there would be a camera with us, and letting her decide whether or not she wanted to be involved. She didn't bat an eyelid at the suggestion. 'No problem, no problem,' she said, and signed the consent form.

It's so hard to negotiate these situations. Even though she was well over eighteen and understood that the TV show would help raise support for the *onga* that would be supporting her, this is yet another example of what I would now consider to be ethically questionable consent.

Mohm had no way of really knowing what it meant to be filmed on an ABC primetime show and how that might affect her life or her younger siblings' lives. We tried our best to make it clear that there was no pressure to agree, but the truth is Mohm was never going to say no. How could she be certain that refusing wouldn't affect CCT's willingness to support her? It meant her consent was really quite meaningless. Unfortunately, I didn't have this insight back in 2009.

I had imagined that they'd just leave the cameras rolling and capture the action as it unfolded . . . but that's not what happened.

When we pulled up in Mohm's village, I got out of the van and walked around to greet Mohm and her aunt, and the commune leaders, village chief and neighbours who were waiting around to see Mohm and the kids off.

Then Ben came up and quietly tapped me on the shoulder. 'Do you mind if we get that again? I want to film the arrival from outside the car, too.'

'You want me to drive away, turn around and come back to say hello to everyone again?' I asked.

'Exactly!' Ben said.

I laughed. 'They're going to think I'm crazy!'

I tried my best to explain to the small crowd that we had to film again, so I would be driving away, coming back again and introducing myself again. They all stared at me blankly, completely bewildered by what I'd just said. 'So when I get back, please can you greet me again like you just did?'

Some of the older ladies chuckled, murmuring under their breath. No doubt they were thinking: *These foreigners are nuts!*

I hopped back in the van and drove away, did a U-turn, then drove up again and introduced myself (again).

Finally we could move on to the real reason we were there.

Mohm and the three kids were packed and seemed happy to go. The cameras rolled as Savenh and the DoSVY officers started doing the paperwork with the commune leaders and village chiefs. That's when I noticed two little kids huddled together under the tree nearby. They were both crying and were obviously extremely upset.

Jedtha and I went to investigate and discovered that the two kids were Mohm's young cousins. Their parents had also died, so she'd been raising them along with her three siblings, but nobody had ever mentioned to us that they even existed.

Jedtha and I exchanged a worried look. We both knew that we couldn't leave the cousins behind, but this was going to put us way over budget. Squeezing in four extra kids was one thing—but six? Meanwhile, the cameras were rolling and the pressure was on. We had to make a decision then and there.

'Okay, they can come,' I said, with as much confidence as I could muster. We'd just have to worry about funding later.

Then it was time for all six of them to say their goodbyes to their old neighbours and leave with us.

We had to film this several times over, too.

Today, I feel terrible about that. It was one thing to slightly embarrass myself by filming multiple introductions, but it was another thing entirely to make traumatised children relive such a stressful event for the sake of the story. In hindsight, I should have set clearer boundaries for the *Australian Story* guys. After all, they're not professionals in child welfare and child protection. Jedtha and I, on the other hand, should have been. It was our responsibility to let Ben and Quentin know what was and was not appropriate.

The other issue here, of course (which I'm sure you've picked up on by now), is that while those cameras were rolling we scooped up six kids and took them away from their village and their community.

It's exactly what CCT does *not* do today. We would have first investigated whether Mohm's surviving aunt, who lived in the village, had the capacity to look after the kids. We would then have helped her provide the necessary care and support to the kids so they could remain in the village, which was like a big extended family to them. We still would have been able to support Mohm to become literate and receive vocational training. And we still would have been able to ensure her younger siblings and cousins had access to quality healthcare and education.

Fortunately, the outcome of Mohm's story is a positive one. CCT supported her in undertaking hospitality training, including a placement in David Thompson's restaurant, *nahm*, in Bangkok. She transitioned into independence, got married, had a baby and is working as a chef in Siem Reap. Her younger siblings have reintegrated out of CCT's foster care and now live with Mohm and her new family. Her two young cousins have also been reintegrated back to their aunt. All the kids are on track to finish school and are doing very well.

~

Ben and Quentin filmed the interviews with Sinet and Jedtha while they were in Battambang, but ran out of time for my 'Big Interview', as they called it. I would have to fly to Sydney to film it, along with a few other re-enactment scenes set in Australia.

Nothing that had happened in Battambang had helped to relieve my nervousness about this interview. To this day, being in the spotlight is my biggest fear in life. When I mention this to people they will often joke: 'Oh, but you love it, really, don't you?'

The answer is: no, I really don't. Even after doing media for more than eight years, I find it as difficult as ever. Unfortunately, generating new funds for CCT is a big job, and appearing in the media is definitely the easiest way to get our messages out there. These days I have tools to help me cope—in part thanks to Brené Brown's iconic 2010 TED talk on 'The Power of Vulnerability', which helped me to realise that part of the reason I struggle so much with being in the spotlight is that, as a perfectionist, I find being vulnerable *extremely* uncomfortable.

In the lead-up to the filming of my Big Interview in 2009, though, I was on my own. I flew back to Sydney, feeling like a death row prisoner about to face a firing squad . . . only to find Carolyn Shine waiting for me at my parents' house.

~

That was a surprise.

Her vivid blue eyes were brimming with compassion. She said: 'I know how hard this is going to be for you. Stay at my place. I've missed you.'

I didn't stop to think about how confusing she was being, or the complications of getting attached to someone who lived so far away. In that instant, all my resentment fell away.

'I've missed you, too,' I said.

~

The *Australian Story* team had set up a space for the interview in a massive, empty studio at the ABC headquarters in Ultimo, Sydney. There were two chairs floating in the middle of the dark room, with a massive spotlight blaring down on one of them.

Oh boy.

You know how when you're really dreading something and getting all worked up about it, people around you say things like: 'It won't be that bad. It's never as bad as you think.'

WRONG. It was that bad. It was worse than I thought.

I was like a deer in the headlights. I dodged the eating disorder questions by admitting to experiencing some mild depression. I fumbled over answers that related to any 'matters of the heart', and finished most of my sentences with 'Um, I dunno. I'm sorry.' I felt like a complete and utter idiot.

It went so badly, the producers had to ask me to do the interview again. They said they'd be able to use *some* of the footage, but they *really* needed me to elaborate on the questions I'd baulked at—which were, of course, the hard ones that were going to make me feel exposed and vulnerable by crying on camera.

They seemed to understand that I'd been too nervous to be able to delve into deeply personal questions. They suggested that perhaps I'd be more comfortable in my own home, speaking with a female journalist?

I agreed politely (albeit through gritted teeth), trying to be as helpful as possible.

So we had our last interview in my parents' living room. Once the cameras were rolling, the journalist started to press me. 'Tell us about your struggles. How did saving the kids impact on your depression? Did helping them help you, too?'

Sure enough, I ended up in tears . . . so I guess they got the emotion they were looking for.

~

Thanks goodness I had Carolyn. She was an incredible support throughout, meeting my fear and anxiety with limitless empathy, warmth and kindness.

We spent every spare moment together in those few weeks in Sydney. I did ask her about Chris, and it *was* complicated. But I was just happy to be with her. I thought she was the most wonderful thing on earth.

The day before I left for Cambodia, we went and sat on a grassy knoll overlooking Sydney's Bondi Beach, watching as the waves crashed up over the rocks. All I could think was how much I loved her and how much I was dreading saying goodbye.

Then the words just fell out of my mouth. 'I love you,' I said, then winced, fearing I'd ruined the moment.

She smiled. 'I love you, too,' she said, leaning in to kiss me. 'The long-distance thing will be a bit tough, but there's no denying how I feel about you.'

I could hardly believe it. Carolyn Shine, the most beautiful woman I had ever known, had chosen me. I felt like the luckiest, and happiest, person alive.

~

I flew back to Cambodia the next morning, still basking in the glow of Carolyn's love, and feeling immense relief that the interviews were over.

We were looking at a few months' respite before the documentary went to air. I had lots of work to get on with to make sure we were ready for what would hopefully be a new influx of support.

The most important task was finding a pathway for CCT to move all of the kids into family-based care. But how would we do that? How would we ensure that all their basic needs were still met, when the reason they were separated from their families in the first place was because of a lack of access to those basic needs? How would we ensure they still had access to the best education and nutrition and healthcare, while addressing all the many complicated issues that result in—and from—intergenerational poverty?

On top of this, things were changing in Battambang. There was a growing concern in the community about the number of gangs of little kids who roamed the streets all day. When I first arrived in Battambang in 2007, I generally only saw kids sniffing glue late at night around the White Rose restaurant and the riverfront area. By early 2010, the numbers appeared to have grown substantially. And the kids seemed to be getting younger, too.

These kids were at great risk of being trafficked, subjected to abuse or ending up in orphanages.

~

I had a stroke of luck when, not long after I returned to Battambang, I went to a birthday gathering at the Balcony Bar and met an American woman in her forties named Barbara.

Barbara and I became instant friends. It was surprising, really, as she was a Christian missionary and I'm, well . . . let's just say I'm the polar opposite of that. But we shared a dry, cynical sense of humour. We fell into a deep conversation and we soon found that, despite our differing thoughts on religion, we were striving for quite similar goals—particularly when it came to keeping Cambodian children with their families.

Barbara had been in Cambodia for four years, working with kids and families in the AIDS wing at the military hospital in Battambang. She had also been working with families living in the Battambang slums. We got talking about the serious lack of support for the children and families in those slum communities.

Like me, Barbara had been alarmed to see the number of 'street kids' in the local area steadily increasing. These kids weren't homeless, though tourists might be told otherwise. They had families, but the families were generally a bit dysfunctional. Because the parents couldn't provide adequate support, the kids had to support themselves. So instead of going to school, they begged on the streets and picked through trash for recycling to sell, usually barefoot and dressed in rags. Sniffing glue killed the hunger pangs—it also evoked sympathy from concerned tourists. Therein lies the paradox of giving (money, food, milk powder or gifts) to begging children: it doesn't help them; it just encourages them to keep begging in high-risk environments, engaging in harmful behaviours like glue sniffing and not going to school.

Barbara and I both agreed that something needed to be done to prevent the problem of Battambang's street kids from getting even further out of hand. We decided to meet with Jedtha so we could put our heads together and see if we could come up with a possible solution.

I was also secretly hoping Barbara could help us figure out that pathway to reintegrating CCT's kids into family-based care. She was certainly just as convinced as I was of its benefits.

~

The slums in Cambodia are dismal places—makeshift villages of tiny corrugated-iron huts, with no running water or sewage systems. Many householders struggle with mental health issues, substance abuse problems, alcoholism, domestic violence and gambling addictions— the legacy of generation after generation trapped in an unending cycle of poverty.

The children born into these communities suffer terribly. The kids we were seeing on the streets were underweight and malnourished, often covered in infected sores, riddled with head lice and scabies. Their hair was often straw-like, patchy and bleached of colour due to malnutrition, and their mouths were full of rotten teeth.

After much thought and debate, Jedtha and I decided to team up with Barbara to launch CCT's first community youth centre for these kids. Our vision was that it would be a place kids could go to access many of the things that weren't accessible to poor families living in slum communities.

We would enrol the kids in their local public school and help their families cover the costs associated with their education like uniforms, pens and pencils, school bags and textbooks. We'd also run supplementary education programs at the centre, and provide nutritious meals, clean drinking water, and access to the shower and bathroom facilities that these kids didn't have at their homes in the slums.

By building these relationships, we'd be able to provide counselling, social work support and medical treatment to the kids and their families, and assist the parents with vocational training and access to employment opportunities.

But the most important aspect of the community youth centre would be that these kids would still be going home to their families every afternoon.

We knew that if the project was going to be a success, it had to be in a location that the kids could easily access. So when a small space in the heart of town came up for rent, we decided it was too good an opportunity to pass up.

We had some funds to cover the set-up, but not for the ongoing operations. But it would be a low-cost project to run, compared to the CCT orphanage, and while we didn't know what the response would be to the *Australian Story* episode, we were fairly confident we'd bring in enough to cover the ongoing operational costs.

We recruited a brilliant Cambodian social worker to run the centre. After it opened, two boys who were heavy glue sniffers started to come regularly. They stopped sniffing glue, cleaned themselves up and brought in their friends, other 'street kids', to check the place out.

In the months that followed, we had sixty street kids, then seventy and then eighty, until they were filling the alleyway that ran alongside the community youth centre.

~

The day the *Australian Story* episode 'Children of a Lesser God' went to air, I was in a state very close to catatonic terror.

It was Easter Monday 2010 and about mid-afternoon in Cambodia. Barbara and I were in Phnom Penh at the time, and I had no intention of actually watching the episode, but Barbara persuaded me to at least try to sit through it. She coaxed me into going to the Java Cafe to access the wifi, so we could watch via a Skype connection with my parents.

I spent the whole time with my head buried behind her back, too horrified to watch. Occasionally I'd stick my head up to see what was going on, but as soon as I heard the sound of my own voice, I'd squeal, clap my hands over my ears and dive for cover again. The other patrons in the cafe must have thought I was bonkers. Even the few seconds I did see were beyond cringe-worthy. I still can't watch it.

I was terrified of what other people would think of me, of being judged by the masses—but, of course, my harshest critic turned out to be me.

~

The response from the Australian public was impossibly kind. And I say 'impossibly' because there's no way any human being could live up to the sorts of things people said about me. The online donations flooded in so quickly that the website fell over for twenty minutes, nearly giving us all a heart attack.

We found out later that 933,000 viewers watched the episode that night.

We all spent the following weeks in the throes of what Peter called 'a crisis of good fortune'. We were not really set up administratively to manage such a massive influx of donations and correspondence. In a matter of days, we had a backlog of over a thousand emails, and they just kept flooding in through the months that followed.

Everyone worked their butts off trying to answer all the emails, respond to all the donation queries, and set up appropriate systems to ensure we were keeping track of it all. It was total madness. It took us nearly a whole year to work through that tidal wave of correspondence.

~

The response from my peers back in Cambodia wasn't quite so positive . . .

At the time the *Australian Story* documentary was filmed, the problems with orphanages in the developing world were not widely known, so none of us thought to include the work we were already doing to reunite siblings and to support families in the thirty-minute program.

But in 2011, a MoSVY/UNICEF report was published. It was called, *With the Best Intentions: A study of attitudes towards residential care in Cambodia.* The study brought to light just how big and deep all these problems were. The facts that it revealed were shocking.

It found that in a five-year period from 2005 to 2010, the number of orphanages in Cambodia had increased by 75 per cent, and the number of children being institutionalised had nearly doubled. This is despite the fact that the number of *actual orphans* in Cambodia had fallen over the same period. The report found that over 80 per cent of children living in orphanages in Cambodia were not orphans, in the traditional sense, but children from poor families. This was the first time I became fully aware of the extent of the problems I had been witnessing up close.

The next shock came when I found out what has been driving this rise in orphanages . . . in fact, it's the main thing that's incentivising the boom in orphanages across the developing world . . .

It's us. The supporters. The donors. The tourists and the gap year backpackers. The well-meaning foreigners from around the world who are unwittingly turning good intentions into a profitable industry.

We are providing the funds and support for these orphanages, which enables more of them to open. To fill these orphanages, more and more children are being separated from their families and institutionalised unnecessarily. It was awful to realise that the laws of supply and demand could apply so widely to the business of orphanages.

~

This problem isn't just confined to Cambodia; J.K. Rowling's organisation Lumos estimates that there are at least eight million children around the world living in institutions. Over 90 per cent of these children have parents or extended family members who could care for them, if they had access to the right support.

Lumos has also reported that young adults raised in these institutions are ten times more likely to become involved in prostitution than their peers, forty times more likely to have a criminal record and five hundred times more likely to take their own lives.

~

Support for orphanages in developing countries is garnered in many different ways, but there's little doubt that the growth in the number of orphanages in Cambodia is correlated with the increase in tourism. One of the main ways the orphanage industry generates funding is via orphanage tourism and voluntourism.

'Orphanage tourism' refers to visiting a residential care facility while on holiday, and 'voluntourism' describes the popular practice of incorporating a short-term volunteer stint as part of a holiday itinerary.

Many orphanages charge for these visits and volunteer stints, or otherwise use them to evoke sympathy from foreigners who will then be moved to donate. The kids are often used to sing and dance, befriend and plead with visitors in order to generate donations. Dodgy and corrupt orphanages will take this even further by deliberately keeping the children in terrible conditions in order to shock visitors, who are then so heartbroken by what they see they are compelled to donate to the kids they believe to be most in need of help—just as I was back in 2005 when I first visited SKO.

These dodgy orphanages are run as businesses in which children are the commodities and donations are embezzled by corrupt orphanage staff. Too often, even goods that are donated to the children (rice, shoes, toys or clothes) are resold after the donors have left. Which is what happened to many of the goods I donated to SKO.

One of the problems here is that, for the majority of well-meaning travellers, visiting an orphanage doesn't seem inherently bad. There's no obvious negative impact, which is why so many people, including myself, have fallen into the trap.

The actual experience feels like this: A few nice people visit an orphanage, trying to do their bit to help; they have a nice day, the kids have a nice day, and everybody's happy. Where's the problem?

You can see the problem when you scale it up. When thousands of well-meaning people visit orphanages year after year, trying to do their bit to help, what gets created is an industry that exploits children in order to make money. In a country where corruption is rife, vulnerable children are everywhere, and affluent, well-intentioned visitors are (naturally) keen to help—the opportunity for exploitation is enormous.

As well as fuelling an industry that tears families apart, orphanage tourism also creates serious child protection risks. Even though the vast majority of people visiting orphanages are kind people who would never dream of hurting a child, the fact remains that not all people are well-meaning and sex tourism is still a serious issue in developing countries like Cambodia. Orphanage tourists, the good and the bad, are mostly not properly vetted, and are given opportunities to interact with kids in an intimate way—for example, playing games, riding the school bus together, hugs and other activities that allow for physical interaction.

Just think about how you might feel in the same situation. What if busloads of tourists were regularly allowed to visit schools, preschools or day-care centres in your home town? What if, on these visits, these tourists were allowed to play and interact with your child?

It comes down to the fact that children are not tourist attractions. They are not animals in a petting zoo and they are certainly not there for the entertainment of tourists and travellers. We don't visit vulnerable children's homes when we're on holiday in Australia, the US or the UK—so why do we feel it's appropriate when we're on holiday in a developing country? This wasn't a question I asked myself when I first agreed to go on a little tour of the local orphanages with Chan back in 2005. But it is a question I ponder a lot today . . .

Orphanage tourism and voluntourism both create serious issues for vulnerable children, but there are some additional problems with voluntourism that are also important to understand.

I am not suggesting that all volunteering is bad, if the definition of volunteering is simply 'doing work for little to no remuneration'. Volunteering in a developing county can be truly life-changing. For many people, it sparks a lifelong commitment to work in the field of social justice. There are skill shortages in many developing countries, especially in Cambodia, where the holocaust had a devastating impact on the knowledge-base held by Cambodian people. Highly skilled and qualified professionals can certainly help by sharing their knowledge and training local people, building their capacity so they are better able to provide quality services. In this way, we are not taking jobs away from local people, but helping them to become even more employable.

It's common to hear voluntourists say 'I swear I got more out of it than the people I was helping!' and for decades this has been lauded as a positive, even charming statement—but this needs to be seriously re-evaluated.

A lot of harm can be done as a result of well-meaning foreigners looking for an experience with the aim of personal growth and fulfilment. The problem is predominantly around unskilled volunteering by tourists who (like me when I first arrived) include a short-term unskilled volunteer stint as a part of their holiday itinerary. These well-meaning people have been convinced that they're helping, but the truth is that unskilled volunteers take the jobs of local people (such as builders, painters, teachers and labourers) who are in fact qualified to do this work to a higher standard.

Unemployment is a huge contributing factor to the poverty levels in developing countries. By working for free in jobs that local people could be doing, voluntourists are preventing local families from accessing jobs they desperately need.

Another problem arises when voluntourists are working directly with children. Many of the kids in these residential care centres have already experienced trauma, even just as a result of being separated from their families, and are already likely to be struggling with attachment disorders. So when voluntourists come in and shower them in love and affection—the love and affection that they *should* be getting from their parents or guardians—they're left emotionally traumatised each time the volunteers leave. The impact of having a high turnover of adults coming in and out of the kids' lives means they re-live that sense of abandonment over and over again.

The real reason so many organisations run voluntourism programs is not because they need a helping hand, but simply to raise money. Voluntourism programs are fundraising initiatives. The cost to the volunteer of carrying out a short-term volunteering stint is a misdirection of funds that could instead be put towards employing local people, with the remainder used to benefit the lives of the organisation's beneficiaries. So while having a personal growth experience is great and a perfectly understandable aspiration to have, it's not okay when it comes at the expense of vulnerable people and developing communities.

I'd like to believe that if everyone understood their efforts were only needed in order to generate funds, we'd all find smarter and much more effective ways to support and add value to the causes we care about.

There are still many other fantastic ways to have fun, meaningful travel experiences in developing countries like Cambodia. Travellers can engage with responsible tour companies that incorporate sight-seeing, cultural immersion and experiential learning opportunities into their tours, while also supporting local community development projects. You can also support ChildSafe initiatives on your travels and choose social enterprise businesses when you're deciding where you'll stay, eat and explore. I've included a few options at the back of this book.

~

Now that you know all this, you can probably understand why my peers back in Cambodia who were already across these issues were deeply concerned about the impact my 'inspiring' story would have.

The *Australian Story* documentary about me had inadvertently told the tale of a young, naïve orphanage tourist, turned voluntourist, turned orphanage founder who went on to facilitate orphanage tourism! And the result of this story was to inspire other young, naïve Australians to make the same mistakes. Oops.

My (now) friend and colleague Daniela Papi, founder of the educational travel company PEPY Tours, wrote a blog about me in 2011 called 'The Dangers of Hero Worshiping (in the Social Sector)', which highlighted the harm that comes from focusing on the 'WHO of social causes and not the WHAT'. She wrote:

> by praising things which make development work look easy,
> which make it seem like any person with no specific training can
> come in and start a successful NGO project, which only focus
> on praising how something started but overlook the discussion
> of the long-term systems in place to ensure a positive impact,
> we are setting up more opportunities for development work
> disasters.

That blog came as a real slap in the face to me in 2011, but of course, she was completely right.

She continued: 'The reason I have this blog is to share the lessons I have learned in order to help prevent people from making the same mistakes I made.'

And that is exactly the purpose of this book. It is the reason I have walked you through the excruciating details of the mistakes I have made.

~

I know it can feel very depressing, confusing and upsetting to learn that helping developing communities and overcoming poverty isn't as simple as we've all been led to believe it should be. But please don't throw your hands in the air and give up!

The problems I've outlined in this book can be reversed and they can be prevented. But it is a mighty task. It requires substantial support and backing, so that governments and reputable NGOs can work together to turn the tide.

If we all work together, I believe that we can overcome poverty. I believe we can put an end to the institutionalisation of children. And I believe we can make sure that vulnerable children everywhere have what all children need and deserve—a family.

Epilogue

I still have mixed feelings about that pro-orphanage *Australian Story* documentary of 2010. On the one hand, a lot of harm may have come from the messages it conveyed to the Australian public. On the other, it is also what generated the funding that enabled us to change CCT's model and close down the orphanage in favour of family-based care. It really has been the springboard for everything that has come since. It's safe to say CCT would not be the organisation it is today without that *Australian Story* and all the incredibly generous people who rallied in support of us.

By 2012, CCT was no longer an orphanage. The story of how we transitioned, and everything that happened in between, could fill a whole other book. But here's a summary of what's happened since 2010:

Within two years of the *Australian Story* documentary going to air, we had successfully moved all the kids into family-based care and were finally able to close the orphanage gates.

Our first step in changing the model was to reintegrate all the children from the CCT orphanage into foster care. That involved selecting kind, caring and trustworthy foster families to care for the kids. We knew many of these families already, as they were our existing CCT staff—including Rouet and her husband, Meah and his wife, and Noit and her husband.

Meanwhile, Savenh and Samnang went on to do further training and formed our social work team, which now has eight members. Together they worked to track down the kids' parents, brothers and sisters, aunts, uncles or grandparents.

The second step was for CCT to help stabilise the lives of the kids' relatives by ensuring they had safe housing. In some cases, we also provided short-term financial support while our social workers helped the families to find ways to generate income and access job opportunities. This all took place while we facilitated family connection—so the kids could slowly get to know their families again.

The third step, which took much more time and in some cases is still in progress, saw the kids move back in with their families or into full independence. This process is always guided by the children and families and only goes ahead when all sides agree. In some cases, such as little Sovanni who was placed with foster parents in infancy, we work towards a permanent plan involving long-term foster care or domestic adoption. Domestic adoption in Cambodia is, however, still a complicated and expensive process. But when it becomes possible, Sovanni's foster parents intend to legally adopt Sovanni.

The fourth step was to make sure the kids and their families are on the path to independence.

All of the children whose stories I have shared in this book— including Makara, Rithy, Akara, Tula and Mao—are now living in loving, stable Cambodian families—some with their biological families, some in kinship care, and some in foster care. The young adults have transitioned into independence.

The community youth centre program that we established shortly before the first *Australian Story* documentary went to air has grown and developed beyond all our expectations. It is now the basis of what we call 'CCT's holistic model'.

The CCT team have all embraced the new model and are now passionate advocates for family-based care.

~

Of course, CCT's efforts remain an ongoing work-in-progress and we constantly push to improve our holistic model to ensure our programs create lasting and systemic change in Cambodia.

We believe this long-term change is best achieved through long-term thinking and a commitment to the honest evaluation of our work and by continuing to adapt and improve what we do. We try to maintain the willingness (and the humility) to keep questioning our assumptions, remain open to new evidence and take constructive criticism on board. That's how we've learned—and continue to learn—valuable lessons.

One of today's biggest commitments at CCT is to keep investing in our people. Development work can be challenging—we see some of the best of humanity, but we also see some of the worst. So it's vital that we support our people—particularly the ones who are out there, day in, day out, changing the lives of kids and families. They are the unsung heroes of CCT. We take every opportunity to invest in them by providing ongoing training and mentoring, and also by fostering a good, supportive team culture.

We also believe in forming alliances with other NGOs who are committed to best practice so we can share what works and reflect on mistakes together and implement effective solutions.

We are currently a member of the UNICEF and Friends International Partnership Program for the Protection of Children Alliance (3PC), the Friends International CYTI Alliance and the Family Care First Cambodia initiative.

One project that the 3PC Alliance is working on is looking to achieve a 30 per cent reduction in children living in orphanages across five provinces in the next three years. Our involvement includes working with another Battambang-based NGO, Komar Rikreay, to provide training and mentoring to the Battambang DoSVY as they complete family tracing and assessments and develop case plans to reintegrate the kids living in these orphanages back to their families.

There are fifty-nine orphanages in Battambang alone, so this is a big job. But, it is my hope that through this process we'll finally see SKO and orphanages like it shut down and the children successfully reunited with their families.

In 2014 the ABC's *Australian Story* filmed a follow-up episode, titled 'The House of Tara', which highlighted some aspects of our new model.

~

The last few years have had their personal highs and lows, too.

In a rather astonishing 'down the rabbit hole' moment, I was named the New South Wales Young Australian of the Year for 2011. Julia Gillard, who was the Australian prime minster at the time, introduced Carolyn and me to the Queen of England. For about five surreal minutes the whole world reduced down to just me, Carolyn, Julia and Queen Elizabeth.

Unfortunately, I was to get a real taste of the dark side of being in the public eye. Throughout 2015 I was stalked and harassed by a woman who saw me on the *Australian Story* documentaries. She is suffering from an obsessive delusion that I am in love with her, despite the fact that I have never met her, or sent her a single email.

I've received hundreds of emails, messages and calls from her, which are extremely disturbing and have been a cause of great distress. Worst of all were the ones that included explicit sexual threats to me and blatant, graphic death threats to my dad, who she believes is standing in the way of our 'love'. It has caused me to genuinely fear for my life and the lives of Peter, Sue and Noni. The threats were so serious that the Australian police took over the case and applied for an Apprehended Personal Violence Order (APVO) on my behalf that prevents her from contacting or coming near me and my family. She didn't agree to the terms of the APVO, so the case was then taken to trial in February 2016. The magistrate gave final orders for a two-year APVO. I fear this won't be the end of the matter, but the police at Rose Bay station continue to be a wonderful support to my family and me. CCT was forced to cancel a fund-raising tour in 2015 as we couldn't afford an appropriate security detail to ensure my safety. Given how uncomfortable I already am with being in the spotlight, this has been a terrible setback for me.

On a much brighter note, I could not be more proud of Sinet. After graduating from high school, she landed a job with BBC Media Action in Phnom Penh as an assistant producer for a radio program about sexual and reproductive health for Cambodian youth. She's since been promoted to the role of producer. She also works with CCT, on a youth mentoring program with our social workers and on our advocacy programs, using her voice to speak out against the dangers of orphanages. She lives a very busy life these days, but on the joyous occasions when we do catch up, I marvel at the woman she's become—zipping around Phnom Penh on a little Scoopy moto, with flaming red hair in wild and wonderful outfits. To be 'different' in Cambodia, to go against the grain in the way she does, requires a lot of courage and self-confidence. She's got more chutzpah, more charisma, and more fight in her than almost anyone else I know.

And her older sister Sineit's 'impossible' dreams did end up coming true! She fell in love with a boy, they got married and had a baby—and both Sineit's husband and her son are free of the HIV virus, as Baz promised. CCT provided Sineit and her husband with vocational training and they are now a healthy, happy little family with a house and a dual income. And their son, now three years old, will never know the poverty that blighted the lives of his parents—the cycle has been broken.

But it certainly hasn't all been sunshine and roses.

SKO continues to operate under Rath's management.

And at age twenty-five, the case of full-blown anorexia I suffered as a teenager came back to haunt me. I was diagnosed with osteo-porosis, a condition in which bones become brittle and are more likely to fracture. It's a disease that I am genetically predisposed to, but the early onset is a result of the anorexia, particularly during the critical time when my body was still laying down bone mass.

If I could send a message to sixteen-year-old me I'd say—I know you feel ashamed, but your eating disorder does not define you. It is an illness that can be treated, so please reach out now and find the help you need. Life is so much better, so much richer, when you are free of it, feeling healthy and strong. And so that, too, is my message to anyone reading this who may be battling an eating disorder in silence. Remember that this illness thrives on secrecy. Be brave enough to start talking about it—whether it be to your doctor, your counsellor, or a trusted friend or family member. There are effective treatment regimes out there—and life is too short to waste another second before taking positive action towards a happier, healthier life.

In the last few years I have also faced some traumatic and heart-breaking events that I could never have anticipated . . .

In 2010, we were on a CCT excursion to the local pool when little Jendar slipped off her lifejacket, just as we were packing up to go home, and jumped into the deep end. We did everything we could to revive her, but it was too late. She was only five years old. Her death had a huge impact on everyone, as Jendar was a real darling of CCT. And it nearly destroyed me. It was really only thanks to Carolyn's love and support that I was able to slowly heal.

Then, in early 2011, Carolyn fell very ill and was diagnosed with appendiceal cancer, a very rare and aggressive malignancy. The CCT team, especially Jedtha and our incredible operations manager at the time, Erin Kirby, did a wonderful job of holding down the fort at CCT so that I could fly back to Sydney. I was by Carolyn's side when she received the horrific diagnosis and while she fought like a cham-pion through massive abdominal surgery and six gruelling months of chemotherapy.

She died in March 2012.

The nine months between her diagnosis and death were nine of the very worst and very best months of my life.

Carolyn's death changed me profoundly.

By the time she died, we were so closely bonded that, in some ways, I feel I know what it's like to be given a terminal diagnosis. I know what it's like to face death, to say goodbye to your life and all the people you love . . .

And yet here I am, alive.

This acute awareness of my own mortality has led to a powerful appreciation of life, of being alive, and a sense of urgency to make the most of the time I get. I made a promise to Carolyn that I would go on after she was gone and live my life to the fullest.

So, for the rest of my days, I'll be striving to honour her memory in the best way I know how—burning the candle at both ends, basking in the light, and trying to leave the world just a little better than I found it.

Cancer fails to get the last laugh

Written by Carolyn Shine in the days
before her death on 10 March 2012

Beings who practise unconditional love are mythical—in my background anyway. It comes from a template not available in the vicinity where I grew up, and I never cease to be dumbstruck by it.

If I hadn't come to know Tara every bit as well as I have, I'd have been suspicious of any thorough description of her personality. Certainly I would have considered it to be lacking in nuance. Where's the shadow? I would ask.

Thrust as she has been, prematurely into a role with enormous responsibilities, I've seen more evidence than I thought amassable that Tara will hang on to someone she cares about with ferocious tenacity, risking her own physical and mental wellbeing if needed, to get them to a safe patch. And bad patches, there have been too many to name.

Like a superhero, she'll be there to help carry me to the toilet in the middle of the night, make a hot drink if she hears an ill dry mouth, a hotpack, if she's heard the tiny restive sound of me rubbing my tummy. With her soothing matter-of-fact voice, she deconstructs the innately terrifying and turns in into almost another step in an adventure.

She's been there for me without fail over the last nine months every time I've grown fearful about having cancer. She does this with an empiric double-pronged approach: unwavering optimism, and plan-building. She made me not only feel sure I would survive my disease, but built glistening edifices in the air that held me in an almost permanent state of thrall. We would travel down the coast to see the horses, we would travel up to Port Douglas, we would see Europe, then we could settle in Cambodia and have a wonderful life there. She talked about the plants I might like to source to make a beautiful tropical garden. Tara leaves no stone unturned in painting a happy picture for someone in need. And she'll follow through, if she can. And while I realise these things won't happen now, for me, because the cancer has won, I still treasure the memories and feel the same frisson of joy when I think of them.

No one can laugh like we can. We managed to turn a year that should be anybody's worst—massive abdominal cancer surgery and loss of many organs, followed by twelve long cycles of chemotherapy, into our greatest year of laughter. How did we do this? I'm not sure. Maybe by sharing a predilection for dark and irreverent humour? By channelling our fear into laughter? Or by laughing in the face of politeness.

My attitude, like Tara's, is that life contains the best and worst of all things, in random parts. I have seen so many of these best parts, and bemoan especially greatly, that my death will preclude me from keeping up to date on science through journals, TED Talks, and podcasts.

That is, unless Tara's pulled strings and exercised her incomparable chutzpah to secure me a spot up the back corner of heaven where all the back copies of *New Scientist* and *Skeptical Inquirer* live and smoking is permitted.

CCT today

We regard our supporters as team-members who deserve to fully understand the complexity of our work. So, when we're explaining our current model to new supporters, we give them a comprehensive presentation that explains all the 'hows' and 'whys' of our work, so they have a genuine understanding of what they're supporting and the impact of their contributions. An early 2016 summary looks like this:

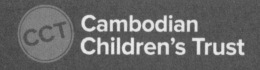

Cambodian Children's Trust

CCT's Holistic Model

PROGRAMS AND SERVICES CREATING IMPACT

The Problem
In order to break the intergenerational cycle of poverty, it's important to understand what drives it.

The poverty trap is created by a tangled web of complex social issues. A lack of access to basic needs such as food, water, shelter and healthcare creates a high-risk environment in which children are prone to illness and malnourishment, and are often forced to spend their days on the streets, begging or working to support themselves and their families. This means many children are only able to attend school intermittently or not at all, and those who are able to attend find it difficult to concentrate due to malnourishment and illness. This leads to poor educational outcomes that result in a low earning capacity in adulthood. Therefore, children who are born into poverty are more likely to grow into adults who are unable to provide for their children's basic needs—perpetuating the intergenerational cycle of poverty.

The immense stress and pressure placed on a family trapped in the intergenerational cycle of poverty often results in family breakdowns. With very few options available to them, parents often entrust their children to the care of an orphanage or residential care facility, believing it will lead to a path out of poverty. However, institutionalisation can have long-term and sometimes irreversible effects on a child's development, resulting in attachment disorders, mental illness, growth and speech delays, and difficulties forming relationships in adulthood. Therefore, growing up in an institution can lead to further incidence of family breakdown in adulthood, as well as an impaired ability to parent their own children—further complicating the intergenerational cycle of poverty.

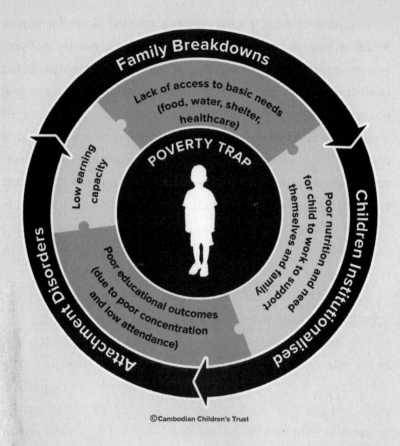

©Cambodian Children's Trust

The Solution

To untangle this complex web of social problems and enable families to break free from intergenerational poverty, it is necessary to recognise and address every one of these problems and provide a holistic solution that is comprehensive, in-depth and tailored to each specific case.

CCT achieves this by delivering a holistic model with a range of programs and services. This solution allows children to remain living with their biological family or, where that's not possible, to stay in family-based care, such as kinship care, foster care or local adoption. We also assist children who have been placed in institutional care to be safely reintegrated into their families or into family-based care. This is achieved while ensuring children have access to education, good nutrition and healthcare, and that their personal safety and other fundamental human rights are not compromised.

CCT's Holistic Model of programs and services operates out of our community youth centres, community preschool, foster care homes and social enterprise. These services include the following:

Social support services: We provide these services while working closely with the local government's Department of Social Affairs, Veterans and Youth (DoSVY), the Commune Council for Women and Children (CCWC), village chiefs and commune leaders. Our team of social workers provides social support services that include:

- assessing referrals and requests for assistance from government and other NGOs
- providing counselling and regular home visits
- facilitating family tracing and family reintegration
- reaching out to children and families living on the streets
- obtaining identification documents for children and families
- assisting parents, guardians and foster carers with behaviour management
- empowering parents to be responsible for decision-making in the best interests of their family and their children's futures
- enabling enrolment in public school.

Crisis intervention: The government child protection system in Cambodia is severely under-resourced. This means there are very few services to support children and families in crisis in Battambang province, where CCT is located. CCT's social workers are on call 24/7 to respond to crisis situations in order to support children and their families during emergencies and times of heightened risk.

Common crises dealt with by CCT's social work team include: children in danger on the streets; missing children; children at immediate risk of trafficking; domestic violence; and mental health crises. CCT's social workers help to develop action plans, source accommodation, liaise with police, de-escalate conflict, provide counselling and, most importantly, ensure the safety of children.

Foster care: CCT's foster care program provides short- and long-term family-based care and support to children who are unable to live with their parents or other biological family members.

Family reintegration: The family reintegration process is focused on family tracing, risk assessments, case planning, counselling, re-establishing relationships, and supporting children to return happily and safely to the care of their biological family. This process involves resolving the issues that originally caused the child to become separated from their family. This may include empowering parents and guardians with income-generation programs or assisting them to access employment and safe housing, and resolving or managing health-related issues. Once the children are reintegrated into their families, follow up is provided by CCT's social workers. Children still have the option to stay enrolled in our community youth centre and preschool programs to receive ongoing support from our social workers and nurses, as well as receiving the benefits of our supplementary education programs.

Healthcare: Cambodian children and families often find it difficult to access adequate healthcare due to the lack of services available and the high cost of medical treatment. CCT keeps children healthy in a number of ways:

- CCT's community youth centres and community preschool provide nutritious meals and clean drinking water as well as preventative healthcare measures, including vaccinations, regular health check-ups and hygiene classes. We also provide treatment for illnesses, injuries and mental health concerns, and support for children and their families living with chronic illnesses such as HIV and hepatitis.

- Hygiene facilities at our community youth centres and preschool include bathroom, shower and laundry facilities, which many children don't have at home. This enables children to maintain adequate hygiene, and prevents many common health concerns, such as lice, scabies, impetigo and infections.

- Twice a year, we run dental workshops in our community youth centres; at these workshops, all the children in our programs are given check-ups and any other dental treatment required, and receive education about dental hygiene.

Education: Our education programs give children a well-rounded education while enhancing their interest and engagement in our programs, ensuring they stay off the streets and enrolled in school.

As well as supporting children to attend public school, we provide comprehensive supplementary education classes to help bridge the gaps in the overcrowded public education system. Children attend academic classes that are aligned to the public school curriculum to help them catch up with their peers, as well as extra-curricular classes in life skills, physical education, self-directed learning such as School in the Cloud and Information Communication (ICT) literacy. To help instil cultural pride and retain ancient art forms, children engage in activities such as Apsara dancing and Lakhon masked theatre.

Many of the children who attend our community youth centres were once at risk of dropping out of CCT's program. Because they were required to stay home and care for their younger siblings, they couldn't attend school. To address this issue, CCT established a community preschool that operates during school hours. This means that children who attend our community youth centres are able to stay in school, and their younger siblings are provided with a safe and nurturing early childhood education. Our preschool program is focused on game-based learning, healthcare, fostering good nutrition, and the development of social and emotional skills in early childhood.

Dependency reduction and income generation: As there is no functioning social welfare system in Cambodia, it is sometimes necessary to provide support to families so that they can cover their basic costs and stay together—for example, elderly grandparents caring for grandchildren, or parents struggling with a disability, which means they aren't able to earn a living to support their children. We believe it is vital that we don't foster welfare dependency, so we have created a model to calculate support payments that is aligned to the realistic cost of living in Cambodia and changes with the family's circumstances. We do this to reduce dependency on support payments and to encourage families to generate their own income wherever possible.

Our social work team assists school-leavers and parents to help them to find safe and non-exploitative employment so that they can support their own families. We achieve this by organising and supporting tertiary education and vocational training, as well as assisting with income-generating activities and access to apprenticeships and employment.

In November 2013, CCT's first social enterprise, Jaan Bai restaurant, opened its doors. Today Jaan Bai provides training and employment for young adults in our programs and is consistently ranked number one on TripAdvisor in Battambang.

The Impact
CCT's Holistic Model achieves positive outcomes for children, families and the wider community:

Health: Over the past five years, the health of children supported by CCT's Holistic Model has greatly improved, resulting in a 40 per cent reduction in the costs of our healthcare program—proving that prevention and early intervention is key.

Retention: We require children enrolled in our community youth centres and preschool to attend daily. This enables our social workers to respond quickly in crisis situations; if children don't turn up to our programs, CCT's social workers will follow up with the family to find out why. Early intervention is vital in crises, such as domestic violence or child trafficking, and our social workers liaise with the family to help resolve the problems or, if necessary, provide short-term crisis care in a foster family. This crisis-response system, combined with our engaging supplementary educational programs, results in very low drop-out rates and ensures the safety of children who are supported by CCT's Holistic Model. Over the past five years we've had an ongoing retention rate of more than 90 per cent at our community youth centres and preschool.

100 per cent family-based care: We believe that every child deserves and has a right to a family. CCT's Holistic Model successfully keeps children with their families or cared for in family-based care, and addresses the primary causes that result in children being trafficked or ending up in orphanages. Our model also means that when children are reintegrated from alternative care (short-term foster care) back into their families, they still have access to vital services such as education and healthcare.

Decrease in street children: The local community in Battambang has reported a significant drop in the numbers of street children begging or trash collecting. Children enrolled in CCT's Holistic Model have access to comprehensive and tailored support services, so they no longer engage in a high-risk lifestyle on the streets.

Scalability: We believe we've developed a scalable alternative to the harmful orphanage/institutional care model prevalent in Cambodia. CCT's Holistic Model can easily be adapted for delivery in other provinces, resulting in more children and families being able to escape the intergenerational cycle of poverty, while ensuring all Cambodian children are able to grow up in a family.

Questions to ask before you support a children's organisation

1. **Do you have residential care?** (Tip: you know it's a residential care facility if the children have rotating carers, if there are lots of children under one roof—more than is common to see in a family setting—and if most of the children are unrelated.)
   Best answer is: NO.
   If the answer is YES, ask the following questions:
   - Why are the children living in residential care rather than with their family? (Tip: poverty or providing access to education is not a good answer.)
   - Have you conducted family tracing and family assessments to find out if the children have family or relatives who could be caring for them?
   - Do you have a plan in place for all the children in your care to be reintegrated into family-based care, i.e. back to their immediate or extended family, into foster care or local adoption?

- Have you successfully completed reintegration? Do you provide follow-up assistance to the family after the children have returned to family-based care?
- Are you registered and licensed with the appropriate government ministries? (Remember: many unregistered homes are operating and being funded by overseas donors.)

2. **Do you allow visits to places where children live?** i.e. dormitories, family homes etc. (Remember: all people have a right to privacy at home and should never be made to feel like they are tourist attractions.)
Best answer is: NO.

3. **Do you allow visitors to interact with children?**
Best answer is: NO.
If the answer is YES, ask the following questions:
- How are these visitors vetted? How can you be 100 per cent sure the visitors interacting with children are not predators? (Tip: ask yourself if you would feel okay about a stranger having the same access to your children.)
- Is the interaction for the benefit of the child or the visitor? (Remember: policy should be drafted only in the best interest of the child, even if interaction does help with fundraising. It is worth noting, though, that it may be necessary for some organisations to allow visitors to observe operations for monitoring, evaluation, and transparency purposes. However, such visits should be kept to a minimum, respect the privacy and dignity of the beneficiaries, create minimal disruption to activities and adhere to a strictly professional agenda.)

4. **Do you have volunteers working for the organisation in roles that have direct contact with children?**
   Best answer is: NO.
   If the answer is YES, ask the following questions:
   - Do these volunteers have relevant, professional qualifications and adequate training for the role? (Remember: unskilled volunteers with inadequate training place children at risk of unprofessional and neglectful care practices. A rotation of adults coming in and out of a child's life contributes to attachment disorders and has negative impacts on a child's development. Therefore, unskilled volunteers should not be working, playing, or interacting with vulnerable children.)
   - Are volunteers adequately screened? (Remember: skilled volunteering for the purposes of capacity building and training of local staff can be a great way to help, but even skilled volunteers should have to provide criminal background checks or a Working With Children Check.)
   - Where do volunteers/visitors reside? (Remember: even skilled volunteers should never stay onsite where vulnerable children reside.)

5. **Do you have a child protection policy?** (Tip: make sure you read it!)
   Best answer is: YES!
   But make sure you ask the following questions:
   - Have all staff been trained on how to implement and abide by the policy?
   - Are local and international staff adequately screened before commencing their roles?
   - Is there a system in place that allows children to safely and confidentially report complaints and concerns?

Remember: you can be part of the solution

Children Are Not Tourist Attractions: Learn why visiting an orphanage is harmful:
www.thinkchildsafe.org/thinkbeforevisiting
Join the ChildSafe movement: Together, we can all protect children and youth from all forms of abuse:
www.thinkchildsafe.org

- **For more information on the situation in Cambodia visit Orphanages, Not the Solution:** www.orphanages.no

- **For more information on the situation globally visit Lumos:** www.wearelumos.org

Reports and studies referenced in this book:

- **Friends International, 'Achieving Positive Reintegration: Assessing the impact of family reintegration', 2014:** http://friends-international.org/resources/research/Achieving-Positive-Reintegration-Friends-International.pdf

- **Lumos, 'Ending the Institutionalisation of Children Globally: The time is now':** http://wearelumos.org/sites/default/files/Lumos%20The%20Time%20is%20Now%20April2014%20FINAL.pdf

- **Lumos, 'Children in Institutions: The global picture':** https://wearelumos.org/sites/default/files/Global%20Numbers.pdf

- **National Scientific Council on the Developing Child, 'The Science of Neglect: The persistent absence of responsive care disrupts the developing brain', 2012:** http://developingchild.harvard.edu/wp-content/uploads/2012/05/The-Science-of-Neglect-The-Persistent-Absence-of-Responsive-Care-Disrupts-the-Developing-Brain.pdf

- UNICEF, 'With the Best Intentions: A study of attitudes towards residential care in Cambodia', 2011: www.unicef.org/cambodia/Study_Attitudes_towards_RC-English.pdf

Want to have an exciting adventure in Cambodia, and learn a whole lot of really interesting stuff about development work while you do it?

Check out these guys:

- **PEPY Tours**
  http://pepytours.com

- **Ayana Journeys**
  www.ayanajourneys.com

- **Learning Service**
  http://learningservice.info

Acknowledgements

(In order of importance . . . just kidding!)

Franky, Rosie and Max, my bestest-ever best friends, you have been there for me, by my side, tails wagging, through it all. I'm only in one piece because of you three and your immense, unconditional love.

Lynda Delacey, thank you for being the most patient, supportive and dedicated co-parent of this book. I'm so grateful to have had such a brilliant writer in my corner. However, if I get any criticism, I'll let them know that that was your bit.

Marnie Walters, for being the greatest friend and 'over-zealous' assistant a girl could ever hope for. Thanks for wrestling through this rabbit-hole life with me and helping to midwife this book into existence.

Erin Kirby, CCT would not be the organisation it is today without you. Your shoes are unfillable.

Sue, my darling Mumzie, I would not be here without you. Literally! I won the lottery finding your womb. But, in all seriousness, I am so grateful for all that you've done for me: your commitment to truth, transparency and authenticity used to embarrass the hell out of me, but now I want to be exactly like you when I grow up. Thanks also for giving me Noni.

Peter, even though I want to punch you in board meetings sometimes, you really are the best dad in the whole wide world. You have the strongest moral compass and passion for justice of anyone I know and have been the most amazing role model in my life. But you were right; from that first moment you met me; I really have given you hell, but I'm pretty sure you have enjoyed the ride. As they say, I am my father's daughter.

Noni, thank goodness I have you to walk through this life with. You're my favourite sister and I'll love you till the day I die.

Jedtha, it's a true honour to lead CCT with someone whose kindness and compassion makes the Dalai Lama look like an average guy. Thank you for believing in me when I was just a dumb kid and no one else did. I hope I did you proud in this book.

Sinet and Sineit, you inspire me like no others. Thank you for showing me what it really means to be brave. And to all the kids who are in this book, your names have been changed but you will no doubt recognise yourselves. Thank you for helping me to tell this story. It is my hope that you have been a part of seeing an end to the unnecessary institutionalisation of children around the world and raising greater awareness of the plight of Cambodia's children. You taught me so much and have made me a better person. I continue to be so proud of all you achieve.

Baz, I am more indebted to you than any other human being on the planet. Thank you for being so wonderfully you. Phoenix rising, baby!

My bestbitch, Hayley Welgus, thanks for being one of the first to read this book and for helping to give me the confidence to be authentically me in the telling of these stories.

My fellow intellectual hooligan Craig O'Shannessy, you have played such a big role in honing my critical thinking skills and in cultivating my ability to embrace vulnerability. In this way, you've shaped my life and the stories in this book in one of the most positive ways possible.

Robert Carmichael, dear friend and author of *When Clouds Fell from the Sky*, thanks so much for lending me your eyes and brain and especially for fact-checking the curly historical bits.

Leigh Mathews, Anna McKeon, Lauren Henderson, Ange Cook, Jane Wilson, Tessa Pacitii and Mark Pacitti, thank you for taking the time to read and provide your invaluable feedback and guidance.

My amazing 'fairy god mothers' Fiona Donato and Trish Doyle, and the wonderful Charlie Teo and Alison Crabb, your support has meant the world to me and to CCT.

Eva Weiner, I am so lucky to have such a wonderful aunty. Thank you for loving me and looking after me like you do.

Rolando Schirato, your unwavering support has helped me through so many tough times. Thank you for being one of the kindest, most generous human beings alive.

Huge thanks to Ben Cheshire, Quentin Davis and the whole team at the ABC's *Australian Story* for being the first ones to bring my story to the Australian public and for making it possible for CCT to become the organisation it is today.

Annette Barlow, Stuart Neal, Angela Handley, Ali Lavau and the team at Allen & Unwin—I'm sorry it was five years late. Thanks for not giving up on me.

Mike Dunne, thanks so much for playing such a huge role supporting Lynda financially throughout the process of writing this book with me. She tells me that your satisfaction comes from knowing it's helping her and CCT. Wish there were more like you out there!

And to all you other crazy cats who have been on this journey with me, to every one of you who has donated, fundraised, advocated, and every one of you who has been a part of the CCT team in Cambodia and Australia, there are simply too many of you to name but you know who you are . . . you have made all this possible. As Simon Sinek says: 'It is not the genius at the top giving directions that makes people great. It is great people that make the guy at the top look like a genius.'

To you, reading this book. Yes, you. Hi there! Thanks for reading and getting to the end. Please help me get the message out: *The unnecessary institutionalisation of children is one form of child abuse we can end in our lifetime. Please redirect your support to organisations who are working hard to overcome poverty, while keeping families together!*

That's all from me now, folks. So long, and thanks for all the fish!